Terence Davies

Published in our centenary year
~ **2004** ~
MANCHESTER
UNIVERSITY
PRESS

BRIAN MCFARLANE, NEIL SINYARD *series editors*

ALLEN EYLES, PHILIP FRENCH, SUE HARPER,
TIM PULLEINE, JEFFREY RICHARDS, TOM RYALL
series advisers

BRITISH FILM MAKERS

Terence Davies

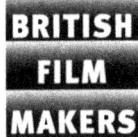

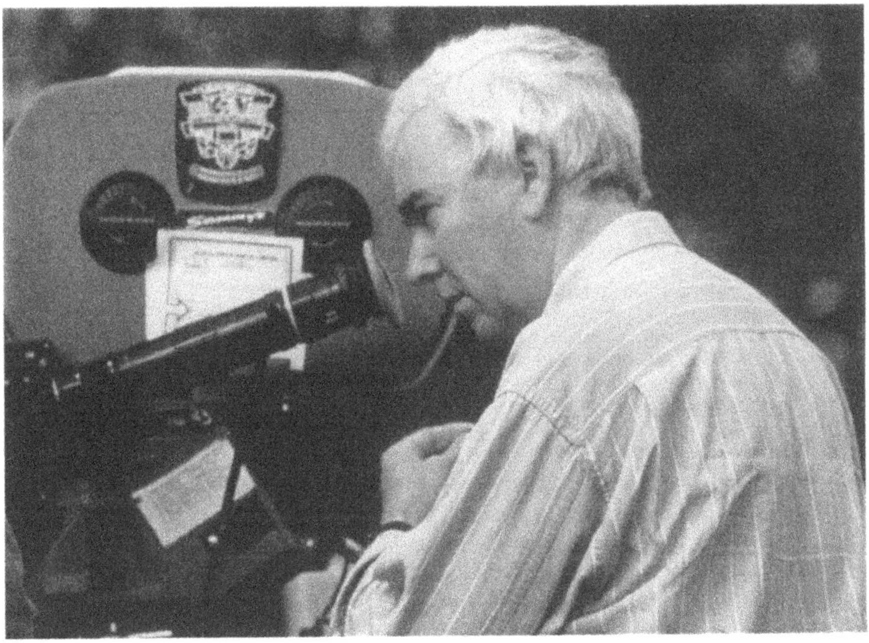

WENDY EVERETT

Manchester University Press
MANCHESTER AND NEW YORK

distributed exclusively in the USA by Palgrave

Copyright © Wendy Everett 2004

The right of Wendy Everett to be identified as the author of this work has been asserted by her in accordance with the Copyright, Designs and Patents Act 1988.

Published by Manchester University Press
Oxford Road, Manchester M13 9NR, UK
and Room 400, 175 Fifth Avenue, New York, NY 10010, USA
www.manchesteruniversitypress.co.uk

Distributed exclusively in the USA by
Palgrave, 175 Fifth Avenue, New York NY 10010, USA

Distributed exclusively in Canada by
UBC Press, University of British Columbia, 2029 West Mall, Vancouver, BC, Canada V6T 1Z2

British Library Cataloguing-in-Publication Data
A catalogue record for this book is available from the British Library

Library of Congress Cataloging-in-Publication Data
A catalog record for this book is available from the Library of Congress

ISBN 13: 978 0 7190 6062 5

First published in 2004 by Manchester University Press

Printed by Lightning Source

For Sybil and Nancy

Contents

LIST OF PLATES	*page*	viii
SERIES EDITORS' FOREWORD		x
Introduction		1
1 Framing the director		6
2 Time, space and memory: the *Terence Davies Trilogy*		34
3 'A pattern of timeless moments': *Distant Voices, Still Lives*		55
4 Mapping the topographies of childhood: *The Long Day Closes*		86
5 Symphony for a new world? *The Neon Bible*		110
6 'A tapestry of small things': *The House of Mirth*		136
7 Music and time: a new dimension		167
8 Close-up: an interview with Terence Davies		201
TERENCE DAVIES FILMOGRAPHY		226
GENERAL FILMOGRAPHY		233
SELECT BIBLIOGRAPHY		235
INDEX		241

List of plates

Terence Davies at work on the set of *The Neon Bible*.
Photograph courtesy of the BFI, reproduced by permission
of   Artificial Eye Film Company Ltd   *frontispiece*

1 'Stasis as drama': Eileen's wedding day, with the family posed
   around the photograph of the dead father. From left to right:
   Freda Dowie as the Mother, Dean Williams as Tony, Angela Walsh
   as Eileen, and Lorraine Ashbourne as Maisie, in *Distant Voices,
   Still Lives*. Reproduced by permission of the BFI   page 83

2 The terrified children huddle under their cart as the air raid siren
   sounds in *Distant Voices, Still Lives*. From left to right: Sally
   Davies as Eileen, Susan Flanagan as Maisie, and Nathan Walsh
   as Tony. Reproduced by permission of the BFI   83

3 Cinema as epiphany. Flanked by his mother (Marjorie Yates)
   and sister Helen (Ayse Owens), Bud (Davies's alter ego, played
   by Leigh McCormack) gazes in delight at the screen. In this
   screen-as-mirror shot, Davies's very identity is self-consciously
   articulated as filmic construct. From *The Long Day Closes*,
   FilmFour International, 1992. Photograph courtesy of the BFI   84

4 Aunt Mae (Gena Rowlands) and the young David (Drake Bell)
   on one of their afternoon walks down Main Street in *The Neon
   Bible*. Aunt Mae is doing her Jean Harlow impersonation as
   she walks. Photograph courtesy of the BFI, reproduced by
   permission of Artificial Eye Film Company Ltd.   84

5 Object of the gaze: Lily Bart (Gillian Anderson) arrives at Grand
   Central Station in *The House of Mirth*. FilmFour International,
   photograph courtesy of the BFI   85

6 The powerful sensuality of unspoken desire: Lily Bart (Gillian
   Anderson) and Lawrence Selden (Eric Stoltz) smoke a cigarette
   together in *The House of Mirth*. FilmFour International,
   photograph courtesy of the BFI   85

Every effort has been made to obtain permission to reproduce copyright material in this book. If any proper acknowledgement has not been made, copyright-holders are invited to contact the publisher.

Series editors' foreword

The aim of this series is to present in lively, authoritative volumes a guide to those film-makers who have made British cinema a rewarding but still under-researched branch of world cinema. The intention is to provide books which are up-to-date in terms of information and critical approach, but not bound to any one theoretical methodology. Though all books in the series will have certain elements in common – comprehensive filmographies, annotated bibliographies, appropriate illustration – the actual critical tools employed will be the responsibility of the individual authors.

Nevertheless, an important recurring element will be a concern for how the oeuvre of each film-maker does or does not fit certain critical and industrial contexts, as well as for the wider social contexts, which helped to shape not just that particular film-maker but the course of British cinema at large.

Although the series is director-orientated, the editors believe that a variety of stances and contexts referred to is more likely to reconceptualize and reappraise the phenomenon of British cinema as a complex, shifting field of production. All the texts in the series will engage in detailed discussion of major works of the film-makers involved, but they all consider as well the importance of other key collaborators, of studio organisation, of audience reception, of recurring themes and structures: all those other aspects which go towards the construction of a national cinema.

The series explores and charts a field which is more than ripe for serious excavation. The acknowledged leaders of the field will be reappraised; just as important, though, will be the bringing to light of those who have not so far received any serious attention. They are all part of the very rich texture of British cinema, and it will be the work of this series to give them all their due.

Introduction

Terence Davies is one of the most important of all contemporary film directors, and his films have the power to fascinate, intrigue and delight spectators of all ages and backgrounds. The fact that until now no single study has been devoted to his work, or that his films are not more widely known and appreciated amongst the British public at large, presents only the first of many intriguing paradoxes that surround him. Davies is neither a straightforward nor an easy director, and the innovative nature of his films, and the way they continually subvert conventional categories and expectations, frequently confuses those critics who seek to pigeonhole them neatly into specific categories; as will be seen, this confusion has had repercussions for the films' wider critical reception. However, this book will argue that it is precisely their tendency to elude classification that constitutes the strength of his films, and that their ability to transcend narrow generic definition not only indicates their startling freshness and originality but also makes them particularly relevant to the contemporary world.

This volume is part of Manchester University Press's exciting new series on British directors, and, given Britain's reluctance to recognise and value its cinema, and my own passionate interest in the work of Terence Davies, I am doubly proud to be associated with this project. What better excuse could I have had for spending so much time viewing and re-viewing these films? And, if that delight has not infrequently bordered on panic, this is only another of those paradoxes mentioned earlier. For the elliptical structure, narrative complexity and intricate and wide-ranging intertextuality of Davies's films means that each new viewing contributes new insight, new understanding, in an endless and all-consuming process. To paraphrase Paul Valéry, it seems that this study could never be finished, merely abandoned and, I would have to add, abandoned on a very temporary basis. Terence Davies's films should perhaps come with a health warning: they are addictive.

The pleasures of writing this book have included spending several hours in conversation with Terence Davies; meeting people such as Jennifer Howarth who have worked with him on various projects; giving papers about and screenings of his work to very different audiences, in different countries, and in widely differing contexts; introducing his films to undergraduate and postgraduate students at the University of Bath, and sharing their sense of discovery and enthusiasm. To all these people, I should like to express my gratitude. The purpose of this volume is to continue and expand the process of discovery, and to communicate my fascination and my findings in the hope that others too will look at Davies's films with similar enjoyment.

Although this study is part of a series devoted to British directors, I have been determined not to restrict my analysis of Davies to a British context, for, if it is important to recognise his debt to the British documentary tradition or to Ealing comedies, it is equally or more important to recognise the extent to which his films reflect past and current trends in European cinema, and to situate his work within a broader context that includes, for example, Bergman, Resnais or Antonioni. Finally, of course, no understanding of his work can be reached without recognition of his youthful passion for the musicals and melodramas of Hollywood.

Structure

The approach I have adopted is basically chronological, to the extent that all Davies's works in turn are analysed in the order in which they were made: thus after a preliminary chapter which provides an overview of Terence Davies, and situates his work in a wider critical, social and cultural context, Chapters 2–6 focus on the *Trilogy*; *Distant Voices, Still Lives*; *The Long Day Closes*; *The Neon Bible*; and *The House of Mirth* respectively. This structure makes it possible to explore ways in which basic themes develop and modulate from film to film, but also to identify the particular differences that substantiate my claim that with each new film that he makes Davies redefines the nature and language of cinema itself. Of course, within this chronological framework, I have ranged freely back and forth in time in response to Davies's own elliptical and fluid approach.

Time

Two major concerns shape the work of Davies, and these will act as threads running throughout this study. The first of these is his fascination with the nature of time, which he directly investigates in all his films up to and, I would argue, including *The House of Mirth*. Tightly related to this preoccupation with the nature of time, is Davies's passion for music, itself a temporal art form of course, and the one which, in Davies's opinion, most closely relates to the medium of film. These twin themes will be examined in relation to all of his work, and the ideas that variously emerge in the different chapters of the book will be brought together and analysed in greater detail in Chapter 7: 'Music and time: a new dimension'.

In place of a traditional conclusion, I have chosen to end the work with an extract from an interview I had with Terence Davies in February 2001 (Chapter 8). It seemed only fair, after pages of my comments and readings, that the final words should be accorded to him, not only because there can be no real conclusion to a work in progress about a film director in progress but also because his infectious humour and repeated self-deprecation serve to bring me firmly back to earth. Moreover, by ending his often harsh comments about the problems of making films with a paragraph describing the intoxication of arriving on set at the start of a new project, Davies reminds us all of the passion for cinema that we share.

The Four Quartets

The themes of time and music that predominate in Davies's work are further highlighted in this study through its repeated references to *The Four Quartets*, by T. S. Eliot, and quotations from this work stand at the beginning of each chapter. Published as individual poems between 1936 and 1942, and in book form in 1943, *The Four Quartets* is widely regarded as Eliot's masterpiece and as one of the key texts of modernism. For Davies, the work is both a delight and a continuing inspiration, and he refers to it repeatedly in conversation, particularly when discussing his own work. Any close reading of his films reveals not only the extent to which Davies is grappling with the same ideas as Eliot concerning the fundamental paradox of time as both relative and absolute, transient and eternal, but also that in so doing he is consciously exploring and reworking Eliot's images and formulations.

The Four Quartets is seminal also in its status as Eliot's attempt to create poetry that functions as music. Here not only the title but the whole structure of the poem is significant. Each of the 'quartets' is composed of five different 'movements', for example, each of which in turn develops and extends an initial theme which thus returns in variations and modulating forms throughout the work. As I shall demonstrate in this book, Davies's own films are similarly structured by musical rather than classical narrative principles, and through them similar variations and modulations can be traced. One of the most fascinating consequences of this approach is the way in which meaning becomes a function of form in a mobile and open-ended process that transforms and transcends traditional narrative strategies.

Time and space

If Davies's preoccupation with time, and with time in relation to space, shapes the structure and form of his films and repeatedly emerges in dialogue and incident, it can also be seen in his camerawork and *mise-en-scène*. Defining visual characteristics of Davies's work, for example, include long motionless takes, and slow, fluid and lyrical tracking shots, often choreographed in relation to music. What is significant about such strategies is that they draw the spectator's attention to the materiality of film, to the nature of the shot and its duration. In other words, by stretching time visibly, they involve the spectator directly in their exploration of time and space, and in so doing demand a creative reading not only of the images that are shown but of the hidden, invisible spaces behind and beyond them. For Davies, cinema is a uniquely privileged medium for exploring what goes on behind and between the images, and, if we can here see further parallels with music (structured by rhythms and notes, but also by the pauses and silences, and by the intervals between the notes), we can also see that any reading of Davies's work must be creative and responsive. Meaning itself therefore is recognised as mobile, unstable and relative.

However, Davies's films are neither pretentious nor obscure, and, by positioning the spectator as co-author, his resistance to mainstream cinema's demands for pace, linearity and closure should be recognised as an act of creative empowerment. Indeed, it is precisely because he himself refuses to make qualitative distinctions between 'high' and popular culture, and between film as art and film as entertainment, that his work is able to appeal to people of different ages, cultures and origins. And if the films provide multilayered collages of sounds and images that individual spectators will understand and enjoy in multiple and different ways, ultimately, and above all, Terence Davies's films are about film; they self-consciously explore and celebrate the form and the potential of the medium in which he feels so privileged to work. Whatever they tell us about ourselves, about Davies, about time, reality, music, literature and art, they are also telling us about the glorious, terrible and powerful nature of cinema and its role in structuring our identity and that of the world we live in.

Framing the director

> Home is where one starts from. As we grow older
> The world becomes stranger, the pattern more complicated
> Of dead and living. Not the intense moment
> Isolated, with no before and after,
> But a lifetime burning in every moment
>
> ('East Coker')

The distinctive and innovative films of Terence Davies (de)construct the shifting times and spaces of identity in fluid narratives whose haunting images are located within a musical architecture shaped by repetition and silence. The films constantly transgress generic and other boundaries, and are thus particularly difficult to categorise or define: hence perhaps the confusion which has so often marked their critical reception.

To date Davies has made five films: the *Terence Davies Trilogy* (1976–83), *Distant Voices, Still Lives* (1988), *The Long Day Closes* (1992), *The Neon Bible* (1995) and, most recently, *The House of Mirth* (2000). However, it is significant that, in Davies's case, even the apparently simple task of providing a total number of films proves somewhat complex, given that his 'first' work, the *Trilogy*, comprises three short films made over a period of seven years: *Children* (1976); *Madonna and Child* (1980); *Death and Transfiguration* (1983); while his 'second' work, *Distant Voices, Still Lives*, is actually composed of two short films, made in 1986 and 1988. No matter how one does the sums, it might be tempting to see this as a modest total for more than a quarter of a century's work, but such a conclusion would be unwise given the nature of the films in question. In turn lyrical, painful, complex, sparse, joyful, despairing or, more precisely, all of these at once, the densely layered narratives and rich visual and temporal textures of these films are as challenging to the spectator as they are rewarding. Each of the films in some way reaches beyond the limits of film itself, restructuring, in so doing, the very syntax of the medium; and while together they constitute a coherent opus to which each film in turn contributes further layers of meaning, individually each film provides an entirely unique and astonishing vision. Whether these films are considered individually or together, it would be difficult to exaggerate the explosive effect they have had upon contemporary cinema.

It is both puzzling and disappointing, therefore, that until now no single study has been devoted to Terence Davies. Of course it is true that articles and chapters dealing with specific films or particular aspects of his work abound, especially in books dealing with contemporary (British) cinema, while short articles and reviews feature repeatedly in film journals and the wider press, and Davies himself makes regular appearances in the media. Indeed, his many interviews, in which he talks revealingly, even obsessively, about his memories, his films, his techniques and his objectives, provide a rich vein of information for any researcher, and a telling indication of his artistic integrity and his modest but passionate belief in what he is doing. Although, as I found during the course of a lengthy interview with him in February 2001, no one criticises Davies's films more harshly than he, nevertheless his comments also reveal his disappointment that his work is not more widely known and appreciated.[1] Davies is in any case far more widely respected than he believes, and even if his films have not always been understood by their critics or viewed by the public at large, they nevertheless do have a passionate and dedicated following across Britain, Europe and the United States, and have won countless prestigious international awards. Moreover, it is clear that his most recently released film, his perceptive and intelligent adaptation of Edith Wharton's novel *The House of Mirth* (2000), has gone some way to introducing his work to a wider public, following its almost universal critical acclaim. If the publicity it generated creates more widespread interest in his work, there is little doubt that Davies's true status, as one of the most important talents of the contemporary era, will at last be recognised. On a more personal level, if this volume contributes to that process in any way, I shall be satisfied.

To date, Davies's work can be divided rather neatly into two parts: the autobiographical films (the *Trilogy*, *Distant Voices, Still Lives* and *The Long Day Closes*), made between 1976 and 1992, and the two literary adaptations, *The Neon Bible* and *The House of Mirth*, which mark his move away from the purely personal. However, even this distinction is less clear-cut than such a statement might imply, given that many of the themes and concerns which structure the autobiographical films recur, albeit in modulated form and voice, in the two literary adaptations, while Davies's passionate love of poetry and music, and the perceptive response to the natural rhythms and the visual potency of language that characterise his literary adaptations, are already a discernible and important constituent of his earlier works.

In addition to his directing, Davies has published two books. The first, *Hallelujah Now*, a mixture of autobiographical memory and fiction, appeared in 1984, and was republished by Penguin Books in 1993. The second, *A Modest Pageant* (1992), brings together the screenplays of all his autobiographical films and includes a short introductory chapter in which Davies discusses the memories and personal references which shape them, and provides a brief description of his (unusual) filming techniques. Whilst *A Modest Pageant* constitutes an essential reference tool for anyone studying Davies's work, it is also fascinating in its own right, clearly revealing his concern with the musicality of language, and with the complex and shifting relationship between words and visual images. The same thoughtful and inventive approach to language emerges powerfully in *Hallelujah Now* which, like the *Trilogy*, is part personal memory, part fictional extension of those memories, and which shares the same three-part structure. Of particular interest, for the purpose of this study, is the dense intertextual framework which links the novel with Davies's autobiographical films.

The three parts of *Hallelujah Now* are entitled 'Songs for Dead Children', 'Letters to a Friend' and 'The Walk to the Paradise Garden'. The third of these, 'The Walk to the Paradise Garden', provided the basis for Davies's radio play of the same name, broadcast on Radio 3 in October 2001. In his broadcast introduction to the play, Davies made reference to *Under Milk Wood*, explaining that, like Dylan Thomas, he wanted to achieve a musical structuring of voices. He also spoke about the particular discipline demanded of a film director attempting to create a work whose visual power must be contained entirely within its language. Both this radio play and *Hallelujah Now* illustrate the range of Davies's creativity, and his fascination with transcending the normal limits of whatever medium he is working in: just as his films can be approached as a form of music whose meanings lie between or behind the images as much as within them, so his writing also explores meaning within a musical structure in which silences and repetitions may be as important as the actual words. There are interesting parallels between his work and that of a number of other writer/directors such as Marguerite Duras, for example, whose films, novels and essays reveal similarly musical structures, or Jean-Luc Godard, whose films interweave particularly dense and complex patterns of visual and cultural references. Indeed, as will be demonstrated, the links between Davies's films and those of his European contemporaries are important, and provide insight that is often lacking when comparisons are restricted to a narrow range of British directors, in particular when in so doing attention focuses primarily upon the socio-realist tradition. Finally, the fundamental eclecticism of Davies's interests, reflected in his continuing experimentation with novel, theatre and interview as well as with cinema, provides a clear indication of his originality, his versatility and his creative complexity.

Biography

There is a dominant autobiographical current that runs through Davies's films up to and including *The Long Day Closes*, and arguably beyond, and which similarly shapes his writings and his various broadcasts. Davies openly acknowledges the centrality of autobiographical memory to his work as well as to his personal identity, so that it is evident that some familiarity with his early years will provide a useful framework in which to situate his films. The intention of the following short biographical account, therefore, is to draw attention to some of the dominant characters, events and concerns which shaped those years, and which are subsequently woven, in various and complex ways, into his memory narratives.

Terence Davies was born in Liverpool on 10 November 1945, and was thus part of the postwar baby boom, a generation growing up in the austere climate of 1950s Britain. He was the youngest of ten children, of whom seven survived, in a working-class Irish Catholic family stretched to breaking point between the poles of an adored mother and a feared and despised father. These opposing influences – maternal love and nurture on the one side, and the violent and repressive Law of the Father[2] on the other – constitute the source of the tensions around which all his autobiographical films and arguably his life and character are structured. His father was a rag-and-bone man, a brutal and unstable sadist who regularly beat his wife and abused his children both physically and mentally. Davies was only six-and-a-half when his father died, but insists that those early years caused him irreparable damage. ('Even my analyst hates my father', he is often heard to mutter.) In an interview published in the *Guardian* to mark the release of *The House of Mirth*, for example, he still refers with passion to the legacy of his traumatised early childhood: 'I'm still acutely aware of atmosphere in a room. When I was a kid I'd run into a room and if he didn't want anyone around, he'd just kick me from one end of the house to the other. You don't make that mistake very often' (Hattenstone 2000: 4). His father suffered from cancer for the two years leading up to his death, and Davies gives us some insight into his protracted illness in a gruelling scene in *Children*, the first part of the *Trilogy*, where the father screams and writhes in agony as he waits for his next shot of morphine. Yet, even within this unbearably painful scene, perhaps the most shocking element of all for us, the viewers, is the violence of the father's sudden outburst against his son. It is not surprising therefore that Davies would tend to associate masculinity with violence and sickness, nor yet that he should still today find it impossible to forgive his father's brutality, for the deep scars remain painful: 'Very often, he screamed at anything and then attacked us as well. It was awful. That happened when I was between the ages of five and seven. That's an awful time for this to happen to a child, because that's when you are at your most vulnerable. When you see things like that, you never forget. It makes you deeply aware of not just people, physically, but the hostile nature of the world and disease' (Falsetto 1999: 76). These memories, and others, still more violent, more terrible, mark the autobiographical films profoundly, and exercise a terrible hold over the spectator.

The counterbalance to the fear, violence and sickness, was of course Davies's mother, and her love and tenderness are identified by him as the source of all that is good. Just as she strove to protect the children from her violent husband, so too she held the family together after his death. Throughout all his work, Davies's mother is represented in a positive way, and in his films she, and indeed women in general (his sisters, his primary school teachers, the hospital nurses), represent the loving and caring side of existence. As we shall see, the powerful tension of the male/female polarity is found at the heart of all Davies's work, on the one hand mother, music, warmth, love, nurture, salvation; on the other father, brutality, inflexibility, violence, corruption, damnation. Moreover, this dynamic shapes his work not only overtly, by being contextualised within the narrative, but also in surreptitious and more complex ways, hidden deep below the surface.

In the almost unrelieved misery of the *Trilogy*, for example, we witness at first hand Davies's suffering and despair and his rage against his father, the Catholic Church, and his own sexuality. But any close analysis of these short films reveals ways in which every aspect of their composition, from their spatial and architectural topography to their visual rhythms and their textures of light and shadow and of sound and silence invites deeper and more complex explorations of this fundamental tension. *Distant Voices, Still Lives,* his second autobiographical film, extends the process still further and reveals not only the dreadful ferocity of the father's violence but also the extent to which the whole family remains traumatised, frozen into immobility and silence, long after his death.

For the young Terence Davies, his father's death marked the beginning of a period of intense happiness, however short-lived and fragile it would ultimately prove to be. Liberated from patriarchal tyranny, the family home was transformed into an essentially female domain; no longer a place of fear and violence, it was positively reconfigured as locus of love and security, and as refuge from the increasingly hostile outside world. It is this period of happiness that is explored in *The Long Day Closes*. Many critics, mistakenly, judged the film sentimental and nostalgic; however, the tensions of the previous films are in fact still present, now lurking menacingly just below the surface of the child's world. And in the quietly observant intelligence of Bud, Davies's young alter ego, we are made uncomfortably aware of the internalisation of his loneliness, fear and misery.

The end of this period of bliss was signalled by Davies's move from the caring environment of his primary school to a tough inner-city secondary school called the Sacred Heart Roman Catholic Boys' School. Within its rigid universe, he was once again subject to the violent Law of the Father, embodied this time by sadistic male teachers, a climate of macho intolerance and the relentless bullying to which he was subjected. Corporal punishment was rife in a system which tolerated neither individuality nor difference of any sort and, for the next four years, Davies was ridiculed, bullied and beaten up on a daily basis, something he revealed to no one at the time (Falsetto 1999: 68–9). Both the *Trilogy* and *The Long Day Closes* recreate this school in all its terror, and chart its role in the erosion of the child's innocence. But additionally *The Long Day Closes* reveals the implacable encroachment of the outside world upon the warm security of home.

Davies's films have frequently been criticised for their failure to engage in any way with the world beyond his immediate family. Such criticism, which reflects a fundamental misunderstanding of the nature of the autobiographical process, similarly fails to recognise that we are, in fact, given considerable insight into the social climate of postwar Britain, but that we must reconstruct this for ourselves from the tiny remembered details of Davies's childhood experiences. For example, the school medical examinations which feature in both the *Trilogy* and *The Long Day Closes* certainly do offer a reflection of the new welfare state and its moves to produce a healthy generation that will in some way compensate for the losses sustained in the war. However, as a child, Davies would of course have had no awareness of this wider social context, and, through his young eyes, we too are made to experience such events as part of a ritual whose sole purpose appears to be his embarrassment and humiliation. On the occasion of the school medical inspection in *Children*, the boys have to wait in their underpants as the doctor calls each in turn to join him behind a screen. Relentless mocking by the other boys makes the experience intolerable for the self-conscious young Tucker (Davies's alter ego). Similarly, in *The Long Day Closes*, the school visit of the 'nit nurse' is relived through the humiliation of being classified as 'unclean', as one of those boys whose hair is infested with headlice. And when, on a later occasion in that film, Bud (the young Davies) visits the school nurse because he has earache, although we certainly notice the fact that he first has to produce his medical card, in another of the tiny but significant glimpses of the social changes taking place at the period, what we, like Davies, are much more likely to remember of that occasion is the nurse's scathing comment 'What nasty little creatures you little boys are'. It is clear that the self-loathing which frequently seems to characterise Davies's response to his own physicality has its origins in just such painful memories. And if the references to the wider world of the 1950s are not highlighted in the narrative it is because, to the child whose world we are exploring, they were merely a backcloth against which painful subjective experiences occurred. The individual spectator must therefore pick up on such clues, and should also be aware that frequently it is through recreating remembered events on screen that the remembering adult too can reach a new understanding of the events which dominated his or her childhood world.

A further interesting example of the multiple and imaginative readings required by autobiographical discourse is offered by the teachers who are the source of so much unhappiness for their young pupils. Clearly, sadistic and unprincipled teachers have played a key role in autobiographical films right from Jean Vigo's memories of boarding school life in *Zéro de conduite* (France, 1932), and they resurface relentlessly in, for example, *Les 400 coups* (Truffaut, France, 1959), *My Life as a Dog* (Lasse Hallstrom, Sweden, 1985), *Hope and Glory* (Boorman, UK, 1987), *Cinema Paradiso* (Tornatore, Italy, 1989), and so on.[3] This element of Davies's films can thus be situated within the generic framework of autobiography. At the same time, such figures are undoubtedly a very real and vivid component of Davies's actual childhood memories. As an adult, he understands the position of these teachers who, as ex-army men, untrained and ill-prepared for civilian life, were, in the aftermath of the war, frequently given teaching jobs for which they were totally unsuited. Almost inevitably, such men chose to model their roles directly upon their experiences of army life (see Chapter 8). In the films, we can actually see the result of this phenomenon in the pseudo-military philosophy of the school and in repeated shots of the boys being made to line up in the playground at a blast of a whistle, and to march, in formation, into or out of their classrooms, and we can identify such scenes as providing further social observation of postwar life. But such indicators must actively be divined by the spectator precisely because they were not part of the child's awareness but an element of the remembering adult's attempt to contextualise or rationalise those earlier experiences.

Given his unhappy existence at school, it is not surprising that as soon as Davies was fifteen and legally allowed to leave, he should do so. He then obtained work as a clerk in what he describes as 'a very Dickensian shipping office', and when the firm closed down, a year or so later, he became a trainee accountant and book-keeper in another Liverpool office. These years, so vividly depicted in *Madonna and Child*, were essentially lonely and boring, but at least Davies had escaped the bullying of school life and discovered some form of independence. Nevertheless (and despite his evident flair for the work involved) the experience was supremely frustrating, and he sought some creative recompense by becoming an active member of an amateur dramatic society, as well as joining a local writers' group. It is a bitter indictment of the class-bound educational system of the time that his considerable literary and artistic talents had not been recognised at all, and that his cultured intelligence was ridiculed or ignored throughout his years at secondary school.

The chance to move away from Liverpool and to escape the boredom of office routine occurred in 1972, when Davies obtained a Local Education Authority grant to study at the Coventry Drama School. Once again, however, his experience of communal education was far from positive. Davies found the atmosphere hostile and the students narrow-minded and prejudiced and yet again he found himself positioned as outsider. He also hated being apart from his mother, particularly since he could not often afford the train journey to visit her. Nevertheless, it was while he was a student in Coventry that he wrote his first screen play, *Children*, which, almost by chance (as a result of a discussion he just happened to hear on the radio), he submitted to the British Film Institute Production Unit. As a result, he was awarded £8,500 to direct the film, which he did during his summer vacation in 1976. But, as we shall see in the next chapter, even this potentially exciting experience proved negative, with Davies plagued by feelings of inadequacy: 'The crew's attitude was "You haven't gone to film school. You haven't made a film. Why should you get all this money from the BFI?" ... They gave me a very hard time and after it was all over, I thought, "I'm never going to do this again"' (Falsetto 1999: 70).

However, more importantly, he had discovered the thrill of looking down into the camera lens, and his future career was decided. In 1983, *Children* won the Bronze Hugo at the Chicago Film Festival, an amazing achievement for a first film by an entirely untrained director. On the strength of this film, Davies moved from Coventry to the National Film School in London, and it was while he was a student there that he wrote and directed the second part of his *Trilogy*, *Madonna and Child*. This film too received international recognition when it was awarded the Golden Hugo at the Chicago Film Festival. The final part of the *Trilogy*, *Death and Transfiguration*, was made after Davies had left the National Film School, with funding from the Greater London Arts Association and the British Film Institute. The *Trilogy* achieved widespread international acclaim, and received a number of prestigious European awards.

In the meantime, Davies's passion for writing continued, and his first novel, *Hallelujah Now*, was published in 1984. His next two films, completed in 1988, were released as *Distant Voices, Still Lives*, winning the International Critics Prize at Cannes in 1988, and establishing Davies's reputation as a one of the most promising young British directors. Four years later, in 1992, *The Long Day Closes* was released, heralded by Davies as signifying the end of his autobiographical cycle. This film explores Davies's childhood after the death of his father, and also, in an original and fascinating move, highlights the central role played by popular culture within the formation of personal identity.

Considerable excitement greeted the news of Davies's next project, *The Neon Bible* (1995), for it was difficult to imagine how a director so closely connected with memory and autobiography would deal with the transition to filming someone else's ideas, let alone cope with the experience of working in the United States. What had first attracted Davies to this novel was its vivid language and powerful visual imagery. Set in Georgia, in the American Deep South, it was written by John Kennedy Toole when he was only sixteen, although it was not in fact published until 1989, some twenty years after its author had killed himself. The novel provides a first-person account of the experiences of a confused and sensitive young boy growing up in a poor, working-class home dominated by a brutal father, and it vividly recreates the claustrophobic society of a small town in the Bible Belt in the 1940s. In many ways, therefore, the narrative finds Davies on familiar territory, and it is likely that one of the reasons why he was initially attracted to the book was that so many of the experiences it traces so closely reflected his own. Moreover, the fact that John Kennedy Toole's work was published at all (his second novel, *A Confederacy of Dunces*, was awarded the Pulitzer Prize in 1981) was entirely due to the determination of his mother (although, for complex legal and financial reasons, she would later relentlessly oppose to the publication of *The Neon Bible*), another factor which might have interested Davies.

A good deal of the criticism levelled at the film when it was first released was that Davies had simply transposed his own Liverpool childhood to the American Deep South (Horne 2000: 14). Such criticism is more than a little unfair, particularly since there are perhaps as many differences as there are similarities in the stories being told. Furthermore, it would seem to ignore both the film's assured inventiveness and the extraordinary resonance and beauty that characterise many of its scenes. Indeed, close analysis of the film's multiple voices and complex textures might lead us to suggest that it is in fact through its transposition of memories, the process of moving inward through someone else's subjectivity, that *The Neon Bible* ultimately achieves its power, and, of course, this process enables Davies to move forwards to his next project: his ambitious and intelligent adaptation of Edith Wharton's *The House of Mirth* (2000).

For this film, Davies returns once again to American literature, adapting Edith Wharton's ruthless dissection of the social mores of New York high society at the turn of the last century. Lily Bart, the film's penniless and beautiful heroine, is played by Gillian Anderson, with Eric Stoltz as her admirer Lawrence Selden, and the film reveals, through masterly close-ups and breathtaking tracking and dissolves, both the independence and fierce inner 'morality' of Lily, and her brittle vulnerability. Its sumptuous images recall the work of late nineteenth-century artists, particularly John Singer Sargent, and its intense and multilayered sound track, often concentrating intently upon the tiniest and most detailed ordinary sounds rather than on music, has evoked widespread comparison with the films of Bresson, Kieślowski and Bergman, in particular. Importantly, the delicate control of detail and the camera's imaginative virtuosity in *The House of Mirth* convincingly demonstrate that Davies is a director who can work just as powerfully with non-autobiographical material.

I commented earlier that one of Davies's most recent projects had been the writing and production of *The Walk to the Paradise Garden*, a radio play, broadcast on Radio 3 in October 2001. I want to return to this work very briefly at this point, because it provides useful insight into his methods of working and indeed to his particular genius. Whilst the narrative is, as we have seen, a reworking of his autobiographical material, specifically the final section of *Hallelujah Now*, as always with his work it is important to consider the interplay of differences and/or modulations which it offers, rather than the similarities. What is strikingly innovative here, in terms of Davies's oeuvre, is the notion that a film director whose primary concern is with exploring ideas through visual images, should chose instead to create images entirely through sounds. In his films, Davies self-consciously uses an eclectic range of music – classical, folk and the popular songs from his childhood – to make the meanings of his images resonate in a way that far exceeds their visual connotation. In *The Walk to the Paradise Garden*, he uses the music of voices, and the refrains of remembered phrases and repetitions from his own past and from his earlier texts and films to replace the visual altogether, or rather to create a form of music that obliges the listeners to visualise the images for themselves through their own personal memories and experiences. 'I've tried to paint for the ear of the inner eye. I've tried to appeal to the eye of the inner ear', he explains (Davies 2001: 4). In other words, if Davies's works offer recurring themes and concerns in constantly shifting harmonies, key modulations occur between sight and sound, between the visible and the invisible and between words and silence, an idea that will be further developed in the chapters that follow. Finally, in this brief survey of Davies's life and work, it is important to note the range of his activities, and the breadth and eclecticism of his cultural interests. Far from being a director who is in some way limited by his intensely personal vision and his obsessive exploration of autobiographical memory, he is in fact someone who uses these apparent obsessions and repetitions in order to subvert traditional generic distinctions, and to explore new and more open concepts of meaning and identity.

Sexuality

The above account, while identifying the male/female tensions underlying all Davies's memories and his (autobiographical) films, does not deal openly with his sexuality, with the confusion and pain that the fact of being gay has always seemed to cause him. This concern, which is a fundamental aspect of his work as much as his life, will inevitably receive more detailed attention in later chapters. However, once again, some awareness, not only that he is gay but of the source and nature of the complex feelings of guilt that surround his sexuality, is important. In *The Long Day Closes*, in which Davies is about eleven, we see the awakenings of his sexuality, and the increasing confusion and fear that result. But in the *Trilogy*, as in his novel, *Hallelujah Now*, we are given a powerful and much more explicit indication of his rage against himself and the world. That Davies has never been able to view his sexuality in a positive light must, of course, be understood within the context of his Catholic upbringing, but equally significant is the part played by the social and moral attitudes prevalent in Britain in the 1950s. It is important to remember that, even between consenting adults, homosexual activity was a criminal offence until the implementation of the Wolfenden legislation in 1967. At the end of the war, homosexuality was widely regarded as a psychiatric disease; indeed, medical treatment of various kinds continued to be given to homosexual men and women throughout the 1950s and much of the 1960s, in order to 'cure' them. *Children* offers us an insight into this attitude through the doctor's comment to Robbie, his patient: 'Still no interest in girls yet, Robbie? ... Well, that may come, son ... that may come' (Davies 1992: 12). Davies, then, would have been coerced into considering homosexuality as some sort of shameful disease (hence, no doubt, some of the anguish reflected in *The Long Day Closes* when the children are pronounced 'clean' or 'unclean' – that is, suffering from nit infestation – by the school nit nurse). Moreover, not only was homosexuality considered a criminal offence in 1950s Britain, but it was increasingly presented to the public as linked with communism and moral corruption (a sort of double plague), and in 1952, under strong pressure from the American government, there was a threefold increase in the number of prosecutions of gay men. In October of that year, on his appointment as the new Commissioner of Police at Scotland Yard, Sir John Nott-Bower promised to prosecute all homosexuals 'with ferocious zeal'. In the ensuing witch-hunt, night-time raids on private houses were commonplace, and so extreme were police tactics that even the discovery of 'incriminating' letters or diaries would inevitably lead to prosecution and imprisonment (Jivani 1997: 98–116). In such a climate, it must surely have been extremely difficult, if not impossible, for anyone of Davies's age and class to develop a positive view of their sexual identity, even without the added complication of Catholicism's condemnation of homosexuality as a mortal sin. And problems were inevitably compounded for children and adolescents by the impossibility of speaking about their sexuality to anyone, both for fear of reprisals and because of the widespread ignorance of the subject that prevailed. The significance and implications of such issues will be further discussed in this book in relation to their relevance to particular films.

Methods of filming

Davies's methods of making films have been frequently described, not least by Davies himself. They are characterised, perhaps above all, by his extreme meticulousness, by the precision and detail of his shooting scripts and by his comprehensive control of every aspect of his subject matter. To extrapolate briefly from the many accounts Davies has given, once the ideas for a film begin to form in his mind (and these will vary from a mere sketch, possibly consisting of little more than a scrap of dialogue and camera movement, to a fully developed scene), he spends a period of ten to twelve months making a series of detailed notes. As the quantity of these notes increases, the narrative gradually takes shape in his head until he is in a position to compose his first draft. Amazingly, in this first draft every track, pan and dissolve, every piece of music and every scrap of dialogue already appears. Davies then leaves the text for four to six weeks, before writing the second, and final, draft. 'That is the script we shoot ... I *never* do a storyboard. The script is both the storyboard and the shooting script. I go onto the film knowing every shot and camera set-up in the movie as well as what is on the soundtrack at any given point' (Davies 1992: x). This method is, to say the least, unusual, and the fact that even before the second draft of the script Davies can visualise every aspect of the completed film in minute detail is astounding. Corroboration of Davies's descriptions of his methods of filming is found in a number of accounts, including Colin MacCabe's recollection of the summer of 1985 when, as the new director of the BFI production unit in London, he first worked with Davies, whose unusual approach clearly fascinated him:

> Davies's scripts detailed every camera movement and angle: the film existed in every detail before any cast or crew were engaged. At the same time every suggestion or alteration was listened to with great care and, occasionally, some minor detail would be altered or changed, but it was clear that this was only after the most intense reflection by Terence: the calculation of how altering one tiny element of one short scene was going to affect the whole film. (MacCabe 1999: 15)

On a practical level, what this means is that Davies's films are invariably made within budget, and according to schedule. What is potentially even more interesting about MacCabe's comment, however, is the implication that Davies creates his films much as if he were a composer; every rhythm, every tonality, every nuance being so minutely scored that, as MacCabe recognises, the smallest alteration will have repercussions for the work as a whole, will irrevocably alter the film's meaning. This observation assumes a particular significance in relation to Davies's concept of the close relationship between film and music, as well as clearly exemplifying the notion of director as *auteur*. And, while Davies never belittles in any way the creative input of the other members of the filming team (all of whom are chosen by him with exactly the same clarity of vision and determination that his shooting scripts reveal), and while, as MacCabe explains, Davies is always prepared to listen to suggestions, nevertheless it is clear that his is the overall vision.

In an interview with Simon Hattenstone following the release of *The House of Mirth*, Eric Stoltz (Lawrence Selden in the film) comments, in particular, upon Davies's sense of vision, and his passionate involvement in his work. Talking about the shock it had been for him, as an American actor used to having his own way, suddenly to be faced by a director who would tell him exactly what to do, and how to deliver each line, he tellingly remarks: 'He doesn't so much direct as conduct. He had the film in his head, and we were there to serve his vision. However much it drove us mad, it also delighted us and intrigued us and fascinated us and we ended up loving him' (Hattenstone 2000: 4). Given Davies's conviction of the links between music and film, I find it particularly fascinating to note how often those who work with him have recourse to musical analogies in their accounts. But comments such as the above again illustrate Davies's utter refusal to compromise. 'Davies absolutely refuses to sacrifice any aspect of his personal vision to the whims of executive producers and/or distributors, while simultaneously remaining resolutely practical in matters of budget and shooting schedules' (Dixon 1992: 20). In my interview with him, Davies recounted tales of many of the battles he had successfully waged in relation to *The House of Mirth*, in retaining both a number of key scenes and even over the form and images featured on the film poster. In the director's commentary on the DVD of the film, he gives a frank and fascinating account of the various cuts and changes that were imposed, and we are privileged to see these scenes in the form he originally intended.

To some extent, working within the financially impoverished European system of film-making may be recognised, at least in some ways, as having been as beneficial to Davies as it has been harmful. For whilst it is true that his job as a director has been made infinitely harder by the need to work within extremely limited budgets (for example, the entire *Trilogy* had a total budget of £46,000, while *Distant Voices, Still Lives* cost £750,000, and *The Long Day Closes* £1.75 million), and by the inevitable, and often soul-destroying struggle to obtain even this minimal support, nevertheless it is unlikely that he would have been permitted to make any of his films within the ratings-conscious and profit-driven constraints of Hollywood. Moreover, the inadequate level of funding has, on occasion, even provoked some of his most brilliant and inventive shots (the transition from America to Europe in *The House of Mirth*, for example, or the stunning plaster and wood recreation of a steam engine that opens that film). Not that this justifies in any way the scant funding or the wholly inadequate distribution and publicity infrastructures available to directors working in Britain. Indeed, given the struggles faced by directors such as Davies, it is little short of miraculous that any films are released, let alone films of such quality and significance as these. It is enlightening to consider that while, in terms of Davies's previous budgets, the £5.5 million he had at his disposal for *The House of Mirth* might seem generous, in fact this total budget represents only slightly more than the cost of a single episode of *The X Files* (the American television series which had made Gillian Anderson famous), and slightly less than the promotion and distribution budget alone for Martin Scorsese's *The Age of Innocence*. And even obtaining this amount of financial support was, as Olivia Stewart (Davies's producer) recounts, a complicated and fraught process involving nine financiers (Constanzo Cahir 2001: 167).

Film-making as group activity

The publication of a series of monographs dedicated to individual directors does, inevitably, encourage an *auteur* approach which may well be susceptible to a certain amount of criticism. Film-making is after all essentially a team operation, as the list of credits for even such low-budget films as those of Davies clearly illustrates, and any evaluation of the strengths and weaknesses of a given film must always recognise the various contributions made by the cast and the crew. While, therefore, it is true that the chapters that follow do tend to concentrate almost entirely upon Davies's films as *his* personal creation, and to analyse them in terms of *his* role in scripting, directing and editing, this is not in any way intended to diminish the contributions of others. Indeed, I shall be including as many references to, and comments by, other people involved in the films as possible. An *auteur*-based approach is however virtually inevitable in the case of Davies, since in all his films, whether or not they are autobiographical, and irrespective of the size of the crew and the experience and renown of the actors, he is always ultimately in control, both composer and conductor of the work in progress. Nevertheless, Davies is the first to acknowledge the enormous creative contribution made by both cast and crew, and it is clear that they deserve far more detailed and sustained attention than is possible here. I compensate to some extent by providing detailed lists of the credits for each film in the filmography, and by including, in addition to brief comments within individual chapters, the slightly more extended discussion that follows.

The cast

Whether working with highly skilled professionals or inexperienced children, Davies has the rare ability to bring out the very best in his actors, often revealing in them unsuspected and previously unrecognised talents. Each of his films contains unforgettable performances although the lack of critical consensus as to just which these are gives some indication of the strength of the cast as a whole. It would therefore seem invidious to limit comments to one or two individuals, particularly since the integrity of each individual performance results, to no small degree, from its generous contribution to the whole. Davies is personally involved in all casting decisions, and has precise and uncompromising views as to whom he wants for a given role, just as he knows precisely how he wants each of those roles to be performed. There is no clear pattern as to how he goes about selecting the cast: sometimes, for example, he may choose an actor with whose stage or film work he is familiar, but equally his initial choice may be made on the mere basis of a photograph. The best-known example of the latter method is his choice of Gillian Anderson to play Lily Bart in *The House of Mirth* because 'she looked like she might have stepped out from one of John Singer Sargent's portraits' (Johnston 2000: 1). Moreover, while Davies frequently uses well-known and highly regarded actors, he is just as likely to select amateurs or semi-professionals, even for major roles. Examples of his use of previously famous actors include Wilfred Brambell, who plays the elderly, dying Tucker in the final part of the *Trilogy*. In this role Brambell gives a harrowing and unforgettable performance whose subtlety might have been hard to predict from his popular British persona as the father in BBC television's *Steptoe and Son*.[4] The choice of Brambell for this demanding role (he is bed-ridden and more or less immobile throughout) clearly illustrates Davies's ability not to be bound by stereotype but to sense some innate quality in an actor that other people may not have glimpsed. To some extent, it may be Davies's isolation from contemporary television culture that gives him a fresh eye, as was so strikingly shown in the case of Gillian Anderson. For although she was known to millions of viewers across the world in her role as an FBI Agent Scully in the American television series about the paranormal, *The X Files*, Davies had never even heard of the series when he chanced on her photograph. It is also true that, in *The House of Mirth*, Anderson reveals a sensitivity and technical versatility that *The X Files* does not even hint at. And it is not uncommon for the performances that Davies inspires in his actors to open new career paths for them; certainly her role in *The House of Mirth* has helped to advance Anderson's serious acting career, just as Pete Postlethwaite's performance in *Distant Voices, Still Lives* had earlier advanced his.

Davies frequently admits to being a stubborn perfectionist on set: 'I know I'm rigorous, and I know what I want. I can tell an insincere gesture or an underfelt line like that. For me, direction is performative. I see myself as brilliant as every single character. I'm a terrific Lily' (Winter 2000: 4). It is perhaps this ability to imagine himself as all the characters which, along with his minutely detailed shooting scripts, imparts such a strong sense of coherence to Davies's films and ensures that the cast are working on his terms and according to his vision, rather than competing individually for success. In this way, the films attain a powerful intensity and focus, while his characters achieve credibility through a simplicity of approach in which every gesture and inflection rings true. This applies to the child roles such as Bud (played by Leigh McCormack) in *The Long Day Closes*, the young Tucker (played by Philip Mawdsley) in *Children*, and both Davids (Drake Bell and Jacob Tierney) in *The Neon Bible*, as much as to the adults. Characters such as the volatile and sadistic father in *Distant Voices, Still Lives*, played by Pete Postlethwaite, or Freda Dowie as the patient and downtrodden mother in the same film, somehow infiltrate the spectator's imagination with an intensity that suggests that they are real people we have actually known, and their expressions and actions continue to haunt us long after the film has finished. In similar fashion, the passionate and exotic character of Aunt Mae (Gena Rowlands) in *The Neon Bible*, and the beautiful, principled but doomed Lily Bart (Gillian Anderson) in *The House of Mirth* create a deep and lasting impact on the viewer that completely transcends any earlier roles with which we may have associated them. Much of this power comes from the thoughtful attention to detail that marks all the performances, illustrated, for example, by the way in which Marjorie Yates, as the gentle mother in *The Long Day Closes*, communicates her extraordinary love and compassion through tiny, ordinary, everyday tasks such as ironing or washing up. But similar comments could quite easily apply to virtually all the characters we encounter throughout Davies's work. The loving and lively brothers and sisters who shape Davies's childhood world, like the neighbours and friends inhabiting the narrow streets of his Liverpool, or even the brittle social set in which Lily Bart tries to survive, succeed in capturing our attention and imagination, and in involving us emotionally and intellectually in their worlds. It is essential to recognise that the personal achievements of all the actors are in no way diminished if we say that their performances are ultimately shaped by Davies's directorial vision.

One of the ways in which Davies obtains consistently coherent and 'truthful' acting is by ruthlessly stripping away from individual performances any mannerisms and inflections that do not ring true, and also by knowing in advance exactly how he wants each role to be interpreted. It is particularly impressive that he contrives to do this without alienating his actors in whom, almost without exception, he inspires respect, admiration and affection. Davies claims that he is well aware of the danger of being too inflexible, and at the press conference held as part of the 2000 Toronto International Film Festival – which featured a retrospective of his work – he explained that, no matter how detailed the script may be, it is only a starting point, and that on set the director must be receptive to any subtle changes the actors themselves may impart to their roles, and be ready to accept these if they ring particularly true. 'They'll look or they'll use a hand gesture or they'll half do something, or forget something, and that's just magic. You can't direct that. No one can' (Walsh 2000: 5). However, the 'truth', of course, coincides with *his* interpretation, and, whilst there is undoubtedly an ongoing exchange of ideas between the director and the actors, nevertheless I suspect that most of it is in one direction. 'He was so passionately involved in the making [of *The House of Mirth*] that we all felt we had to live up to his imagination, which is boundless – how he pictured us in the roles. It was a challenge. A curious way to work. We were a lot of surly actors, we're pretty much used to doing whatever we want. And he wouldn't stand for that. It was a great experience', comments Eric Stoltz (who plays Lawrence Selden), at that same Toronto press conference (Walsh 2000: 4). Praise indeed from one of a group of already highly successful actors who, in order to work in Davies's film and on Davies's uncompromising terms, had been prepared to accept far less money than they would normally earn.

It is important to recognise that 'sincere' and convincing acting is not necessarily the same as 'realistic' acting. Given Davies's insistence on the unity of form and meaning, and his constant preoccupation with the rhythmic and visual structure of his films, it follows that his characters must function as signifiers in much the same way as the music or the camera. A number of critics found the slow and deliberate delivery of Gillian Anderson too 'artificial', by which they meant that it was not what they would call 'realistic' (in much the way perhaps that Davies's autobiographical films were earlier criticised for their excessive formalism and lack of 'realism'). But, as will repeatedly be seen, Davies never confuses his films with reality and as an intelligent and self-conscious director he not only recognises but actively foregrounds the fact that they are explorations of the nature of film and art as much as they are narratives. In *The House of Mirth*, therefore, the character of Lily Bart is conceived not only as the product of a particular society and morality but also as a filmic construct, a fictional identity whose origins are situated within the delicately ironic and deliberate language of Edith Wharton's novel.

The crew

If individual performances are subject to Davies's overall vision, the same is essentially true of those who work alongside him in making the film, since each member of the crew must be prepared to work on his terms, to achieve his vision. I said earlier that Davies was particularly miserable during the filming of *Children*, because the crew assigned to him (as part of the BFI award) made him feel inexperienced and inadequate. Given his legendary sensitivity, it is possible that this reaction was exaggerated, but all the same the experience was not positive, and from his second film (*Madonna and Child*) onwards, he has always selected individuals with whom he could empathise. As a result, a close bond generally develops between director and crew and this is reflected not only by the warmth with which Davies refers to them but also by their willingness to work together repeatedly (much in the European *auteur* tradition). If we take as an example the team working on *The Long Day Closes* – Mick Coulter (director of photography), Monica Howe (costume designer) and Christopher Hobbs (production designer) – we can see that they were originally chosen not only for their considerable skill and experience but perhaps also because they share certain background affinities with Davies (Coulter is a Glaswegian from a Catholic background; Hobbs and Howe grew up in the same period), and, significantly, they again worked with Davies on his next film, *The Neon Bible*. Similarly, Olivia Stewart, who was the producer for *The House of Mirth*, had earlier produced both *The Neon Bible* and *The Long Day Closes*, for she and Davies have developed a close bond of trust. In the detailed listings of the cast and crew of each film provided at the end of this book, it is fascinating to note these and other examples of overlaps between the films.

Essentially, in Davies's films, factors such as design and visual composition are just as vital to the construction of meaning as are the actors and the script. This point is acknowledged by Pat Kirkham and Mike O'Shaughnessy in a short but fascinating *Sight and Sound* feature on *The Long Day Closes*. 'Design in film is often neglected, but in the case of *The Long Day Closes*, together with the music, it is design that is largely responsible for the film's affectivity, making a significant contribution to its overall meaning and appeal' (Kirkham and O'Shaughnessy 1992: 13). In support of this claim, they quote Christopher Hobbs (production designer – see above), who explains that the cinematography in *The Long Day Closes* does not set out to re-create 1950s Liverpool, but to represent Davies's own very personal memories of place and time, 'I therefore went for a memory realism, which is not the same as real realism, and tried to create a child's eye vision of the world'.

The concept of memory realism, drawing attention to the way that external space functions as a metaphor for inner subjectivity, is particularly apposite in handling Davies's films, for it pinpoints a key characteristic of his technique which is the coincidence of inner and outer realities. In other words, it helps us to appreciate that in all his work the settings, like the costumes and props, constitute a vital component of the film's meaning and are never there merely for decoration or historical veracity. And it is within this context that Davies's apparently obsessive concern with colour and texture can be understood. It is well known, for example, that Davies chose to film *Distant Voices, Still Lives* with a coral filter, and then to process the film using a complex bleach bypass technique to desaturate the colours and create the appearance of hand-tinting. It is perhaps less widely appreciated, however, that he did not do this in order to achieve an accurate recreation of postwar Liverpool so much as to articulate his own experiences of what he remembers to be the period's inherent bleakness and fragility. And if the only primary colours in the film are the reds of his sisters' lipstick and nail varnish, this too has less to do with verisimilitude than with involving us on his terms in his experience of the feminine as the unique source of warmth and affection.[5] In collaboration with Coulter once again, Davies returned to the bleach bypass process for *The Long Day Closes*, but this time in such as way as to obtain a warmer and more glossy finish, with greater contrasts of light and shade. Thus from the most nuanced and subtle differences in tone and texture we can identify essential differences between the nature of the memories being explored in the two films, *The Long Day Closes* being, to a considerable extent, an exploration of a world shaped by the films and songs that so delighted his younger self. In *The Neon Bible*, Davies's first Cinemascope film, he and Coulter again worked together to create their version of a small town in the American Deep South by using the saturated vibrancy of the Technicolor films of Davies's childhood, the colours with which *Gone With the Wind*, in particular, had mythologised the region's history. It is often the case that Davies approaches mood and atmosphere by referring to remembered films, to photographs or to the work of particular artists. Rembrandt and Vermeer are frequently his inspiration for lighting and texture, and in preparation for the shooting of *The Long Day Closes* he and Coulter spent considerable time analysing reproductions of their paintings, as well as studying a series of 1950s Kodachrome photographs of Lancashire. In *The House of Mirth*, much of the inspiration for characters, costumes and interiors originated in the work of contemporary artists, particularly the society portraits by the American John Singer Sargent.

Editing and music

Terence Davies is passionate about music and will spend hours knowledgeably discussing his favourite symphonies or string quartets. This passion emerges through the range and variety of music he includes in his films, and the central importance he accords it (never relegating it to a mere background role, for example). However, the influence of music is perhaps even more significantly revealed in Davies's understanding of film itself as a musical form. The importance of this idea will be explored in greater detail later in this book, but it is worth commenting briefly at this point that, in any close consideration of how Davies structures and edits his films, the predominant principles can be recognised as musical, rather than reflecting a more traditional narrative logic. Therefore, when Davies speaks of editing as the source of the rhythmic structure (and inner meaning) of the film, he evaluates its success in terms of whether or not the film in question ultimately 'sings'. And when he embarks upon an analysis of a scene with which he feels somehow dissatisfied, as for example the Revivalist meeting in *The Neon Bible*, he does so by explaining that somewhere it has a missing 'beat'. Moreover, as was suggested earlier, Colin MacCabe's comment that in Davies's films the slightest alteration to one single element will inevitably have repercussions for the whole clearly supports the notion that the film itself functions as a musical composition since its meanings cannot be disassociated from its form.

Davies is of course not the only director to recognise the close affinity between music and film. While a whole range of other directors, notably including Tarkovsky, Bergman, Leos Carax and Angelopoulos draw similar analogies in relation to their own work, it would equally be possible to trace the notion back as far as Eisenstein's theories of montage, for instance, or to the motifs, repetitions and thematic modulations that structure early dada and surrealist works such as *L'Etoile de mer/Starfish* (Man Ray, France, 1928), or René Clair's exploration of visual rhythm in *Entr'acte* (France, 1924).[6] For his part, the French director Leos Carax believes filmic structures to be inherently musical, and this approach is best illustrated in *Les Amants du Pont Neuf / The Lovers on the Pont Neuf* (France, 1990), whose composition and editing were directly modelled upon Kodály's Cello Sonata Opus 8: 'I really wanted to construct the film like that sonata' (Thompson 1992: 11). Bergman's diary entry for 15 August 1970, written when he was in the process of planning *Cries and Whispers* (1971), reveals the extent to which he too conceives of film in musical terms:

> There is going to be a theme and different movements. For instance, the first movement will be about 'this tangle of lies'. It will probably turn out that each of these women will represent one movement, and the first movement will be a variation on this theme: 'This tangle of lies' will go on for twenty minutes without interruption. The words will ultimately become meaningless, and the behaviour will be out of sync; illogical forces that one cannot account for will come into play. It's possible to take away all the explanatory parts, all unnecessary and supportive lines and positions. 'This tangle of lies.' First movement. (Bergman 1994: 89)

Bergman's comments are particularly interesting, given Davies's long-standing admiration of his work and the widely acknowledged affinity between *Cries and Whispers* and *The House of Mirth*, and it is fascinating to note just how many characteristics these two directors share. Not only is Bergman influenced by particular artists when he is working, but his striking use of colour also serves to express inner feelings and emotions ('I have thought of the colour red as the interior of the soul'), while he conceives of silence and minute everyday sounds as key components of narrative meaning. In fact the work of a number of European directors in the 1960s and 1970s offers sustained and systematic investigations of the possibility of creating film according to specific musical principles. Significant examples might include Straub and Huillet's *Chronik der Anna Magdalena Bach / Chronicle of Anna Magdalena Bach* (Italy/West Germany, 1968), Delvaux's *Rendez-vous à Bray / Meeting at Bray* (Belgium, 1971) and Robbe-Grillet's *L'Eden et après / Eden and After* (France, 1971). Earlier, I referred to Marguerite Duras (who was responsible for some of the most challenging and haunting films produced at that time) as someone whose work may usefully be approached as a form of music, and I have argued elsewhere the possibility of seeing her films as examples of fugue (Everett 2000: 21–35). Recognising this quality in Davies's films provides a clearer understanding of their dynamics and their emotional power, and offers insight into the way they create meanings using a whole range of different 'voices' (which include but are not limited to those we have noted so far: acting, dialogue, colour, texture, rhythm, music, sets, props and so forth). Once this technique is recognised, the true complexity of the inner structures and inflections of Davies's films can be appreciated. The relationship between Davies and music will be discussed, in varying degrees, in the chapters that follow, and will be systematically developed and explored in Chapter 7.

Reception

A brief examination of the reception accorded to Davies's films makes it possible to situate him more precisely within the broader context of contemporary European film-makers and indicates dominant critical trends that will emerge in later chapters. I commented earlier that, given the originality and undoubted importance of Davies's films, it was difficult to understand why no single monograph had thus far been devoted to them. This situation would be inconceivable were he, for example, a French director, working in France, and I suspect that we may to some extent conclude that in Britain there is a certain hostility towards British-directed 'art house' movies. Of greater significance, however, is the fact that Davies's films are difficult to categorise as either realist or formalist, a feature that has led to a degree of critical wariness or frustration.

From realism to aesthetics: the key debate

The widespread enthusiasm that greeted the release of *Distant Voices, Still Lives* in 1988 served to kindle new interest in Davies's earlier *Trilogy*, as well as leading to his wider assessment as one of the most promising of contemporary British directors. For Geoff Andrew, for example, writing in 1989, Davies is 'arguably the most ambitious and most promising director currently working in Britain' (Andrew 1989: 72). But what chiefly characterised the British response at this period was the categorisation of Davies's films as essentially 'realist' by virtue of their subject matter, northern working-class settings, use of amateur or inexperienced actors, location shooting, unobtrusive camera and long focus. Moreover, Davies's working-class background and his marginalised sexual identity have frequently served to argue the 'authenticity' of his work. An article by Tony Williams written in 1993, 'The masochistic fix: gender oppression in the films of Terence Daves' (Williams 1993), foregrounds these two elements, as does Geoff Eley's essay 'The family is a dangerous place: memory, gender, and the image of the working class' (Eley 1995). However, in the 1980s, in a climate in which 'art' film still tended to be defined as the antithesis of realism, it was impossible to ignore the formal complexity and self-consciousness of the films, and lively debate about their identity continued for more than a decade in journals such as Screen (Neale 1981; Keighron 1991).

The release of *The Long Day Closes* in 1992 served to intensify this debate by making it increasingly difficult to apply the social-realist label. Key articles of the time, such as Caughie's 'Halfway to paradise', in *Sight and Sound*, were critical of the film's 'ironic self-consciousness', and its 'aestheticisation of drabness' (Caughie 1992: 12). In other words, the formalist concerns of the film were seen as an essential dilution of the (superior) realism of Davies's earlier work. The legacy of Caughie's article remains clearly visible for quite some time, resurfacing, for instance, in comparisons between the 'hard-edged' narrative of the Bill Douglas *Trilogy* and the blander cinema of 'nationalist nostalgias and clearer ironies' typified by Davies (Dick, Noble and Petrie 1993: 204), as in Sarah Street's description of Bill Douglas's work as 'much harsher', and less prone to 'aestheticised nostalgia' than that of Davies (Street 1997: 185).

Whilst indicating the shift in focus towards questions of memory and identity that mark critical debate at the end of the twentieth century, nevertheless what such comments reveal most clearly is not that Davies's films lack integrity in their treatment of the past but that they break the rules of realism as much as they satisfy them. However, instead of acknowledging and investigating the hybridity of their narratives, critics dismissed the non-realist elements as nostalgia. For quite some time, Davies was uncomfortably positioned within the British 'heritage' tradition, even if this required further qualification, as in the case of Powrie's 'alternative Heritage' (Powrie 2000: 317). On the other hand, if the 'personal revelation' and 'abstract imagery' of Davies's films did undoubtedly set him apart from the British documentary tradition (Quart 1994: 64), these same qualities also enabled him to escape the worst excesses of 'British parochialism' (Friedman 1993: 10), and the 'facile class conflicts' of 1960s British kitchen-sink realism (White 1993: 14). They also made it possible to position him within the wider

European tradition, later characterised by Orr as a cinema of 'spiritual and perceptual ambiguity' (Orr 2000: 53–4). In this move, Davies is linked with Jarman and Greenaway rather than with Bill Douglas, in a canon which generally includes Antonioni, Bergman, Bresson, Ozu, Resnais and Straub (Dixon 1992: 20; White 1993: 15).

General works about cinema

Confusion about the nature of Davies's film language is apparent also in more general volumes about cinema where his treatment is in any case patchy and erratic. There is, for example, no mention of him at all in *The Sunday Times 1000 Makers of the Cinema* (Morgan and Perry 1997), or in Robert Sklar's *Film: An International History of the Medium* (Sklar 1993), despite the latter's claim to provide a 'complete analysis of the major films, directors, and national cinemas'. This exclusion, in itself, reveals something of Davies's perception in Britain as a maker of 'difficult' and 'arty' films.

In all 766 pages of *The Oxford History of World Cinema*, published in 1996, and claiming to provide the 'definitive history of cinema world-wide', there are only two brief references to Davies's work (pp. 612; 613). The first places *Distant Voices, Still Lives* alongside *The Draughtsman's Contract* (Peter Greenaway, UK, 1982) and *Caravaggio* (Derek Jarman, UK, 1986), as examples of films funded by the BFI as part of its policy shift towards 'more *accessible* cinematic forms' (my emphasis), while the second links *The Long Day Closes* with *The Crying Game* (Neil Jordan, UK, 1992) and *Orlando* (Sally Potter, UK, 1992) as examples of 'art cinema' that have helped to sustain what it calls 'the last vestiges of British cinema'. Here art cinema, British cinema and accessible cinema are intriguingly and unusually brought together. Two years later, in *The Oxford Guide to Film Studies* (1998), Davies receives a single mention (p. 17), which places him, alongside Jean-Luc Godard, François Truffaut, Michelangelo Antonioni, Bernardo Bertolucci and Theo Angelopoulos in a list of examples of directors whose works attempt to create a counter-cinema that resists the dominant Hollywood structure. While this comment is uncontentious, as is the assertion that all these directors were influenced by Bazin, the explanation that such 'counter'-cinema is created by the directors' concentration upon 'the complex gaze of the camera rather than editing to construct their mise-en-scène' (p. 17), is unhelpful. Nevertheless, such comments continue to situate Davies within the broader European context.

Autobiography

Orr was one of the earliest to recognise that considering Davies's films as examples of autobiography might well permit a reconciliation of the perceived contradictions within his work. In *Cinema and Modernity*, he identifies the Douglas *Trilogy* and *Distant Voices, Still Lives* as part of an 'alternative' British cinema whose 'thoroughly modern' realist discourse rejects mainstream conventions of storytelling. More particularly, 'as autobiographical memory films reconstructing the past', he notes, 'they draw on the heritage of the British documentary, the highly charged poetic power of John Grierson and Humphrey Jennings. But they do so because they are part of the wider age of modern European cinema.' In other words, it is the discourse of autobiography that enables Davies's work to straddle British realism and the European art films, and 'the idea of a pristine 'realist' tradition hence becomes an unworkable fallacy' (Orr 1993: 47).

Orr's implicit suggestion that autobiography provides a form of 'crossover' narrative shows a degree of perception often lacking even among those critics who raise the autobiographical issue. Certainly, in Britain, autobiography has frequently tended to be confused with nostalgia and heritage, a stance that takes little account of its status as an inherently paradoxical form whose purpose, far from being a desire to escape from the present into a static, idealised past, must rather be understood as an attempt to understand present identity through the past. Autobiography is thus concerned with the constantly shifting relationship between past and present selves, and with the complex and multilayered processes of remembering, and its fluid and elliptical discourse is characterised by viewpoints which shift constantly through space and time. It is moreover an intensely self-conscious and self-reflexive discourse in which selfhood itself is understood as a filmic construct. Even this brief account, indicates clear parameters in which Davies's work can be viewed, and suggests that a helpful approach is to position him within a lengthy filmic tradition (stretching back at least as far as Jean Vigo's *Zéro de conduite / Zero for conduct* (France, 1932), and arguably even further), but whose true significance became apparent only through the rapid increase in the production and popularity of such films in Europe in the last quarter of the twentieth century. A clarification and development of the basic principles of filmic autobiography will therefore play a central role in the following chapters.

Notes

1 An edited version of this interview is included as Chapter 8 of this book, and is referenced henceforth as Everett 2001b.
2 This term, which is of current usage in contemporary film theory, is borrowed from the work of the French psychoanalyst Jacques Lacan (1901–81) who, in his analysis of the development of individual identity, pinpoints the significance of the male child's desire for its mother (Freud's Oedipal phase). As the authoritative figure in the family, the father prohibits the child's desire, imposing his rule linguistically, and it is this repressive and authoritative 'No' that is defined by Lacan as the Law of the Father.
3 For a more extensive list and discussion of autobiographical films sharing this and other characteristics with Davies's work see Everett 1996: 103–11; Everett 2001.
4 'Steptoe and Son' was a black comedy series about two rag-and-bone-men, which was first commissioned by the BBC in 1962 and was so successful that it continued to run until 1974, by which time it was into its eighth series.
5 In *Au revoir les enfants* (France, 1987), Louis Malle's autobiographical account of his life in a boarding school in northern France during the Occupation, we find a similar example of expressive colour. The entire film is restricted to a range of greys and blues as articulation of the cold, bleak memories he has. And the only red in this film is seen in his mother's lipstick, revealing her as the sole source of warmth and affection for the child.
6 Clair is one of the first to attempt to define the nature of filmic poetry and visual rhythm see, for example 'Cinéma pure et poésie' (Clair 1970: 145–56).

References

Andrew, G. (1989), *The Film Handbook*, Harlow, Essex: Longman.
Bergman, I. (1994), *Images: My Life in Film*, London: Bloomsbury. Translated by Marianne Ruuth.
Caughie, J. (1992), 'Halfway to paradise', *Sight and Sound* 2/1 (NS), May, 10–13.
Clair, R. (1970), *Cinéma d'hier, cinéma d'aujourd'hui*, Paris: Gallimard.
Constanzo Cahir, L. (2001), 'The House of Mirth: an Interview with director Terence Davies and producer Olivia Stewart', *Literature/Film Quarterly* 29/3, 166–71.
Davies, T. (1992), *A Modest Pageant*, London and Boston: Faber and Faber.
Davies, T. (1993), *Hallelujah Now*, London: Penguin Books. Originally published 1984.
Davies, T. (2001), 'Four songs at twilight', *Guardian*, 13 October, Saturday Review, 4.
Dick, E., Noble, A. and Petrie, D. (eds) (1993), *Bill Douglas: A Magic Lanternist's Account*, London: British Film Institute/Scottish Film Council.
Dixon, W. W. (1992), 'The Long Day Closes: an interview with Terence Davies', *Cineaste* 19/2–3, December, 20–3.
Eley, G. (1995), 'The family is a dangerous place: memory, gender, and the image of the working class', in Rosenstone, R. (ed.), *Revisioning History: Film and the Construction of a New Past*, Princeton: Princeton University Press, pp. 17–43.
Everett, W. (1995), 'The autobiographical eye in European film', *Europe: An International Journal of Language, Art and Culture* 2/1, Spring, 3–10.
Everett, W. (1996), 'Timetravel and European film', in Everett, W. (ed.), *European Identity in Cinema*, Exeter: Intellect, pp. 103–11.
Everett, W. (2000a), 'An art of fugue? The polyphonic cinema of Marguerite Duras',

in Williams, J. S. (ed.), *Revisioning Duras: Film, Race, Sex*, Liverpool: Liverpool University Press, pp. 21–35.
Everett, W. (2001), 'Film', in Jolly, M. (ed.), *Encyclopedia of Life Writing*, London and Chicago: Fitzroy Dearborn, pp. 323–4.
Falsetto, M. (1999), *Personal Visions: Conversations with Independent Film-makers*, London: Constable.
Floyd, N. (1988), 'A pebble in the pool & ships like magic', *Monthly Film Bulletin* 55/657, October, 295–6.
Friedman, L. (ed.) (1993), *British Cinema and Thatcherism*, London: UCL Press.
Hattenstone, S. (2000), 'First steps in show business', *Guardian*, 6 October, Review, 2–4.
Horne, P. (2000), 'Beauty's slow fade', *Sight and Sound* 10/10, October, 14–18.
Jivani, A. (1997), *It's Not Unusual: A History of Lesbian and Gay Britain in the Twentieth Century*, London: Michael O'Mara Books Limited, by arrangement with the BBC.
Johnston, T. (2000), 'Even my therapist hates my father now', *Independent*, 1 October.
Keighron, P. (1991), 'Condition critical', *Screen* 32/2, Summer, 209–19.
Kirkham, P. and O'Shaughnessy, M. (1992), 'Designing desire', *Sight and Sound* 2/1 (NS), May, 13–15.
MacCabe, J. (1999), *The Eloquence of the Vulgar*, London: BFI.
Morgan, R. and Perry, G. (1997), *The Sunday Times 1000 Makers of the Cinema*, London: Thames and Hudson.
Neale, S. (1981), 'Art cinema as institution', *Screen* 22/1, 11–39.
Orr, J. (1993), *Cinema and Modernity*, Oxford: Polity Press.
Orr, J. (2000), *The Art and Politics of Film*, Edinburgh: Edinburgh University Press.
Petrie, D. (ed.) (1992), *Screening Europe: Image and Identity in Contemporary European Cinema*, London: BFI.
Petrie, D. (2000), 'The new Scottish cinema', in Hjort, M. and Mackenzie, S. (eds), *Cinema and Nation*, London and New York: Routledge.
Powrie, P. (2000), 'On the threshold between past and present "alternative heritage"', in Ashby, J. and Higson, A. (eds), *British Cinema, Past and Present*, London and New York: Routledge, pp. 316–26.
Quart, L. (1994), 'Wartime memories', *Cineaste* XX/3, 63–4.
Radstone, S. (1995), 'Cinema/memory/history', *Screen* 36/1, Spring, 34–47.
Sklar, R. (1993), *Film: An International History of the Medium*, London: Thames and Hudson.
Street, S. (1997), *British National Cinema*, London and New York: Routledge.
Thompson, D. (1992), 'Leos Carax', *Sight and Sound* 2/5, September, 10–11.
Walsh, D. (2000), 'Terence Davies's *The House of Mirth*: a comment and a press conference with the director'. Reposting of a review by David Walsh, originally published 9 October 2000 as part of a series of articles discussing the 2000 Toronto International Arts Festival, and including an interview with Terence Davies. World Socialist Web Site: the International Committee of the Fourth International (ICFI), www.wsws.org/articles/2000/dec2000/mirt-d28.shtml.
White, A. (1993), 'Remembrance of songs past', *Film Comment* 29/3, May/June, 12–15.
Williams, T. (1993), 'The masochistic fix: gender oppression in the films of Terence Davies', in Friedman, L. (ed.), *British Cinema and Thatcherism*, London: UCL Press, pp. 237–54.
Winter, J. (2000), 'Terence Davies on the cruel inventions of *The House of Mirth*', *The Village Voice*, www.gauk.net/archives/2000/villagevi.html, 1–4.

Time, space and memory: the *Terence Davies Trilogy*

> Time present and time past
> Are both perhaps present in time future,
> And time future contained in time past.
> If all time is eternally present
> All time is unredeemable.
>
> ('Burnt Norton')

When, in 1976, during the summer vacation of his first year at drama school, Davies directed his first film, *Children*, with a British Film Institute grant of £8500, he was entirely untrained, with no previous experience in the medium, other than as a spectator. He still recalls with some bitterness the stressful and humiliating nature of the experience, claiming that nearly everyone in the crew hated the script, and resented his role, given his inexperience and technical incompetence. Luckily, of course, he also remembers, perhaps even more vividly, the intoxication of looking down the camera lens for the first time, and the excitement of actually creating the film's dramatic structure through the editing process (Falsetto 1999: 70).[1]

Shot in black and white, with a predominantly professional cast, *Children* may in many ways be recognised as the work of an inexperienced director who is learning the trade. Davies himself refers to it as his 'apprenticeship' film, pointing out that, with 46 minutes running time, it is slightly too long, and that its internal rhythms are not always entirely successful. He cites, as an example, his 'angora sweater' shot ('because by the time it runs through the projector, you can knit one'): a long, static shot of the mother and child on a bus which, lasting 2 minutes 20 seconds, is judged by Davies to be just too slow, held for just too long (Falsetto 1999: 73). One might equally argue that the camera is rather too static throughout the whole film; that the mood is too uniformly bleak and that the assured fluidity which would later become one of Davies's stylistic hallmarks is only rarely visible here. Nevertheless, the film is overwhelmingly powerful: its stark black and white images and dramatic use of chiaroscuro, particularly in its close-up shots of faces, along with the raw edginess of its visual compositions, convey the director's rage and despair with an often unbearable intensity, famously leading to one American critic's comment that 'it makes Bergman look like Jerry Lewis' (Kennedy 1988: 16). Moreover, in its intercutting between past and present and its thoughtful interrogation of the temporal and spatial constructs of memory, the film refutes any attempt to categorise it as 'merely' the work of a novice director. Rather, it emerges as the key statement of theme or subjects which Davies will continue to develop in varied and modulated form throughout his subsequent works.

In any case, *Children* should be considered not in isolation but within its immediate context as the first in a series of three autobiographical films (generally referred to as 'The Terence Davies Trilogy'), for it is obvious that it gains considerably more significance and impact from this position. The second film in the series, *Madonna and Child* (1980), was made by Davies as a graduation project while he was a student at the National Film School in London.² The *Trilogy* was completed with *Death and Transfiguration* (1983), which Davies filmed shortly after graduating. Almost from the beginning, therefore, Davies seems to have had something in mind which was further-reaching than the limits of a single film, and the overwhelming importance of this autobiographical project (which would not, of course, finish with the completion of the *Trilogy*) is overtly and repeatedly acknowledged. It is clear that for Davies the desire to make films, and the need to understand and come to terms with a painful past, are inseparably linked: 'The reason I began making films came from a deep *need* to do so in order to come to terms with my family's history and suffering, to make sense of the past and to explore my own personal terrors, both mental and spiritual, and to examine the destructive nature of Catholicism' (Davies 1992: ix). Thus, we can recognise in the films' bleak images a direct transposition of the topography of Davies's own experiences, in which key elements, already signalled in the previous chapter, stand out as clearly identifiable landmarks.

The three films which compose the *Trilogy* trace, more or less chronologically, the life of Tucker, a solitary, unhappy figure, tormented by his sexuality, and by the guilt bequeathed by his Catholic upbringing. Like Davies, Tucker lives and works in Liverpool and the spatial topographies of the city echo or articulate his own, a point to which we shall shortly return. Unlike Davies, however, Tucker cannot escape, although his doomed existence, which is explored in the narrative of the *Trilogy*, should be recognised as the route that will ultimately enable Davies himself to escape. (And it is, of course, significant that Davies was able to make these films only once he had actually left Liverpool.)

Tucker's childhood, depicted in *Children*, takes place (as did Davies's own) in a working-class quarter of Liverpool in the 1950s, and he too experiences the misery of a life terrorised by an abusive, brutal father at home, and by systematic and relentless bullying at school. Like Davies, Tucker must struggle alone and unaided to make sense of his growing awareness of his homosexuality, which was particularly difficult given its condemnation by the Catholic Church as a mortal sin, and by the state as a serious crime, so that it was a subject that could never be discussed or even acknowledged within his family or his social group.[3] The film includes the death of Tucker's cruel and abusive father, and vividly depicts the simultaneous terror and relief this event provokes in the child. *Madonna and Child* takes up the narrative some twenty or so years later, depicting a middle-aged Tucker as a solitary, depressed figure, employed in a local office, and living alone with his elderly mother. The hopeless future foretold in *Children* has now become a reality. The adult Tucker remains tightly imprisoned in his existential despair; his boredom and frustration at work; his increasingly furtive sexual desires and encounters; and his all-encompassing sense of guilt. What little gentleness there is in the film emerges through the filming of the mother, of whom the camera provides a series of softly lit, loving and delicate portraits; and the only moments of contentment occur when Tucker and his mother are together. Otherwise, the narrative is overwhelmingly bitter and angry. The film draws to a close with Tucker's nightmare vision of his own death and damnation, a sequence which is directly followed by a shot taken from the quayside where he catches the ferry to work each day. This shot, which visually mirrors the film's opening, is also accompanied by the same music, thus underlining the inescapable circularity of Tucker's unhappy existence.

A fade to black leads directly into the opening sequence of *Death and Transfiguration*. In this, the final and arguably the most complex chapter in the *Trilogy*, Tucker is portrayed as old and frail; he is physically immobile and unable to communicate. In this way, the isolation and mental paralysis which marked earlier depictions of the character reach their bitter conclusion. And, as if to foreground the overall stasis of trauma, the film's narrative is framed or contained by two deaths: it starts with that of Tucker's beloved mother, and ends with his own, lonely and unloved, in a bleak hospital ward. The three films together map an entire existence which, from the first, is portrayed as doomed; and despite their stylistic differences, and the increasingly assured and fluent techniques that signal Davies's evolution as a director, the mood remains predominantly black throughout, and the powerful undercurrents of rage and despair persist.

Even this brief and necessarily descriptive account of the narrative structure of the *Trilogy* does, however, indicate something of the originality which immediately marks the films as having a significance way beyond their status as early examples of a young director's work. For instance, it is clear that Davies not only recognises the multiple viewpoints and tenses of autobiographical discourse, exploring both his past and present selves, but also invents a future self – which is both real and fictional, both hypothetical and inevitable. Furthermore, the films also articulate his fantasies and his deepest fears and nightmares: 'In the Trilogy I was not only exploring literal truth – my relationship with my mother and father, my religious and sexual guilt – I was also examining my terrors', he explains (Davies 1992: xi). Through their stark and undifferentiated combinations of memory and hypothesis, of the experiential and the imaginary, of the oneiric and the routinely trivial, these films interrogate and contextualise the multiple and shifting tenses, moods and viewpoints of memory, in a reflexive and creative process in which, as we shall see, the spectator is directly implicated. And given that, as Davies repeatedly and insistently maintains, content always dictates form, it is clear that it would not have been possible for him to do this within a straightforward chronological narrative.

The structures of memory

Let us explore this idea further. If, earlier, I described the films as having a 'chronological' structure, I did so warily, and in only the most general of terms. For while there is undoubtedly a loose chronological framework – Tucker's journey from childhood to death – the actual narratives of the films, both individually and in relation to each other, are not linear. Rejecting the rules and established codes of classical découpage – or continuity editing – which require a seamless transition from one shot to the next, and function to ensure spatial and temporal contiguity and unambiguous, unproblematical narrative coherence – Davies instead brutally juxtaposes diverse times and spaces within a fragmented discourse which (re)creates the very processes of remembering and the multilayered temporality of memory.

It is here that we can recognise the relevance of the opening lines from T. S. Eliot's *The Four Quartets* which are quoted at the beginning of this chapter, and which could well serve as Davies's underlying hypothesis both within and beyond the *Trilogy*: that past and present are part of the future, and consequently that the future is already contained within the past. And like Eliot, whose poetry he so admires, Davies is exploring in his work the nature of time and memory in relation to identity, and is reaching similar conclusions. Throughout all three films, the apparent divisions between past, present and future, or indeed between the real and the imaginary, are entirely fluid and unstable since, like the deeply embedded processes of remembering, the narrative development is associative rather than linear. The diverse temporal and spatial loci of the films are thus tightly imbricated, one within the other; moreover, they are all depicted as equally 'real', and are all perceived by the spectator as equally present.

If we look more closely at the structural intricacies of this work, we can see, for example, that in *Children* the narrative constantly switches between Tucker as an adolescent and Tucker in his thirties, using unmarked, unexplained, irregular cuts that abruptly juxtapose the two periods within what appears to be the same spatio-temporal frame, in clear defiance of the classical norm. Moreover, although Davies's written script refers to the scenes where Tucker is in his thirties as 'the present', thereby seeming to identify other scenes as 'the past' (as we might expect in an autobiographical work), that is not necessarily the way in which the film is perceived; indeed we might equally, or even more easily, read it as being set in Tucker's childhood, with a number of intervening flashforwards. This reading is particularly plausible given that the majority of scenes depict Tucker as a child, and tend, on the whole, to be individually of longer duration than those in which he is an adult. The immediacy which is one of the specificities of the filmic image, of course, automatically suggests a continuous present tense to the spectator before whose gaze the action is actually occurring on the screen. To be read as past events, therefore, images must traditionally be contextually situated through editing, using such techniques as the dissolve or fade, with further and unambiguous support provided by a range of linguistic, visual and musical indicators. Davies, however, refuses to provide us with such pointers in that he uses exclusively unmarked jump-cuts to move from one period or place to a different one. The temptation might therefore be to consider that the techniques he employs in this film are fundamentally simple, given that the camera itself is almost uniformly static, and the focus almost always close. However, it seems to me that this formal 'simplicity' in fact provides a powerful indication not only of Davies's willingness, from the start, to disregard or flout all the accepted traditions of narrative film-making with which his passion for the Hollywood cinema of the 1950s would certainly have made him familiar, but also of his complex understanding of the nature of time and memory; of the way that the past intrudes constantly upon the present; of his recognition of the perhaps unique ability of film to affirm the presentness of the past. Despite its status as an 'apprentice' film, *Children*, then, should be recognised as innovative and original; the apparent simplicity of its editing creates a complex and multilayered temporality, just as the apparent 'realism' of its exterior images is – as will be seen – both construction and manifestation of a complex and multiple interiority.

I have described Davies's camerawork in *Children* as overwhelmingly static, reflecting the frozen trauma of the world he is exploring. However, it is interesting to note that there is one single occasion on which his camera provides an indication of the fluidity which will later become a hallmark of Davies's directing: in the closing sequence of the film, the child stands at the window crying. The camera moves outside, fusing in a single movement interior and exterior spaces, and revealing the child's tight containment within the domestic interior (he is tightly framed by the window), before it draws gradually upwards and away, to the accompaniment of the song 'Barbara Allen'. The child, the window, the house are thus placed into a wider perspective; we look down on the street, a tightly crammed geography of narrow terraced houses, narrow back yards, washing lines, tiled rooftops and smoking chimney stacks. Indeed this shot may be seen to provide a slight foretaste of the vertical travelling shot which establishes the internal topography of childhood in *The Long Day Closes*. However, the crane shot in *Children* does not create an equivalent sense of perspective or release: the events are still too close, too painful for that to occur. Nevertheless, in its uncompromising depiction of Tucker's entirely trapped existence, we see both the judgement of the remembering adult and his continuing anger.

It is true that this constricted childhood world expands slightly in the following film, *Madonna and Child*: individual shots are visually bolder and more dynamically textured than in the earlier film, with a more dramatic contrastive use of light and darkness, and a sense of potential release is signalled right from the opening sequence in which the camera reveals a new mobility as it follows the swooping flight of a seagull. However, any intimation of hope is quickly countered by our first sight of the now middle-aged Tucker since both his hopeless bearing and the screen's rigid framings show him to be frozen into a despairing immobility, as does the camera's immediate return to its former stasis. The narrative itself is almost entirely structured by abrupt and dislocating jump-cuts, and once again these are unmarked so that they conflate the different times and places of memory and imagination.

Even more brutally than in *Children*, Davies creates whole series of disturbing juxtapositions which vividly communicate the overwhelming sense of rage that underpins Tucker's guilt and despair. In particular, the most violent fracture is now situated in the relationship, or rather the dislocation, between visual images and sounds, a technique which enables Davies to endow his film with a new sense of spatial depth (as we shall shortly discuss), as well as constituting a powerful source of irony.

In *Death and Transfiguration*, Davies again uses the technique of direct and dislocated or dislocating cuts through time and space as reflections of Tucker's own fragmented identity. However, this last film is by far the most fluid of the three, in terms of both its camerawork and its editing techniques, as the narrative ranges restlessly through remembered times and places, from early childhood to old age, to which the dying man responds, but which remain entirely hidden from us. The concluding shot of the Trilogy shows Tucker, as a young boy, walking away from the camera, hand in hand with his mother as we hear her singing 'You're still the only boy in the world'; in other words, its conclusion (the death of Tucker, therefore an event located within a fictional future) actually leads us further back in time than the narrative has previously allowed, not only underlining, in so doing, the relentless circularity of subjective time, and suggesting perhaps 'an imaginary transcendental union with the maternal realm' (Williams 1993: 238), but also pinpointing the love between mother and child as a key element of transfiguration, possibly in relation to music; a point to which I shall return.

Unmarked jump-cuts and fragmented narratives have, of course, increasingly become part of the language of directors whose concern is memory and identity. One of the earliest and best known examples of this technique is found in *Hiroshima mon amour* (Alain Resnais, France, 1959), which intercuts, jerkily and without explanation, the heroine's present in Tokyo with her past in Occupied France, and thus faithfully recreates the processes of remembering and the nature of individual experience, as well as reflecting the subjective nature of identity and time. (The specific focus, in this example, is the painful and involuntary recall of suppressed and traumatic memories.) At the time when *Hiroshima mon amour* was made, its temporal dislocations were perceived as enormously challenging, both to accepted cinematic language and to audiences themselves, and, although the technique has now become reasonably familiar, none the less mainstream film still tends, on the whole, to provide various codes and pointers which will serve to avoid audience confusion. Even today, however, Davies's temporal dislocations in the *Trilogy* strike us as particularly brutal and disturbing, and this is at least partly due to that fact that they fragment not only the linear progression of the narrative but also the very close spatio-temporal relationship which is a characteristic of filmic discourse. For example, in these films abrupt jumps through time do not necessarily involve spatial change; it is as if the circularity of time is so overwhelmingly powerful that it contains space itself, or possibly that the containment created by the space is so powerful that it controls even the movement of time. It is important, therefore, for us to look in greater detail at the *Trilogy*'s use of space, and at the way Davies explores the spatio-temporal relationship.

Time and space: the geographies of memory

If the preoccupation with time as a complex phenomenon, illustrated of course in the work of writers and thinkers such as Proust, Bergson and T. S. Eliot, is generally considered to be fundamental to modernist thought, the postmodern period is frequently characterised by its concern with space or, in particular, with the complex relationship between space and time. Foucault, for example, sees this concern as a dominant feature of the contemporary period which he characterises as 'the epoch of space' (Foucault 1986: 22), while for David Harvey (1989) the radical changes in cultural, political and economic thought which signal the start of the postmodern era may be best understood as the direct outcome of dominant new ways of experiencing space and time (Harvey 1989: vii).[4] Fundamental to this new awareness is the recognition that space is at least as complex as time, quite possibly even more so. In other words, it is no longer possible to envisage space as the straightforward attribute of factors – such as area, volume or distance – that can be objectively and precisely measured and described. Instead, it must be recognised not only that our individual experiences and mental mappings of space are as subjective and complicated as our temporal awareness, but also that what we perceive as space is itself a social, mental and historical construct, something therefore which is inherently unstable and fragmented.

This debate assumes a particular significance when applied to film, given that the space/time dynamic is fundamental both to camera movement and to the editing process which, by juxtaposing static frames so as to achieve a dynamic reading, enables the director to range at will through time and space (Harvey 1989: 308). It is the very movement of its images that, disrupting the coherence and fixity of perspective, creates filmic space as dynamic and multiple (Heath 1981).

A beautiful example of the camera's ability to range freely through space and time is provided in *The House of Mirth*, in which a single and extended travelling shot transports us and the narrative from the rain of America to the sunlit shores of Monte Carlo, deliberately foregrounding the spatio-temporal dynamic. In the *Trilogy* too, the relationship between time, space, history and place is directly and variously posed, and Davies draws the viewer's attention to its complexity through a landscape of fragmented spaces, sounds and times. Through its framings and divisions, as well as through the images it projects, the screen presents us with a topography of mental spaces and subjective mapping; an architecture constructed and inhabited by impression and imagination, by memory and fantasy; a complex and fluid inner/outer world.

Liverpool

The setting for this inner/outer world in the three films we are looking at is, of course, Liverpool, and it is significant that the *Trilogy* is frequently referred to as the 'Liverpool Trilogy', in a (largely undeveloped) acknowledgement that Liverpool itself plays a major role in the films' narrative. It is interesting that when Liverpool does receive particular critical mention, it tends to be in articles which are concerned with Davies as a 'realist' director, with his relationship with the British documentary movement, and his social and sexual polemic. (As we have seen, such readings, which posit the film's engagement with concepts of evidence and mimesis, frequently reflect a misapprehension of the nature of filmic representation, as well as a failure to understand fully the autobiographical context of Davies's early works.) It is important, therefore, not to seek in Davies's films a faithful study of life in working-class Liverpool in the postwar years, since the viewpoint provided by his first-person camera will create something altogether different. Of course it is true that Liverpool is the context for the narrative, the container in which Davies's memories are quite precisely situated; and we can see how powerful he himself felt its controlling presence to be when, recalling his unhappy years as a drama student in Coventry, he remarks, 'it was not a particularly good experience *but at least I had got away from Liverpool*' (Falsetto 1999: 69, my emphasis). And, as I remarked earlier, it was not until he managed to escape from Liverpool that he was able to begin the process of making films, and in so doing to find the creative voice which would ultimately constitute his own salvation. But, crucially, the Liverpool that these films re-create is a subjective townscape which simultaneously shapes and is shaped by Davies/

Tucker. As locus of memory, the city we discover is thus both very limited in scope and very large in scale, reflecting on the one hand the extreme narrowness which marked Davies's formative childhood experiences, and on the other what Boorman, writing about his own autobiographical film *Hope and Glory*, refers to as 'the extreme close-up vision of infancy' (Boorman 1987: 19).

All urban space is rigidly subdivided into areas delineated by class, money, race, ethnology and so forth, and thus structured by a series of oppositional dialectics. In these terms, Davies's Liverpool is white, Catholic and working-class: it is composed of a close community, situated in a tight network of narrow streets and identical terraced houses. Reflecting his own childhood experience (and that of Tucker), the topographical parameters of *Children* reduce this small subsection of Liverpool still further, since within it the child's existence is entirely mapped in and between the confines of school, home and church. What we therefore see is a geography of containment, a landscape framed by buildings whose purpose is the social training of the child, the need to teach him his place in the world. And yet, as far as Tucker/Davies is concerned, he does not fit into these buildings or indeed into their vision of the future, for they offer, quite literally, no room for individuality, creativity or difference. The very configuration of the urban spaces in the film thus automatically positions Tucker as misfit (and we shall see how the prime cause of this as presented in the *Trilogy*, his homosexuality, can find expression only in the non-spaces of the city: subterranean, dark and hidden from view). Whilst the inclusion in the narrative of *Children* of shots of Tucker as an adult might be expected to extend the viewpoint somewhat, the spaces such shots reveal, the interior of a doctor's surgery, and the pavement of a busy road, for example, increase temporal distances without contributing any wider spatial perspective. And, significantly, both these two additional spaces are equally cramped and uncomfortable for Tucker, both serving to confirm yet again his position as social misfit. The only glimpse of even the possibility of a wider geography occurs, as has been seen, in the closing sequence of *Children*, but even here the camera is unable to rise above roof-top level, and cannot escape from the immediate surroundings of the domestic space in which the child himself remains transfixed. I remarked earlier that, at this point, the child is crying. He is actually crying for his dead Father from whose tyrannical and brutal Law he is still unable to escape, and the fact that his internal space and the domestic space of the home cannot here be separated clearly articulates the subjective (adult) viewpoint of the camera. There is one other occasion in *Children*, a bus journey, which might be expected to establish some sense of a wider perspective; to contribute some clearer awareness of the geography of Liverpool. However, although the bus moves, the camera does not. Positioned inside the bus, it concentrates, in a lengthy and static close-up (in fact, the famous 'angora sweater' shot) on the mother and child, both of whom are framed and trapped within the physical geometries of bus and window just as surely as they are isolated from the external world by their own internal despair. The subjective and reflective camera does not therefore allow us to focus upon the outside world, and the passing streets remain blurred, unreal and without definition.

It is true that *Madonna and Child* broadens these horizons a little to reflect Tucker's adult status by including his daily ferry trips across the Mersey on his way to and from work, and of course the daily routine of the office itself. I have already noted the new-found mobility of the camera which, in the film's opening sequence, tracks the movement of seagulls in flight. That, along with the fact that we focus on the fluid movement of the water and are also allowed a skyline view of Liverpool, would seem to indicate a widening of horizons and perspectives. However, this indication is misleading since even these clearly recognisable exterior spaces are flattened and contained within the two-dimensional framing of the screen. The very river seems devoid of its usual connotations of escape and change, not only for the protagonist whose isolation appears to make him oblivious of the changing flow of the water, but also for the spectator whose vision cannot break free of the tight framings. Seated on a bench on the moving ferry, Tucker sits hunched in an attitude of immobile despair, weeping silently as he will once again within the claustrophobic confines of the office. Moreover, the tall nineteenth-century buildings that border the River Mersey appear alien, distant and unfriendly. Indeed, all the important architecture of Liverpool configures the city as a distinctly masculine space, designed by male architects to be occupied and used by male merchants and traders. The capital and power that created Liverpool as a successful port and a major centre for Britain's colonial dominance in the nineteenth century remain firmly located in its public sphere in the mid-twentieth century.

That the struggle for representation within the spaces of the city is both social and architectural, as well as a key element in the articulation of identity, is recognised by Rob Lapsley in an interesting essay on cities and film, in which he states that:

> The politics of the city is a matter not only of capitalism's inequitable distribution of satisfactions and misery but also of the struggles around such issues as gender, ethnicity, age and religion, struggles in which

images and representations informing our sense of both self and reality are a crucial factor in the reproduction and contestation of existing social practices. (Lapsley 1997: 187)

Recognition of the importance of such struggles for representation, within the specific context of gender and sexuality, is fundamental to Susan Hayward's essay on representations of the corporeality of Paris in contemporary French cinema. She too notes the fundamental masculinity of its public architecture, and comments that women simply have no space or representation outside private, domestic places. In Davies's Liverpool, we see that one of the main spatial oppositions his films articulate is between the close intimacy of the women's spaces, hidden behind the net curtained windows of the terraced streets on the periphery of the town, and the wide-open, masculine confidence of the public spaces at its centre. Hayward also comments upon the virtual absence of gay and lesbian spaces either within French cinema or in the streets of the capital itself, and she notes that the two films which, in her opinion, constitute something of an exception in this context (*Les Nuits fauves/Savage Nights* (Cyril Collard, France, 1992) and *Gazon maudit/French Twist* (Josiane Balasko, France, 1995)) both situate homosexual identity entirely 'within the night time economy of the city' (Hayward 2000: 32). This observation is, of course, true in relation to the representation of gayness in European cinema in general, as well as having close links with representations of sexual desire in a number of *films noirs* of all nationalities; Davies's film too operates in a similar manner, for it is clear that the only space in which Tucker can express and situate his sexuality is in the hidden recesses of the city at night, down dark alleys and in subterranean public lavatories. And it is this geography of night and darkness, of the underbelly of the metropolis as locus for Davies's sexuality, that provides the only significant addition to the landscape of *Madonna and Child*. Moreover, neither of the two spaces whose representation in the final film of the *Trilogy*, *Death and Transfiguration*, widens the now familiar litany of school, home, Mersey, office, and the alternative hidden dark spaces of night could be said to broaden our perspective in any positive manner: the first is the crematorium in which Tucker's mother's funeral takes place, and the second the drab hospital where Tucker himself lies ill and dying.

Stasis, anguish and death frame and colour Davies's *Trilogy*, and if it articulates the inescapable circularity of time through its restricted range of settings and tight containment, the overwhelming sense of spatial enclosure or entrapment is powerfully reinforced by his use of editing. Abrupt and unmarked jump-cuts through space and time dissolve the boundaries which separate even the apparently discrete loci of memory: schools, church, hospital, the terraced house of childhood, the high-rise flat of the adult Tucker, boat, bus, public lavatories and tattooist shops are tightly imbricated, one within the other, fused inextricably as in Tucker's memory. It is not Davies's intention therefore to provide either a geographical or a sociological study of Liverpool in the 1950s, and, for all the apparent 'realism' of their images, the urban spaces his films articulate are the subjective spaces of Tucker's personal identity.

Architecture

> Architecture provides the articulation, the 'coupling', between mathematical or physical space and social space since every building occupies and restructures, outside and inside, a little bit of physical space and at the same time contributes to the production of social space, that is to say the mapping of the structures of social and economic space onto the physical world. (Forgacs 2000: 101)

In the *Trilogy*, architectural structures assume particular importance, dominating individual frames as well as projecting Tucker's history and suggesting his fate. In other words, the subjective identities of memory are contained and expressed by the buildings and places the films explore. Forgacs's account of architecture as the meeting point of physical and social space is not, therefore, entirely adequate, because it is equally important to recognise in this conjunction the spaces of memory, imagination and subjectivity. The *Trilogy* is not attempting a documentary-style verisimilitude, and for all the apparent mimetic realism of its shots of streets, buildings, and interiors it is essential to recognise these as reflections or representations of a subjective and personal universe. An interesting corollary is that, for the spectator too, access to this inner world is granted through the films' repeated shots of the particular buildings and sites that shape and contain it.

Through its deliberate, even painstaking detailing of the architecture of these places, Davies's camera explores and unravels the intricate and multiple layers of meaning they contain. We have already noted, in terms of Tucker's identity, the significance of the alien masculinity of the public architecture of Liverpool. Upright, rigid, complacent, such buildings automatically define Tucker as 'other', and position him outside their space. A further striking example of the alienating nature of architecture in the *Trilogy* is the secondary school which plays such a major part in Tucker's life. We are introduced to this building right from the first, since *Children* opens with a fade into a static shot of the school building whose large and forbidding exterior entirely dominates the screen. In his published screenplay, Davies describes it as 'an ageing piece of rambling Edwardian Catholicism', thus imbuing this space with a personal reading it would not necessarily otherwise impart (it is a *Catholic* building) (Davies 1992: 3). By using this building as the establishing shot, Davies intentionally foregrounds its significance within his autobiographical discourse, and its status as locus of trauma is further emphasised by the camera's intense and motionless concentration; we perceive it initially in what appears to be a still photograph, and this frozen image only gradually moves more fully into its function within the filmic narrative. The building we observe appears to be deserted. The road in front, leading nowhere, since it is contained as a short diagonal by the framing of the shot, is bare, empty and eerily silent. There are no sounds of traffic to support its function as road; it is a frozen space within the frozen shot. Yet somehow the very absence of people from what is immediately identifiable as a social space suggests a presence. And when we hear, off-screen, the indistinct sounds of children's voices, we do not know whether they are real or merely the ghostly memories contained within the building. It is impossible to identify their temporal status in relation to this deserted, even derelict building. The school is situated outside time; it is simultaneously and inescapably part of Davies's past, his present and his future existence.

In his essay on the films of Michelangelo Antonioni, 'The space between: photography, architecture and the presence of absence', Ian Wiblin discusses the way that, in his own photographs, it is buildings rather than people that shape his perception, buildings that provoke his initial response. The intensity of this response, he explains, reflects the fact that particular buildings constitute the discernible presence of their anonymous, transient, invisible inhabitants: 'The final photographs depict spaces where the people are both imaginary and absent' (Wiblin 1997: 106). What particularly interests him is 'the narrative potential that is somehow stored in seemingly empty architectural space', since this potential establishes a key link between photography and cinema, evoking in the spectator a creative and emotional reading of these spaces (Wiblin 1997: 107).

Wiblin's ideas may usefully be applied to Davies's use of architecture. By using a still shot of an empty building as the start of his autobiographical trilogy, he thus situates his narrative within its deserted premises, and invests his memories with its symbolism, while at the same time using it as an ironic distancing device signifying the judgement of the remembering adult. Form and content are thus brought together within its space, as are different times, tenses and viewpoints.

In a comment which can be directly related both to Eliot and to Davies, Wiblin notes how filmed architectural space appears not only to occupy the depicted present but, also to project a past and a future (Wiblin 1997: 108), and, as will become increasingly clear, Davies's films offer repeated illustrations of this phenomenon.

Perhaps the most striking feature of this opening shot is the powerful sense of menace and anguish that it imparts. Unlike Davies, we, the spectators, cannot at this point tell the narrative significance of the building (although its social status and standing are immediately recognisable), but nevertheless, we perceive this memory space to be curiously forbidding. Wiblin too recognises the sense of menace that is projected by buildings which have been 'witnesses of events and history, their resilient presence of symbols of a humanity evolving, decaying or unresolved. Such an edge must be inherent to buildings deliberately constructed as objects of oppression and intimidation' (Wiblin 1997: 107). Within the terms of Davies's narrative, there is absolutely no doubt that this building has been constructed as a place of oppression and intimidation; and it is fascinating that he has already prepared us for such an understanding through his long and motionless establishing shot, so that we are, at least partly, ready for the anguish occurring within its walls, which is where the camera leads us as it moves into the playground where Tucker is being abused by a group of bullies.

Like the concrete playground, the interior of the school is made up of rigid and inflexible barriers, shadows and angles which are simultaneously realistic and expressionist, reinforcing the confinement and inevitability of Tucker's life. The classrooms are dominated by rigid rows of desks; there are no curves, no hint of creative potential or flexibility. The spaces between the classrooms, mapped by long and menacing corridors and flights of steps, are entirely contained; the outside world is banned from this building, kept at a distance through high barred windows which offer no view. The learning process to which Tucker is subjected is equally rigid and inflexible, since it seeks to impose a 'macho' uniformity, based on violence and the repression of any form of difference or individuality. Within this aggressively male universe, Tucker's particular differences cannot be tolerated, and he is subject to constant physical and mental abuse. Even his attempts to appear to conform, his excessive politeness and subservience towards his teachers, and his determined application to his work, merely accentuate his difference.

If the story of Tucker's life begins with the architecture of the school, it ends with another social and public space, the hospital: and the two institutions are shown to have a great many features in common. Like the school, the hospital has a forbidding exterior, which clearly indicates its status and function, and is heavily redolent of the various histories that have occurred within its brick walls. Like the school, its interior functions as a rigidly controlled container; a mathematical and sanitised space that swamps and dominates the lives of those within, and shows little concern for individual sensibilities. In order to emphasise the close relationship between the spaces of hospital and school, Davies repeatedly cross-cuts between the two, and this cutting further heightens the sense of inevitability surrounding Tucker's situation, since temporal change is tightly contained within spatial stasis.

The interior of the hospital entirely dominates the patients it contains, emphasising their insignificance through its towering ceilings and rigid layout. The wards are structured by symmetrical rows of identical beds which depersonalise the patients in a process further enhanced by their treatment by medical staff who discuss them in an impersonal voice-over, as little more than collections of symptoms. The wards are joined to each other and to the various treatment rooms by a confusing labyrinth of seemingly endless and identical corridors, and again isolated from the outside world by high and sightless windows. But there is, nevertheless, an important difference between the hospital and the school we see in *Children*, for the rigid masculinity of the hospital space is subverted by the nurses, by the women who, as carers, align themselves with the maternal figure and thus with salvation. However automatically and efficiently they carry out their nursing duties, and however apparently scant their regard for their patients as individuals, it is they, for example, who decorate the ward for Christmas, allowing something creative and emotional to subvert its rigid interior, and it is a solitary nurse who chooses to watch over the dying Tucker. It is also significant that although Davies chooses, by cross-cutting, to imbricate school and hospital, the school in question is not the sadistic secondary school which opens the *Trilogy*, but an earlier one, the more gentle, caring primary school, run by soft-voiced nuns, that he attended between the ages of five and eleven. This male/female opposition, which is directly linked to the paternal/maternal divisions of home, will be a key structuring element of all Terence Davies's autobiographical films, illustrating what he sees as 'the enduring constancy of my mother, juxtaposed with the enduring, malign influence of my father (Davies 1992: xi).

Whilst Tucker's homosexuality as primary source of alienation and estrangement is only indirectly explored within the school and hospital scenes, it is openly dealt with in the film's scathing indictment of the Catholic Church. Like the other institutions we have looked at, the

Church is initially approached through its architecture, and again we have outside shots which reveal its social standing, and interior scenes where we observe more fully the Church in action. And although the Church constitutes a powerful (negative) presence throughout all three films, its interior spaces, its hypocrisy and its inflexibility are articulated in greatest detail in a lengthy sequence in *Madonna and Child*. I have already noted the anger felt by the adult Davies towards Catholicism's condemnation of homosexuality as a mortal sin, and for the sense of guilt and despair its teachings fostered in him from early childhood. In the extraordinarily complex and multilayered sequence in question, the adult Tucker is in church with his mother, in order to take confession. The sequence begins with the camera's fluid exploration of the church's vast and beautiful interior space. As it pans slowly round, it pauses briefly on a number of altarpieces, triptychs and icons, a series of representations of the Madonna and child. These provide direct reflection of the title of the film, as well as a self-conscious comment on the narrative content of the sequence in question, and the nature of the relationship between mother and son which is foregrounded in all Davies's autobiographical work. Davies also uses these icons and images to express his rage at the hypocrisy of the Church's teachings, and the ultimate failure of the institution to help either him or his mother. The radical innovation offered by this sequence is created by Davies's dislocation of sound and image. At first, as we are shown the interior spaces of the church, we hear sacred organ music, both architecture and music together defining the internal space of the church as place of sanctuary and worship. However, Davies then exposes the ultimate hypocrisy of this sacred space, by revealing its distance from, and indifference to, the world outside, to the real problems of its parishioners. Abruptly, and without disturbing the slow gliding camera movements, the soundtrack cuts to an explicit, angry, despairing telephone conversation between Tucker and a tattooist, as the former pleads and bargains for his genitalia to be tattooed. The lengthy conversation, crammed with crude Anglo-Saxon vulgarities, is rendered particularly shocking through its angry violation of the hushed interior of the church, and it automatically forces the spectators to acknowledge and explore the region between seeing and hearing, in its demand for a creative response. A further dislocation of sound and image occurs slightly later, and to similar effect, as Tucker himself takes confession. As the priest murmurs the ritual prayers, we actually see Tucker and an unidentified man engaged in oral sex. Again, the brutality of the juxtaposition shocks us into an active response. By conflating the inner spaces of church and the inner desires of Tucker's sexuality, Davies condemns the narrow inflexibility and the hypocrisy of Catholic doctrines, while the violent dislocation of sound and image creates a sense of depth, a new off-screen, non-representational space which the spectator is insistently required to explore. Significantly, this space also reflects an ironic and critical perspective which is entirely that of Davies, since Tucker, as we have already seen, is unable to escape the narrow confines of his existence. He feels anger and despair, but cannot escape his own sense of guilt, and therefore lacks sufficient critical distance to judge.

We have already remarked upon the identification of Tucker's sexuality with dark, hidden spaces, and it is now necessary to consider this again in relation to the architectural constructs of the *Trilogy*. As we have repeatedly seen, the dominant social buildings which structure so much of Tucker's life seem automatically to exclude him simply because he does not fit. In other words, they define Tucker as misfit because they are not sufficiently flexible to allow for individuality or creativity. Davies himself had to escape the containment of Liverpool before he could, through these very films, find the way to express his own identity. Since Tucker has no such possibility, he is condemned to remain a perpetual misfit. Within the strict confines of respectable Liverpool life, the only spaces which tolerate his difference are hidden, unacknowledged: the dark underground non-spaces of the city. Whereas the other landmarks contouring the narrative can therefore be examined in terms of their architectural construct and their roles as container, the subterranean spaces where Tucker wanders cannot be mapped. Tucker, like the spectator, is excluded even from the one gay club he knows (itself, of course, a non-place operating outside the law and hidden away behind walls and closed shutters), and is condemned to lurk in furtive shadows, in dark corners and sordid public conveniences. In one scene in which the camera follows Tucker as he heads despairingly for a public lavatory, it focuses entirely upon his feet, as he walks along the pavement and then, significantly, descends the steps which lead him under the ground, and out of sight. The anonymity imposed by the camera's concentration on his feet continues as it remains resolutely behind Tucker and the man he meets at the urinals. However, even within the domestic space of his home, Tucker does not have the freedom to express his identity or his sexuality, whether because of his father's violence, when he is a child, or his concern for his mother, in later years. His desires must remain secret; in his room, photographs of male wrestlers must be carefully hidden from view, shut away inside a wardrobe; at night, dressed in the black leather that replaces his daytime clothes, he tiptoes furtively down the stairs and out into the darkness in search of some form of freedom.

By using architectural structures as both exploration and articulation of subjective identity and viewpoint, Davies reveals the extent to which our childhood experience shapes our spatial awareness, contours our individual worlds, 'floods private and public spaces, [undoing] their readable surfaces, and [creating] within the planned city a "metaphorical" mobility' (de Certeau quoted in Jenks 1995: 82). It is obvious, therefore, that any attempt to seek in the *Trilogy* a recreation of working-class life in postwar Liverpool, that is, to attempt to use the films as a form of social documentary, is fundamentally misguided, since it is not Liverpool that the films re-create but the Liverpool of a particular childhood experience. However, it is worth remembering that the use of apparent mimesis to articulate subjective viewpoint is in any case a fundamental characteristic of film discourse. Lacking abstraction, the concrete and apparently realistic images of film must always be recognised as representation not reproduction; the concrete images which the film director must work with thus constitute what Deleuze calls 'a language system of reality', in which the false semiological distinction between the object as mere referent and the image as component of the signified breaks down (Deleuze 1989: 128–9). As Orr points out, it is essential to recognise that 'subjectivity is conveyed through the objective shot, not the POV (point-of-view) shot' (Orr 1998: 2–3). It would seem that the failure to recognise this fundamental point was responsible for the fact that a good many British critics, faced with the apparent 'realism' of Davies's stark world, chose to situate the *Trilogy* within the British documentary tradition.

The question of just where Davies's films should be situated, of the influences that shape his vision, is fascinating and complex, and is one that will repeatedly feature in this study. And whereas it is impossible not to recognise, particularly in his later autobiographical work, the repeated homage to Ealing comedies, and to the overwhelming centrality of American popular culture within his childhood world, the films in the *Trilogy* are somehow too raw, too bitter in their exploration of experienced and imagined misery, to permit any such positive memories. In reviewing the question of influences upon his early work, Davies himself is somewhat reticent, claiming, for example, that, at the time of making *Children*, he had limited experience of films outside mainstream English and American. However, any analysis of his syntax and imagery almost inevitably leads to a frame of reference which includes such directors as Bresson, Bergman and indeed the whole European tradition of experimental, subjective and retrospective narration. But it is no less important to recognise the vast range of other cultural influences and concerns which underpin all of Davies's films; explicit and implicit references to literature, theatre, music and art play an equally vital role within their complex narratives.

Despite all this, it is the intense originality of Davies's work that constitutes its greatest fascination and this originality is apparent right from his earliest films. Thus, the *Trilogy* provides a vital insight not only into the themes and subject matter which will continue to dominate later works, but also into the actual development of Davies's innovative style and techniques. We have already noted the films' complex narrative and temporal fragmentation, for example, and the slow, fluid and contemplative camera movements which will characterise all his work. We have also discussed examples of the way in which, by radically dislocating sound and image, he imbues the film with a powerful off-screen space in which conflicting viewpoints and ironies, which are the hallmarks of autobiographical memory, can be articulated. If the *Trilogy* provides a bleak account of suffering and hopelessness, of anguish and despair, it is must also be recognised as the vehicle of salvation, as the final scene of *Death and Transfiguration* seems to suggest. The *Trilogy* has been seen as 'a grave, intelligent, and strangely uplifting account of the human soul's capacity to triumph over physical degradation' (Andrew 1989: 73), but the key to any such 'triumph' is of course film itself. Davies will almost obsessively return to his painful past in his next two films, *Distant Voices, Still Lives* and *The Long Day Closes*, but as in music, which his films so closely resemble, the familiar themes and subjects will appear in modulated forms, and these changes through time will enable us to chart Davies's increasing control not only of his medium but of the very memories which the films articulate: 'involved with past and future. Only through time time is conquered' (Eliot 1959: 16).

Notes

1 Despite the atmosphere he found so difficult at the time, Davies frequently acknowledges his gratitude to Sarah Ellis, who was his editor on this project, for her unfailing patience and guidance.
2 Jennifer Howarth, a fellow student at the National Film School, and his future producer for *Distant Voices, Still Lives*, recalled, in an interview with the author in 2001, how Davies's work already shone out from that of his fellow students at the time.
3 As was seen in the previous chapter, homosexuality remained a criminal offence in Britain until the passing of the Sexual Offences Act in 1967, following the publication of the Wolfenden report. This act decriminalised homosexual acts between consenting adult males in private in England and Wales. However, it was not until 1992 that the age limit was lowered to eighteen.

4 Key theorists on space include Gaston Bachelard, Walter Benjamin, Noel Burch, Henri Lefebvre.

References

Andrew, G. (1989), *The Film Handbook*, Harlow, Essex: Longman.
Boorman, J. (1987), *Hope and Glory*, London and Boston: Faber and Faber.
Davies, T. (1992), *A Modest Pageant*, London and Boston: Faber and Faber.
Deleuze, G. (1989), *Cinema 2: The Time-image*, London: Athlone Press. Translated by Hugh Tomlinson and Robert Galeta.
Eliot, T. S. (1959), *Four Quartets*, London: Faber and Faber.
Falsetto, M. (1999), *Personal Visions: Conversations with Independent Film-makers*, London: Constable.
Forgacs, D. (2000), 'Antonioni: space, place, sexuality', in Konstantarakos, M. (ed.), *Space in European Cinema*, Exeter and Portland, OR: Intellect, pp. 101–11.
Foucault, M. (1986), 'Of other spaces', *Diacritics* 16/1, Spring, 22–7. Translated by Jay Miskowiec.
Harvey, D. (1989), *The Condition of Postmodernity: An Enquiry into the Origins of Cultural Change*, Oxford: Blackwell.
Heath, S. (1981), 'Narrative space', in *Questions of Cinema*, London: Macmillan, pp. 19–75.
Jenks, C. (ed.) (1995), *Visual Culture*, London and New York: Routledge.
Kennedy, H. (1988), 'Familiar haunts', *Film Comment* 24/5, September–October, 13–18.
Lapsley, R. (1997), 'Mainly in cities and at night: some notes on cities and film', in Clarke, D. (ed.), *The Cinematic City*, London and New York: Routledge, pp. 186–208.
Orr, J. (1998), *Contemporary Cinema*, Edinburgh: Edinburgh University Press.
Wiblin, I. (1997), 'The space between: photography, architecture and the presence of absence', in Penz, F. and Thomas, M. (eds) (1997), *Cinema & Architecture: Méliès, Mallet-Stevens, Multimedia*, London: BFI.
Williams, T. (1993), 'The masochistic fix: gender oppression in the films of Terence Davies', in Friedman, L. (ed.), *British Cinema and Thatcherism*, London: UCL Press, pp. 237–54.

'A pattern of timeless moments': *Distant Voices, Still Lives*

> Time past and time future
> Allow but a little consciousness.
> To be conscious is not to be in time
> But only in time can the moment in the rose-garden,
> The moment in the arbour where the rain beat,
> The moment in the draughty church at smokefall
> Be remembered; involved with past and future.
> Only through time time is conquered.
> ('Burnt Norton')

Davies's obsession with time and memory, and his overwhelming need to address his past, continue into his next film, *Distant Voices, Still Lives* (1988), an astonishing work, 'a pattern of timeless moments' (Davies 1992: 74), in which the camera slips freely through time and space, weaving in and out of memories and viewpoints in a composition which is far closer to music than to conventional narrative, but whose heart is the silence and stillness of its title. If in the *Trilogy* Davies experiments with the circularity of time by 'remembering' his future, in *Distant Voices, Still Lives* he 'remembers' a time which, at least for the most part, preceded his personal experiences and observations. The autobiographical project is thus rendered increasingly complex, here being less the articulation of Davies's direct personal memories than those of his mother, his two older sisters, Eileen and Maisie, and his older brother Tony. For Davies, their stories of this period, repeatedly told to him as a child, were so vivid that they entered his imagination, becoming to all intents his own (Davies 1992: xi). *Distant Voices, Still Lives* thus presents a fascinating blend of personal memory and myth, of subjective involvement and distance, which creates a multiplicity of layers and meanings that is far more complex than anything achieved in the *Trilogy*, and demonstrates a new fluency and a new sense of artistic perspective.

As the title implies, *Distant Voices, Still Lives* is actually constructed from two distinct, yet entirely interrelated films, which were made in 1986 and 1988 respectively. The setting, once again, is Davies's native Liverpool, and the subject matter is domestic, focusing upon his family in a period which, in *Distant Voices*, ranges from 1940 to the mid- (and, on one occasion, late) 1950s, and, in *Still Lives*, concentrates on the late 1950s. Davies does not represent himself in the narrative, which, as suggested earlier, is instead composed of the fragmented memories of his mother and older siblings (so that the dynamics of tense and viewpoint are particularly fascinating). Each of the two component films is framed or shaped by the rituals of traditional family life: *Distant Voices* centres on Eileen's wedding, which is tightly interwoven with the funeral of the father, while *Still Lives* opens with the birth and christening of Maisie's daughter, and ends on the evening of Tony's wedding day. As I have already implied, there is no conventional narrative development (because, as Davies explains, 'the film is about memory, and memory moves in and out of time all the while'), and the temporal and spatial slippages are unmarked and unexplained ('I had to find a way of saying, you're not going to see "what happens next"') (Floyd 1988: 295). Once again, therefore, the viewer is obliged to participate creatively and directly in the experiences of the film. Davies would argue that the 'arbitrary' and elliptical structure of the film is an inevitable consequence of its subject matter since memory does not move in a logical or linear way; its circular and repetitive patterns reflect the emotional importance of events, not their chronological sequence (Davies 1992: 74). In a study of the films of Jean-Luc Godard, Sterritt provides a useful comment about this attribute of memory, pointing out that its very arbitrariness 'makes it an antidote to the calculated strategies of "normal" storytelling, and an exciting source of material for a filmmaker who values cinema as a vehicle for intuition, speculation, and discovery' (Sterritt 1999: 231). It is clear that *Distant Voices, Still Lives* can be seen in just such terms.

Background

Before we look in more detail at the narrative and formal composition of *Distant Voices, Still Lives*, it is helpful to understand something of the film's context, both within Davies's developing career, and in relation to British cinema of the time.

Distant Voices, the first of the two films, was made in 1984, with financial backing from the British Film Institute Production Fund. This fund provided an essential lifeline to young British directors at the time, having, since the late 1970s, concentrated its support on precisely the sort of experimental low-budget feature films that they were making. Examples of such films include *Radio On* (Chris Petit, 1979), *The Gold Diggers* (Sally Potter, 1983) and *The Draughtsman's Contract* (Peter Greenaway, 1982). Given the Thatcher government's antagonism towards cinema, its refusal to view film in artistic or cultural terms, its implacable opposition to any form of subsidy, its abolition of the Eady Levy, and its closure of the National Film Finance Corporation (NFFC), it is somewhat ironic that so many retrospective accounts of British cinema in the 1980s present the period as an exceptionally exciting one.[1] In Colin MacCabe's account of taking over from Peter Sainsbury in 1985 as head of the Production Division of the BFI we find a vivid description of a period which was characterised, on the one hand, by an intense creative output and, on the other, by the extreme underfunding and staff shortages which were the direct result of Thatcherite policies. MacCabe also notes the particular irony of the fact that it was the increased final tranche of funding heralding the abolition of the Eady Levy that allowed the making of such key and – ironically – oppositional works as Jarman's *Caravaggio* (1986), Greenaway's *A Zed and Two Noughts* (1985) and, of course, Davies's *Distant Voices, Still Lives* (MacCabe 1999: 12–14). And it is within this context that MacCabe records at length the making of *Distant Voices, Still Lives*, starting with his recollection of the immediate impact of *Distant Voices* when he first watched it, early in 1986:

> Although I had thought the script brilliant, nothing prepared me for the force and violence of Terence's memoir of his working-class family. The trilogy of short films he had already made had shown Terence a talented director but with real resources at his disposal he proved himself a genius. There was only one problem. The film was only 45 minutes long and, although it could be assured of a very successful life on the festival circuit, it would never reach any wider audiences. I knew, however, that Terence had always wanted to make a companion piece on the family (set some ten years later) and if one put two 45-minute pieces together one would have a film that could be shown in cinemas round the world. The risk, however, was enormous: we would sit on a great film and let no-one see it while Terence wrote a new film from scratch which we would then have to finance, shoot and edit. If I had any doubts they were soon dispelled. The Board was adamant we should go for a feature. Channel 4 were equally clear that they would provide additional money to pay for most of the second half. Over the next two years, as other films came and went, I was conscious that we had a work of genius up our sleeve – although there were bad 3-o'clock-in-the-mornings when I feared that

the actors might die or that Terence would lose his touch. Such moments were rare and were more than compensated for when in May 1988 we screened *Distant Voices, Still Lives* in the Director's Fortnight at Cannes to tumultuous acclaim. With the International Critics Prize under its belt, the film went on to be one of the art-house hits of the year around the world. (MacCabe 1999: 16)

With MacCabe's encouragement, the extra funding provided by the BFI and Channel Four thus enabled Davies to write and film *Still Lives* as the sequel to *Distant Voices*, and to obtain the wider distribution that is essential if a director is to become known. In this and other ways, he was fortunate. The whole purpose of the Production Board at that time was to enable talented directors to reach their potential without needing to take account of commercial constraints, so that, although his budget was relatively small (£750,000), Davies was able to make the film he wanted to make, without needing to compromise. (As has already been seen, his methods of filming do, in any case, always take scrupulous account of the finance and time available.) Moreover, in any terms, £750,000 represented a considerable advance on the total budget of £46,000 he had for making the *Trilogy*.

Reception

MacCabe's account gives a clear indication both of the qualities he immediately recognised in Davies's film ('a work of genius') and of the widespread success which greeted its release. The award of the International Critics Prize at Cannes where, in the words of one of one of the film's reviewers, 'it outshone almost every other movie' (Kennedy 1988: 13–14) was only the first of a host of prestigious international prizes, and the film quickly achieved a cult status, which it retains today.[2] *Distant Voices, Still Lives* therefore should be recognised as the film which brought Davies's work to the attention of a wider national and international public, and did much to establish his reputation for 'unnerving originality' (Kennedy 1988: 14). Orr considers it to be 'one of the great films of the 1980s', inviting comparison with Bergman, particularly in its depiction of family as 'collective subject' (Orr 1998: 11), and it is because of this film that Davies was recognised not only as 'Britain's most exquisitely gifted film-maker' (Horne 2000: 14) but as one whose work was fundamentally 'revolutionary' (Hattenstone 2000: 2). In this context, it is fascinating to learn that when Jean-Luc Godard, in conversation with Colin MacCabe in the early 1990s, commented that there was no longer such a thing as a British film industry, and that in any case 'the British were never very gifted movie-makers', he acknowledged a single exception to his sweeping and dismissive judgement: *Distant Voices, Still Lives* (Petrie 1992: 102).

This is not to say, of course, that, at the time of its release, the film was given a unanimously positive reception, nor even that it was necessarily widely understood. It is perhaps a measure of the film's complexity and its power that it has spawned a whole host of contradictory critical readings, varying from the eulogistic to the acerbic, and that, at the same time, it should have directly affected such a wide range of spectators; for, as Davies comments, 'people all over the world have said that they've seen their own childhood on the screen' (Floyd 1988: 296). It is also significant that the debate still continues, thus making it possible to trace the dominant critical trends of the past decade through the various readings of this film.

One key area of critical debate concerning *Distant Voices, Still Lives* centres, not surprisingly, on realism and the British social documentary tradition. As was seen in the previous chapter, the *Trilogy* was widely considered to be a realist film, located firmly within this tradition by its stark black and white images and its 'realistic' portrait of working-class Liverpool in the 1950s. But I also noted how misleading such treatment could be, given its tendency to ignore both the essential subjectivity of the screened world and the complexity of the filmic construct. Once again, the subject matter of *Distant Voices, Still Lives*, its harrowing memories and minutely detailed domestic setting, encouraged critics to locate it within the British documentary or realist tradition. Such readings could find support in Davies's claim that his intention in the film had been 'to show life the way it was back then' (Kennedy 1988: 16). Furthermore, the film appeared to fulfil the widely accepted criteria of 'realism': deep focus, long shots, location filming, social subject matter, northern working-class setting, lack of stars and so forth. Indeed, in comparison with the 'realist' cinema of the British New Wave films of the late 1950s and 1960s, *Distant Voices, Still Lives* seemed somehow *more* authentic, *more* true to life, because of the social origins of its director. Critics repeatedly commented on the fact that Davies was working from within the working-class culture rather than from outside (see, for instance, Dixon 1994: 251), a suggestion which Davies himself seemed to support: 'I can't think of any film that really captured what it felt like to be working class because working-class people didn't make movies' (Williams 1996: 66).

Nevertheless, any readings of the film as exemplifying social realism were forced to take account of both its extreme self-consciousness and its formal complexity, those very qualities which were traditionally used to define 'art' film as the antithesis of realism (see for example, Neale 1981: 11–39). One typical response was to view the non-realistic elements of *Distant Voices, Still Lives* as a fundamental flaw in its make-up. Street, for example, compares Davies's work unfavourably with that of Bill Douglas, whose films she finds 'much harsher', and less prone to what she calls 'aestheticised nostalgia' (Street 1997: 185). Caughie too seems not altogether convinced by what he calls the film's 'aestheticised drabness' (Caughie 1992: 12). And, less subtly, the author of a review of *Distant Voices, Still Lives* in the *Washington Post*, failing to reconcile the film's uncompromising realism ('a funeral would be a day at the beach in comparison') with its formal complexity, simply gives up, exclaiming: 'Oh no! Form versus content!' (Howe 1989).

Almost every analysis of the critical reception accorded to *Distant Voices, Still Lives* seems to reveal evidence of the struggle to resolve the apparent conflict between its realist and its formal characteristics: on the one hand, it is seen as 'a mirror held up to a country, a family, and a time' (Kennedy 1988: 14), 'a gruellingly matter-of-fact document of everyday cruelty' (Barker 1988: 294) or a 'finely constructed study of working-class life' (Eley 1995: 25), on the other as a 'daring aesthetic experiment', characterised by 'brilliant formal stylistics' (Falsetto 1999: 67). And, quite often, there is the suggestion that the two approaches are simply not compatible, that 'rigorous formal composition', for instance, inevitably indicates a lack of concern with cultural, historical and psychological explanations.

It is tempting to suggest that our perceptions of the nature of filmic realism have altered so radically since the 1980s that such reactions would no longer occur. After all, looking back at the last two decades of the twentieth century, Higson points out 'the eclipse of the realist discourse in British film criticism and the ascendance of auteurism' (whereby, he would argue, even 'realist' directors such as Ken Loach are perceived as *auteurs*). For Higson, this shift is part of a general recognition that tensions between social and aesthetic features have *always* existed within so-called realist films (Higson 1998: 504). In similar vein, Christopher Williams suggests that the dominant British film tradition was never, in fact, realism, but social, or more precisely a form of 'social-diffuse' cinema, and his suggestion that most of the films made in Britain in the 1980s should be characterised not as either 'realist' or 'art' cinema but as 'social art cinema', a new and more hybrid form which brings together traditional social realist discourse within the more self-conscious narratives of the European art cinema (Williams 1996: 190–200). Many of Williams's ideas were later developed by Martin Hunt in an article entitled 'The poetry of the ordinary: Terence

Davies and the social art film' (Hunt 1999). Hunt argues that Davies's work is central to the 'new mode of British film practice' identified by Williams, but that it is, above all, his postmodern aesthetic that allows his films to operate successfully within both the British and the European traditions.

However, despite the increasing flexibility and broader readings that mark much recent thinking, British critics are still sometimes uneasy about the attempt to reconcile 'realism' and 'art' cinema. One typical example can be found in an article published in *Screen* in 1991, in which Peter Keighron sets out to study the response of left-wing critics to *Distant Voices, Still Lives* and *A Very British Coup* (Mick Jackson, 1988), films made in the same year and confronting a range of issues of 'class and politics in British society and history' (Keighron 1991). This is an interesting piece of research, which raises a number of useful points in relation to film criticism and political debate. However, a certain confusion is revealed from the start, as Keighron examines the responses to *Distant Voices, Still Lives* provided by what he classifies as 'dominant right wing' or 'mainstream' criticism. The first point to note is that, whilst he presents these two categories as synonymous, he fails to explain his reasons (the reviews he quotes from are taken from *The Times* and the *Mail on Sunday*, for example, but also from the *Observer* and the *Guardian*); however, the defining characteristic of both would seem to be evidence of any attempt to approach the film in terms of its artistic or formal identity, particularly if, in so doing, the reviewer suggests a universality of appeal or meaning that transcends the film's particular working-class context. Thus, both David Robinson's suggestion that *Distant Voices, Still Lives* can be viewed as 'a metaphor for the human condition that strikes universal chords', and Philip French's belief that 'films that appear most local and concentrated are often the most universal in their appeal', are treated by Keighron as examples of criticism operating as 'the denial of the social world'. Equally suspect, in his opinion, are any attempts to situate the film within a broader artistic context, alongside, for instance, the writings of Lawrence, Eliot or Proust, or the films of Bresson, since to do so, he maintains, presupposes a familiarity with other texts and artists that automatically excludes the working class for whom the film was made.

Although we might wish to take issue with a number of areas of this argument, not least that art necessarily smacks of privilege, and that the working class is incapable of dealing with broader perspectives or references, the significance of this article is that it provides a clear example of the desire to impose a narrow specificity on both the film and its critical treatment. It can be argued that Keighron's discovery that even the reviews in 'core' left-wing journals (interestingly *Socialist Worker* and *Morning Star* seemed to be the only two he could find) show both an unwillingness to use the film to initiate political debate, and a tendency to applaud its universal and aesthetic values, does not so much reflect the fact that 'the mainstream operates a hegemony in the area of critical discourse' (as he concludes) as that it is simply not possible to approach this (or indeed any) film in quite such polarised and unambiguous terms.

It is the need for more flexible readings of *Distant Voices, Still Lives*, able to reflect the film's combination of the historical and the sociological with the aesthetic and the stylistic, that provides the starting point for Tony Williams's essay, 'The masochistic fix: gender oppression in the films of Terence Davies' (Williams 1993). For Williams, the film's eschewal of traditional realism in favour of more self-conscious and stylised representations provides proof of Davies's recognition that traditional British cinematic discourse could not effectively oppose Thatcherism, and that such opposition necessitates the creation of an 'alternative' form of British cinema (Williams 1993: 239). In other words, for Williams, *Distant Voices, Still Lives* is a film in which Davies deliberately contests the dominant political discourse of the 1980s. Within his thesis, the most obvious site of this opposition is situated in the film's masochistic associations which create 'a cinema based upon unpleasure rather than the typical cinematic mechanism of pleasure'. He argues that *Distant Voices, Still Lives* cannot therefore be understood outside the immediate context of Thatcherite policies based upon traditional family values and reflected in her virulent attack on all manifestations of the 'permissive society', especially single-parent families and gays.

This essay too makes a number of useful and interesting comments, particularly within its context of a work about film and Thatcherism. Moreover, its attempt to reconcile the apparent conflict between content and form by positing them as a conscious oppositional move on Davies's part does provide a way out of the sort of critical impasse noted above. And, of course, it is certainly true that this period of British film history offered a striking proliferation of what might loosely be branded 'oppositional' films, and it is possible that the political climate of the 1980s which, in so many ways, reflected that of the 1950s (similarly characterised by a government focus on 'traditional' family values) might have increased Davies's personal bitterness at being marginalised by his sexuality, and given an added impetus to his desire to explore his past. Nevertheless, it is misleading to suggest that his film was made with a specific and dominant political purpose, and it is vitally important to bear in mind both Davies's concern with form as content and the film's avowed autobiographical status.

However, the consideration of *Distant Voices, Still Lives* as a representation of working-class life in the 1950s has proved a popular approach in recent years. In an interesting essay on memory, gender and the image of the working class in *Distant Voices, Still Lives*, for example, Geoff Eley (1995) breaks away from the issue of the film's combination of realism and formalism, arguing that all film is representation, a matter of artfully constructed images. What is of particular concern to him is the way in which *Distant Voices, Still Lives* contributes to, or directly challenges, traditional representations of 'working-classness' in British cinema. Whilst he does acknowledge, from the first, the film's status as autobiography, or, in his terms, 'working-class autobiography', its main interest lies in its 'finely constructed study of working-class family life'. That this study is incomplete, in that it contains, as he points out, no description of the neighbourhood or the other inhabitants of the street, no wider context of adult friendship, no references to the world of work, or indeed to national or local politics, is, despite Eley's acknowledged recognition of the film's autobiographical status, still presented as a weakness; and he remarks quite critically that the fact that the film is set in the 'distant past' reduces its potential to disrupt or subvert. The article is astute, and undoubtedly makes a useful contribution to literature dealing with *Distant Voices, Still Lives*; nevertheless, it is disappointing that it too seems to be assessing the film in terms of what it is not rather than what it is. Indeed, this approach is even more prevalent in the response to *The Long Day Closes*, as will be shown in the next chapter. For the moment, the point I wish to make is that a film whose narrative is classified, however loosely, as 'realist', continues to create a number of fairly consistent critical expectations, and that these sit confusingly with the notion of autobiographical discourse.

The coincidence of form and meaning is an appropriate starting place for this chapter since it helps to clarify a number of the issues raised above as well as suggesting ways in which *Distant Voices, Still Lives* can be seen as both specific and universal in its appeal, both realist and self-conscious in its composition, and can fit equally well into both the European *auteur* and the British documentary traditions.

Form and meaning

If I have suggested that much of the critical treatment of *Distant Voices, Still Lives* is confused, and that any narrow focus upon the film as primarily a sociological or political document or even as an example of high art or social realism inevitably highlights internal contradictions or inadequacies, it is because I think it essential, in any reading, to foreground the film's autobiographical status, and to approach its undoubtedly multiple discourses within this context. By shifting the focus in this way, it is immediately clear that the various conflicts and contradictions identified above can be unproblematically accommodated as defining features of autobiographical discourse itself: lack of linear chronology; blending of truth and fiction, of reality and imagination; unstable and shifting temporal and spatial viewpoints; complex combinations of narrow subjectivity and universal understanding; and the self-conscious foregrounding of the processes of its own construction, for example, all coexist within this genre (Everett 1995).

Given that *Distant Voices, Still Lives* is acknowledged by Davies to be autobiographical, an inevitable consequence for him is the impossibility of using a traditional linear narrative since memory itself does not function in such a manner. In the light of some of the critical comments considered above, it is somewhat ironic that, even as early as the 1950s, Gusdorf had pointed out convincingly that in autobiographical discourse, 'temporal perspectives ... seem to be telescoped together and to interpenetrate one another', and that the subjective 'truth' of the individual could be articulated only in a form which rejects the linear chronology of historical time (Gusdorf 1956: 43–4). For Davies, the narrative structure of the film must recreate the fluid circularities of the process of remembering: 'The film constantly turns back on itself, like the ripples in a pool when a stone is thrown into it' (Davies 1992: xi). This comment reflects the fact that almost anything in the present can serve as a memory trigger, can transport us suddenly into the past: smells, tastes, sounds (especially music), words, sensations and even images, for example, may all function in this way. But equally, each individual memory once recalled may trigger other deeper, less accessible memories. Autobiographical memory can thus be understood to be composed of multiple layers which are elaborately interleaved, or tightly nested one within the other, so that remembering is less a matter of retrieving a single record than of moving gradually through a highly complex structure in which each remembered fragment may lead to others, in a process which is entirely fluid and open-ended. In consequence, autobiographical films invariably present themselves as a self-conscious and open-ended part of this process, and recognise that the very act of re-creating the past on screen will automatically change both that past and the way it is remembered in the future. Moreover, just as it is possible to approach the shifting tenses and non-linear structures of the film as part of the generic features of autobiography, so too its multiple and shifting viewpoints can be viewed in the same way, for the autobiographical self is inevitably both subject and object of the gaze, both self and other, and viewpoint, like tense, is thus unstable and inconsistent. If *Distant Voices, Still Lives* is viewed as autobiography, the formal elements which have so frequently been seen as contrived and self-conscious, and as detracting from the realistic memory narrative, can be shown instead to be fundamental to the film's meaning.

Nevertheless, accepting that this film is, on the one hand, a 'mirror held up to a country, a family, and a time' and, on the other, a film about the functioning of memory, or possibly even a film about making a film about memory (Kennedy 1988: 14), with all the formal complexity and self-referentiality this implies, is only a starting point. It enables us to escape narrow critical agendas because it shows how film is not one thing or the other but a mix, and it thus frees us to look afresh at its personal and innovative qualities and to begin to be able to unravel and understand some of its complexities. What is it about this film that makes it so particularly powerful and convincing? How is it that *Distant Voices, Still Lives* cannot be seen as 'just' another autobiographical account, but instead as a fresh look at cinema itself?

Movement and music

In *Distant Voices, Still Lives*, the camera glides through and between memories, twisting and turning upon itself in complex patterns which if not chronological or plot-driven may instead be recognised as musical and harmonic. In other words, as Davies so frequently remarks, like music, the structure of the film *is* its meaning. And because this film glides not only through Davies's personal memories and the stories and myths that created those memories but also through the memories of different members of his family, the shifting viewpoints and perspectives that accompany its temporal and spatial slippages are particularly complex and intricate. Through the diverse rhythms and harmonies such slippages create, the film's meanings proliferate and extend, as even a brief examination of the opening sequences of *Distant Voices* will reveal.

The film opens with the background sounds of thunder and heavy rain, over which we hear the measured tones of a male announcer reading the shipping forecast. The screen itself is black, with the title, *Distant Voices*, written across it in white. Already, it seems, the spectator has been plunged into a world which is familiar (textured by easily identifiable everyday sounds) and yet disturbing, since the screen remains blank and the pictures that accompany the sounds we hear must be formed by us, inside our heads. Thus the mutually supportive relationship between image and sound is disrupted, and both listening and viewing are posited as essentially individual and creative acts. Moreover, it is impossible to identify with any certainty the period into which the film is transporting us; the shipping forecast, our only clue, being essentially timeless.[3] It is interesting to record that, for Davies, the shipping forecast is a mantra, a magic incantation that acts as music rather than meaningful language, and thus has a potent ability to recall the remembered past. 'The shipping forecast was like magic because I didn't understand what it meant – I still don't – so it was like a kind of ritual, an incantation,' he explains (Floyd 1988: 295).

The establishing shot which follows is of the outside of a terraced house in the pouring rain. The camera pauses in close-up, focusing on the front door and downstairs window, denying us any broader context, and providing an essentially restricted, domestic viewpoint. Unlike the long static shot of the school building that opens the *Trilogy*, however, there is no suggested menace here. The camera's gaze is level and neutral, and the architecture is not public and imposing but private and intimate. This house as feminine and marginalised space (in contrast with the masculine and public spaces of central Liverpool discussed in the previous chapter) is thus identified as the setting for the film, and the camera's close attention reflects both the close-up vision and the restricted locus of memory. If, as the central space of the narrative, the house itself is signalled as container of memories, what is particularly interesting is the way in which the layers of memories which it contains will proliferate and develop for the spectator throughout the film.

After some seconds, we see the mother open the front door and stoop to pick up the three pints of milk from the doorstep in a gesture which is both overwhelmingly banal (every day starts in this household with this action), and richly symbolic (mother as source of nurture; the three bottles echoing the three children).[4] A cut then transports us into the front passageway of the house. Directly in front of us is a narrow flight of stairs, and the mother pauses at its foot to call out that it is seven o'clock, before moving out of shot to the right and, we presume, into the kitchen. For its part, the camera remains static, its focus still on the stairs. The mother re-enters the shot, calls once more, and again returns to the kitchen. Still the camera waits, still fixed on the stairs. And as we

'A PATTERN OF TIMELESS MOMENTS' 67

continue to focus on the empty flight of stairs, we hear the voices and footsteps of Tony, Eileen and Maisie rushing down, and chatting to their mother.

It is worth pausing on this brief, apparently simple and almost banal sequence to consider quite why and how it is so powerful. As the opening to a film it is confusingly non-specific: it could be any morning, at almost any time (and this supports the notion of the film as exploration of time and the process of remembering). And as in the credit sequence, Davies presents us with a haunting combination of emptiness and sounds; of absence and presence. Disembodied, as yet non-specific, these then are the 'distant voices' of the film; the voices of memory, perhaps the ghosts of the past that still fill the stairs and passageway of the Liverpool house. The scene itself is often considered to be abstract and formally challenging, and it is certainly true that the spectators must create their images from the sounds that are heard, even though the locus of the film is there on the screen.[5] Moreover, if the voices that reach us are indeed those of memory, it is impossible to tell whose memory is being explored, although inevitably the spectators' memories will be involved. Davies himself denies that the scene is at all complex, recounting how, when he was a child, each day started with him lying in bed listening to the familiar noises of the house waking up – the milk bottles, the footsteps, the chatter (Floyd 1988: 295) – so these memories could quite simply be his (although he himself does not feature directly in the film). On the other hand, they may (also) be those of other people whom we have not yet met, or they may in fact be part of a more abstract exploration of the ways in which sounds of the past are both contained in, and able to reconstruct, the landscapes of memory.[6] (Later, towards the end of *Still Lives*, the silent house is again filled with the voices of children as the mother sits dreaming by the fire, their absence made presence through their remembered voices.) Since Davies denies the spectator any temporal or other guidance, the film constantly demands a creative, active response: 'The difficulty of assembling scenes in a logical temporal order means that the audience is forced to participate in the process of remembering, and to experience it as an attempt to impose order on a confused totality of memory which is ever-present in the characters' minds' (Barker 1988: 294). But ultimately it also acquires a particular fascination as it resonates within the spectator's imagination.

If meaning is no longer an attribute of plot or story, the spectator must be responsive to alternative strategies and, in particular, must be sensitive to ways in which meaning is inherent in form. Patterns of repetition, for example, which play an important role in *Distant Voices*,

Still Lives, are not merely stylistic devices but a vital component of the narrative. Thus, for instance, the passageway and stairs in which the opening sequence is set will recur repeatedly in *Distant Voices, Still Lives*, as they will again in *The Long Day Closes*, each time acquiring new and deeper resonances, in a process which replicates that of memory (each act of remembering changes in some way the memory that is recalled). The process also reflects the way that a repeated refrain in a piece of music changes our relationship to that music as it becomes absorbed into our personal memory. Visual and thematic repetitions and modulations are particularly important in Davies's work, occurring both within and between individual films, and between his films and his writing. Other examples we shall notice in *Distant Voices, Still Lives* include the static family groupings in the parlour, and the repeated threshold images of doors and windows. (These last are inherently ambiguous spaces, of course, since they frame and contain the characters while, at the same time, functioning both as access into the family and as potential escape from it.)

The idea that Davies uses musical structures in his films will be further developed in Chapter 8, which will also consider the role and function of music within the individual soundtracks. But any analysis of *Distant Voices, Still Lives* must recognise the role music plays in the creation of its narrative meaning. For example, music is heard for over half the film's total running time, and is never accorded a 'mere' background role but is always foregrounded so as to be least as important as the dialogue, images, and narrative action. Indeed, we are obliged to recognise that music is one of the primary 'voices' or signifiers in the film. The clear-cut stark opposition between moments when music is heard and moments when it is not must be recognised as a vital component of the film's meanings, particularly in relation to the father's traumatising violence. This is clearly demonstrated by the fact that whereas the mother's presence is almost always marked by music, especially song, the inarticulate violence of the father is signalled by oppressive silence, and the songs and music that shape the landscapes of memory are almost only heard when he is absent (although as we shall see, their function transcends the simple binary division this might suggest).[7] Similarly, much of the contrast between the stark suffering of *Distant Voices* and the more muted anguish of *Still Lives* is actually expressed by the absence or presence of music.

If we can consider both images and sounds (including music itself) as different voices within the film's remembering process, it is important to be aware of the way in which the shifting relationship between the two also determines meaning. Thus, at times they function

'A PATTERN OF TIMELESS MOMENTS' 69

together, in harmony, at others they diverge, so that visual memories are replaced by sounds, or sounds by images. And, occasionally, there is strident discord (as when we watch the mother being beaten by her husband to the sentimental strains of 'Taking a Chance on Love', for example). Essentially, neither image nor sound automatically takes precedence; both are equally important, and meanings proliferate in the tensions between them. A brief return to the opening sequence of *Distant Voices* provides a telling example. As we saw a moment ago, the staircase remains deserted despite the sounds we hear. When the voices of these unseen people fall silent, they are replaced by the song 'I Get the Blues When it's Raining', which we hear in its entirety. Not to be deflected, the camera retains its intent focus upon the empty stairs, in fact intensifying its gaze by gradually moving closer to them, before tracking right through 180 degrees to focus once again on the hallway and the front door, but this time from inside. An entire space is thus created, defying the two-dimensionality of the screen. It is an intimate space which positions us inside the memory of the unknown narrator, but also an empty space whose dimensions are irrevocably marked by the music and lyrics that we hear. Previously, from outside the house, we watched the rain falling as the shipping forecast created its own off-screen vistas; then we stared at an empty staircase as we heard feet rushing down it, and voices suggesting a specific occasion that we could not identify ('Are you nervous, love?'), then that static, intimate and silent space was given mental and physical shape by a song whose lyrics about rain and sadness replace the actual rain we had been watching. And central to this establishing sequence is the emptiness of the hallway and the stairs.

This concept of shifting signifiers and voices, and of the spaces and tensions behind and between what we see and hear, provides a key pointer to Davies's innovative techniques, for, like the intervals and silences that shape a piece of music, such spaces are at the heart of the film, structuring its narrative rhythms and meanings. But silences and spaces are essential to the film's mobility in a number of other ways as well.

Stasis and silence

The suggestion that the structure of *Distant Voices Still Lives* can be likened to music in its fluidity and its essential self-reflexivity goes at least some way to explaining the film's emotional power and its ability to generate complex meanings at a variety of levels. In the foreword to his published screenplays, *A Modest Pageant*, Davies describes the film's narrative structure as a 'mosaic of memory' created from 'a pattern of timeless moments' (Davies 1992: 74), and this comment is particularly interesting in its insistence on the notion of stasis in relation to time. Given the fluidity of time, and the open-ended process of remembering, as well as the essential mobility of film itself (elsewhere described by Davies as 'movement and rhythm through space *and* time'), one might have expected him to describe the fragmented patterns of the past as kaleidoscope rather than mosaic, and so it is at this stress upon stillness within motion that I now want to look.

A clue is already provided, perhaps, in Davies's description of the way in which the film constantly turns back on itself like the ripples in a pool when a stone is thrown in. The ripples, he explains, are the memories, spiralling outwards in fluid and changing patterns and reflections. The pebbles are the moments outside time, the shards of memory at the heart of the movement. In Davies's film, these 'timeless moments' are positioned quite literally *outside* the flow of time by being depicted as still or frozen poses which disrupt the temporal and spatial movement of the film itself. Such moments, in which film appears to imitate still photography, are often approached in this way although Davies himself is resistant to such readings, insisting that the only photograph referred to is the actual one of his father standing beside a horse; this framed photograph is centrally positioned in the parlour, where it dominates and structures the various family groupings, just as the memory of the father dominates and structures all other memories and experiences. He thus rejects the notion that he is otherwise structuring the film around photographs or tableaux.[8] And whilst it is helpful to explore a number of issues in *Distant Voices, Still Lives* through the relationship between photographic and filmic images, particularly with regard to trauma, memory suppression and death, it is essential to recognise this apparent pausing of the natural flow of film as a self-conscious technique in Davies's filmic depiction of 'stasis as drama' (Davies 1992: 103).

Davies suggests that the main event in the film, the 'pebble' or point of origin of its complex ripples of memories, is Eileen's wedding: 'It seems to me that 7/10ths of the film is in that first scene: it's the day of her wedding, she remembers her dad. That's the pebble dropped in the pool, and then there are those ripples of memory, which is what the film is all about' (Floyd 1988: 295). Whilst it is true that this scene (the second of the family groupings in the parlour) does provide the starting point for the narrated memories, once again Davies is not admitting the film's full complexity, for there is in fact a deeper starting point, one that is not directly articulated but buried far below the surface, and is the real cause of the stasis we observe. Nevertheless, this scene offers a key to understanding the underlying structure of the film. The wedding group is the second of the family group scenes in the parlour (although it is in fact set up *before* the first of these by the mother's voice asking Eileen whether she is nervous). It depicts, from left to right, the mother, Tony, Eileen and Maisie, smartly dressed in their wedding clothes, standing in a line in the parlour, two on each side of the black and white photograph of the father. The scene is one of those frozen moments, with both camera and group being almost entirely static. Eileen speaks first saying, tearfully, 'I wish me dad was here'. Any suggestion of sentimentality or nostalgia that might be suggested by such words is, however, quickly countered as Maisie, in voice-over, responds, 'I don't. He was a bastard and I bleedin' hated him!' At this point, a cut moves us directly into Maisie's memory, in an extremely disturbing scene in which, made to scrub the cellar in order to be allowed to go to a dance, she is first humiliated and then violently beaten by her father. To the sound of her screams during his frenzied attack we cut directly back to the silent parlour as Eileen repeats 'I don't half wish me Dad was here', so that we are irrevocably drawn into the silent tension between the two images. We then immediately cut once again through time to another scene of violence. This time, we are in Tony's memory as he screams at his father in what Davies describes as 'a paroxysm of rage and hurt'. Tony, who has run away from the army and is desperate for help, has cut his hands badly on the broken window pane, but his father still refuses to acknowledge his presence, and the disturbing scene ends as Tony is beaten and bundled into a van by the military police. From these two memories of physical and mental abuse, all the others will flow as we move seamlessly and without guidance through different times and memories.

A number of interesting points immediately arise from this stark and dramatic episode. In terms of space and architecture, it is important to notice the significance of the cellar in Maisie's memory sequence. This space under the house entirely escapes the female intimacy of the building that we noticed earlier. As the hidden side or underbelly of family life, the cellar is a place of darkness and fear, a place where the father's power is absolute. The fact that this dominance tightly relates material power with masculinity is made clear through the father's gesture in flinging on to the ground the coins that will enable Maisie to go to the dance, just before he begins beating her. Maisie is on her hands and knees in a position of total subservience. As the father fishes in his pocket for the loose change, the camera observes in close-up his hand inside his trouser pocket, in a shot that tightly associates masculinity, violence and power.[9] The same relationship is at the heart of Tony's flashback too, as the son flings his last coins into the fire as a symbol of his (impotent) rejection of the Law of the Father.

At the same time, more complex relationships are being set up between these incidents and the other memories that shape *Distant Voices, Still Lives*, but also between this film and Davies's other works, and this relationship will irrevocably influence the response of the spectator to the scenes and events that are encountered. For example, the cellar in Maisie's flashback will inevitably recall Tucker's descent into the public lavatory and other dark subterranean spaces in the *Trilogy*. Moreover, the traumatic violence we witness will help us to understand the particular significance of cellar as the site of Bud's only tears in *The Long Day Closes*. A similar example of the potency acquired by objects and places through such recurring memory patterns is the particular menace that underlies the gesture with which the father seizes the poker to push the coins further into the flames in Tony's flashback, inevitably recalling the scene in the *Trilogy* where he uses the poker to beat his wife, and where we share the child's terror as, alone in his room, he listens helplessly to his mother's screams.

From the violent ending of Tony's memory sequence, we again cut directly to the frozen stillness and silence of the wedding group, as they are about to leave for the church. In other words, not only does this scene develop a complex range of intertextual references that extend the film's impact to include other works by Davies as well as the spectator's own memories and imaginings, but it also sets up a dynamic which is created not from forward impetus but from stark contrast or conflict. Indeed, all the spiralling memories of *Distant Voices, Still Lives* could equally be approached as a series of oppositions: movement/stasis; silence/music; maternal/paternal and so on. Film, like the identities it explores, becomes an intersection of opposites at the heart of which is fragmentation and absence.

Absence and presence

Although Davies identifies the wedding scene as the pebble that sets the memory ripples in motion, the ripples themselves reveal more powerful undercurrents deep below the surface; the hidden point of origin of the stasis and trauma the wedding scene portrays. It is therefore significant that the sequence in which this scene occurs is composed of two distinct family occasions: the father's funeral and Eileen's wedding, so that the wedding itself is firmly imbricated within the funeral that directly precedes it. The impossibility of separating the two occasions is ensured by the way the film fuses together different times and spaces with a series of dissolves, and by the rhythmic pattern and duration of the song which we hear throughout (a recording of Jessye Norman singing 'There's a Man Goin' Round Takin' Names'). In contrast to the visual and musical fluidity that constructs the sequence, however, both the funeral and the wedding scenes are depicted as virtually static; both scenes assemble the same four characters, and in both the central image is a framed black and white photograph hanging on the wall. Our gaze is immediately drawn to this photograph because of the way it appears to dominate and structure the family group, and its central importance is underlined as the camera moves in to frame it in extreme close-up as the family leaves the room for the funeral. The photograph itself seems innocuous enough: a man poses beside a horse, while another less distinct figure can be seen in the background. Nevertheless, the power it exerts is tangible, and is made particularly disturbing by the stillness the photograph seems to impart to the family group that surrounds it. At first, it seems as though we are perhaps looking at a (real) still photograph within a (posed) still photograph, an aspect Powrie describes as a 'mirror effect', which positions 'the father as a photographic image within a pseudo-photographic image' (Powrie 2000: 21). A number of critics have identified the 'freeze' effect in such shots as a reference to the family photographs which, as Sontag comments, have increasingly become 'a rite of family life', the means used by a family 'to construct a portrait-chronicle of itself – a portable kit of images that bears witness to its connectedness' (Sontag 1977: 8). Eley, for example, exemplifies this approach, noting the 'stylised, static, photograph-like quality of many of the shots (frequently the main characters are posed in a tableau, as if for a photograph)' (Eley 1995: 26). Barker too draws the family album analogy, claiming that *Distant Voices* 'animates the snapshots in this family's album' (Barker 1988: 294), and Elsaesser draws together ideas of photographs and memories in his analysis of Davies's style, as characterised by his 'spare, formal, snapshot memories' (1988: 292). In a review of *Distant Voices, Still Lives* published in the *Washington Post* in September 1989, Hal Hinson even suggests that old family photographs might well constitute the inspiration for Davies's visual strategy, and claims that the repeated positioning of his characters in a straight line across the frame serves the same commemorative function (Hinson 1989). John Orr, taking a similar viewpoint, claims that the film's static images are reflections of family photographs, and that the memories depicted in the film 'spring to life out of still photographs', in his brief and somewhat confused analysis (Orr 1998: 11). Somehow, however, such explanations are unconvincing given the two events in question: funeral and wedding sit uncomfortably together in the family album, particularly in relation to the predominance within each of the photograph of the father. Moreover, not only does Davies himself insist that he is not referring to the notion of the family photograph anywhere in the film's so-called tableau shots (a term he also dismisses); he insists that there was, in any case, no tradition of taking photographs in his family.[10] Nevertheless, it is important to understand both the role in the film of this single, isolated photograph and the significance of the apparent freezing of the family group (and indeed the film itself) in proximity with it.

The photograph which shows a man standing beside a horse is, as Davies told me, an actual photograph of his father.[11] Thus it establishes a link with a 'reality' which lies outside the normal parameters of film, and serves yet again to emphasize the hybrid status of autobiography. As the still point at the centre of the memories the film will explore, the photograph testifies to the existence of the father, thus exemplifying the photograph's traditional role as a form of ontological proof, and establishing, in Barthes's terms, 'the that-has-been, or the having-been-there of the object depicted' (Barthes 1977: 44). For Barthes of course, the photograph inevitably speaks of death and loss, for it tells us not only that its subject is now dead but also that, at the time it was taken, he was going to die (Barthes 1984: 96). And the aorist tense that Barthes identifies as being that of the photograph seems to fit particularly well with the conflicting temporalities of autobiography itself: the father is already dead, but he is very much alive within the film's past-as-present narrative. Nevertheless, even within that past, we are aware that he is going to die. (Tellingly, the wedding scene, which provides footage of the 'live' father, is preceded by his funeral, and immediately followed by a scene of the family grouped around the hospital bed on which he lies dying). In its inevitable association with death, its status as *memento mori*, the photograph could appear to be performing the sort of commemorative act that Hinson suggests. Indeed, such a reading is set up by Eileen's wish that her father were alive, uttered as the photograph places him just behind her, in the centre of the screen. However, the violent juxtaposition of Eileen's words and the flashback memories of Maisie and Tony denies us the possibility of any such reading. This photograph is not a consolation but a menace, and the absence it speaks of is experienced by us, through the family, as what Sontag calls a 'pseudo presence' (Sontag 1979: 16).

Any oppositions or conflicts inherent in the temporal status of the photograph are intensified by positioning it within the moving images of a filmic narrative, and it is in the complex relationship between still and moving images to which it draws attention that the significance of Davies's photograph may be grasped. For Barthes, the essential difference between still image and film is first of all mechanical: 'in the Photograph, something *has posed* in front of the tiny hole and has remained there forever ... but in cinema, something *has passed* in front of this same tiny hole: the pose is swept away and denied by the continuous series of images' (Barthes 1984: 78). The consequence of this basic difference is that, whereas the photograph testifies to the past by freezing time, the constant flux of filmic images, whereby each in turn interrogates and modifies the previous one, accords them all a transitory and unreliable status. Further differences follow: the static, unchanging time-slice of the photograph cannot play an active role within the ongoing process of remembering since, frozen in time, it can neither restore memory (Barthes 1984: 91) nor transfer grief into mourning, its active equivalent (Sontag 1979: 73). On the other hand, as we have already seen, the perceived present tense of film allows it to function as memory, arguably making it an ideal form for the creation of autobiographical discourse (Everett 1996: 107).

What role then does this particular photograph play? Davies certainly did not need to include it to establish the truth of his father's existence since the flashback sequences recreate his presence for us far more convincingly than any photograph could. Nor does the photograph contribute to the film's sense of period authenticity which is created more effectively through devices such as *mise-en-scène*, colour and music. (For example, to recreate the authentic atmosphere he sought, Davies filmed *Distant Voices, Still Lives* using a coral filter; he removed any primary colours (apart from red lipstick and nail varnish) from the sets and costumes, and processed the film using a complex bleach bypass technique so that the finished print would acquire desaturated colours and the appearance of hand-tinting (Baxter 1988: 14; Floyd, 1988: 295).) And whilst the interplay between still and moving images within a filmic narrative may undoubtedly prove a powerful device for confronting the passage of time, the inclusion of still photographs inevitably slows down the pace of a film, and focuses attention on the materiality of the medium. This is particularly true of the scenes we are considering, and it is perhaps here that we can begin to understand the real significance of the photograph.

Trauma, stasis and the photograph

'Trauma', from the Greek word for wound, is used to refer to the experience caused by extreme terror or shock, and its mental scars frequently include problems in articulating or even remembering the original experience (Gilmore 2001: 885). If we look briefly at the inclusion of still photographs in films, it is significant that, as well as slowing the rhythm and drawing attention to the materiality of the medium, they very often serve to represent some element of the past which it seems impossible to assimilate comfortably into the present of the narrative. Perhaps the best-known example of this is the powerful dialectic between stark black and white photographs of the atrocities of the concentration camps, and the colour footage of these camps in the present, in Alain Resnais's documentary about the Holocaust, *Nuit et brouillard / Night and Fog* (France, 1955). Similarly Georges Perec's documentary about the experience of Jewish migration, *Récits d'Ellis Island: histoires d'errance et d'espoir / Ellis Island Revisited: Tales of Vagrancy and Hope* (France/USA, 1979), a film itself 'haunted by death', also reflects Perec's own 'deeply-felt preoccupation with the processes of memory', particularly his own traumatic absence of memory (Wagstaff 2000: 37). Perec too depicts the past using still photographs, self-consciously displayed against the walls of the now deserted buildings of Ellis Island, so that, as the camera moves slowly across their surface, it deconstructs the very fabric of film. In such cases, when the trauma of the past makes memory impossible, it is the photograph's 'strange stasis, the stasis of an *arrest*' (Barthes 1982: 91, his emphasis) that seems appropriate, rather than the moving images of the film.

Barthes sees the stasis of the photograph as intrinsically violent, not because it shows violent things but because 'in it nothing can be refused or transformed' (Barthes 1984: 91). And it is this quality, in particular, that seems to be the key to the photograph's function in *Distant Voices, Still Lives* since, as point of violence and stasis, it has the ability to stop time, to rupture the flow of the film and thus to enact the moment of trauma. If the frozen attitude of the family reveals the extent of their continuing trauma, so powerful is this trauma that it has the power to halt the film, to take away the very movement that defines it, to disrupt its process of articulation.

However, there is in this film a far more significant absence than that of the father, which is, of course, that of Davies himself. Thus the key element in understanding this film is not the father's representation as photograph, or even the ability of that photograph to disrupt the narrative, so much as the absence from the narrative of the person whose autobiography this is. Clearly, Davies had no problems in creating his alter ego in either the *Trilogy* or *The Long Day Closes*, so why does he remove himself so entirely from this narrative? How are we supposed to read a portrait of the self from which the self is missing? It is of course true that several of the memories explored in the film precede Davies's birth, and have been collected by him from the family stories he heard when growing up. But equally he was present at a number of the events the film depicts, and we know from both the *Trilogy* and his many writings and interviews that he was, and still remains, directly traumatised by his own early experiences of paternal violence. Nevertheless, he chooses not to include himself in this film.

One possible explanation might be that, by leaving himself out of narrative, Davies is able to create a greater discursive space or distance in which he can experiment more freely, and it is certainly true that there is a wider perspective and a freer and more experimental approach than we find in the *Trilogy*.[12] It is equally true that such a strategy enables Davies to situate his identity within the broader context of the family. He of course describes this process as a homage to his family, as it undoubtedly is, particularly in its treatment of the mother. Nevertheless, in its quiet observation of the family dynamics, the camera articulates both the observant child and the evaluating adult, and as such must inevitably involve an assessment of Davies's identity as shaped by his family context. And, given that research by psychiatrists such as R. D. Laing had in the 1960s identified the link between mental states such as schizophrenia and family environment (explored, for example, in Ken Loach's *Cathy Come Home*, UK, 1966), Davies would inevitably have used the mirror of family life as a way of reflecting his personal trauma: 'Trauma is never exclusively personal; it always exists within complicated histories, both individual and collective' writes Gilmore, adding that 'the difficult articulation of trauma entails situating a personal agony within a social and cultural context ... This implicit evocation of a sense of shared experience goes to the centre of first-person accounts' (Gilmore 2001: 886–7). This idea ties in neatly both with the problems of articulation revealed by the stasis of the family group in relation to the photograph and with the fact that, for Davies, the trauma caused by paternal violence is tightly bound up in the trauma of his sexuality and his resulting sense of alienation. For in many ways the most surprising absence we might identify in this film is any representation of the homosexuality which so strongly colours all his other autobiographical work. Puzzled by this, a number of critics have chosen to see Tony as Davies's alter ego. In this reading, for example, Tony's tears as he stands outside the house on his wedding night indicate his shame at being forced to conceal his true sexuality by contracting a conventional marriage (Powrie 2000: 30). While it is doubtless true that elements of the director/author may be traced in all the characters he creates, nevertheless such a reading is certainly oversimplistic, not least because the film provides scant evidence in its support. Moreover, nowhere does Davies impute homosexual desires to his brother. From the evidence within the film, Tony's tears are more likely to relate to his fear of contributing to the pattern of unhappy marriages that we see throughout the film, and to his impotent rage against the Law of the Father (Davies 1984: 51; Everett 2001b). If, on the other hand, we read the tears as those of Davies himself, we are more likely to find in them his despair at the inevitable breakdown of the family, and his overwhelming fear of the future. 'And dread comes over me as the house echoes in the dark, as Fridays become as cold as Sundays ... And mother and I are left entirely, utterly alone. The house rattles and calls, the house with its rich, its voluptuous memories, crumbles into disrepair as the rats gnaw in the cellar and the distemper in the bare, empty rooms cracks' (Davies 1984: 52).

What this incident presents is a combination of all these ideas, marked by Davies's own overwhelming sense of alienation. And it is interesting to note that contemporary autobiographies (particularly, but not uniquely female narratives) frequently use similar strategies of distancing in their handling of memories that cannot be articulated easily. For example, writers such as Nathalie Sarraute, Marguerite Duras, Gertrude Stein and Annie Ernaux (as a fairly random selection) position their own lives and identities in the gaps between the words, the spaces that are not spoken, and the fragmented self is frequently articulated through multiple, competing voices and characters. It seems that Davies too, is not able to represent himself directly in this narrative, but that through fragmentation and alienation he instead positions himself in the non-spaces, in the tensions and gaps, in between the words and the melody.

And yet, whereas the pseudo-presence of the photograph of the father reflects his absence, Davies's apparent absence reflects his overwhelming presence. The camera provides his gaze, the film explores his critical and emotional awareness, and his self-conscious exploration of the nature and power of cinema is also, and overwhelmingly, an exploration of his identity.

Film as identity

If autobiography is a largely fictional project, the constant invention of the self, for Davies that self is essentially a filmic creation. And although he might claim that *Distant Voices, Still Lives* is about other people's memories, his own presence is revealed not only in the self-consciousness of the film but also, dramatically, through the film's direct homage to cinema. One of the most lyrical sequences, for example, begins with a glittering shot of umbrellas, from above, tightly clustered in the heavy rain. Their shining dark blues and greys fill the screen in a sumptuous and glorious collage, as the romantic orchestration of 'Love Is a Many-Splendored Thing' swells to a climax. This shot is Davies's reference to *Singin' in the Rain*, the first film he ever saw (Floyd 1988: 296). As the camera pans up the brick wall behind the umbrellas (the exterior of the cinema), it passes two film posters advertising, on the left, *Love Is a Many-Splendored Thing* (Henry King, USA, 1955), and, on the right, *Guys and Dolls* (Joseph L. Mankiewicz, USA, 1955). Both are dramatically lit from above, by two spotlights. As the camera dissolves outer and inner spaces, moving into the auditorium of the cinema, we watch not the screen but the audience, all of whom are beautifully back-lit, their faces transfixed by the film in front of them. Davies's sisters, like some of the other women, are in tears. It is significant that Davies chooses not to show us what they are watching; instead we marvel with him at the power and beauty of the medium in which he works. Through his film's exploration of the power of cinema, Davies overcomes trauma, and can articulate his identity without the threat of stasis.

Such scenes, of course, also reveal the ironic judgement of the adult who is remembering this past, and underline the gap and tensions between the romantic view of heterosexual love purveyed by Hollywood and the grim reality which *Distant Voices, Still Lives* unflinchingly explores. This we must read, for example, through the sequence which follows, as we look vertically down as George and Tony fall (from the scaffolding) through a glass roof. The slowness of the images, and the continuing strains of 'Love Is a Many Splendored Thing' transform the drama into a glorious ballet as fragments of glass float and spin in changing patterns across the screen. But an abrupt cut transfers us with a sickening jolt back to the reality of the accident, and to the men, lying critically injured in a hospital ward. Davies's film is never sentimental, it is too intelligent, too aware, hence the brittle fragility of the shattering glass. But it does recognise the emotional and sentimental power of music and images to transform our lives, for better or worse, and, in so doing, it gives him a voice to express his identity. This supremely important awareness of self as inseparable from its filmic articulation will lead him, and us, to his next film: *The Long Day Closes*.

Notes

1 The Eady Levy consisted of a levy upon exhibitors' earnings whereby a proportion of box-office takings in British cinemas was made available to British producers with the purpose of encouraging the British film industry. The levy was first devised by the Treasury official Sir Wilfred Eady and introduced on a voluntary basis in the 1950s. It was later made compulsory, under the Cinematograph Films Act of 1957, and was administered by the British Film Fund Agency until abolished by Thatcher's Films Bill 1984-85, in her attempt to apply stringent market principles to the film industry (for further information about the levy, see, for example, Hill 1999: 31-52). This system closely resembled the one that continues to function so successfully in France as part of its general funding strategy. (For a wider view of funding mechanisms across European cinema see, for example, Finney 1996: 114-38.)
2 Other prizes include: The Golden Leopard at the Locarno International Film Festival (1988); the International Critics' Award (FIPRESCI) at the Toronto International Film Festival (1988); the LAFCA Award for Best Foreign Language Film in the Los Angeles Film Critics' Association Awards (1989); and the Amanda in the Norwegian International Film Festival (1990).
3 Of course, the accent and tones of the announcer do suggest the 1950s or early 1960s, although the forecast itself would be difficult to date with any precision.
4 It is difficult also to avoid reading into such a shot a whole range of other autobiographical references, such as, for example, the moment in Truffaut's *Les 400 coups* when Antoine, starved of maternal love and support, steals and drinks a bottle of milk.
5 A fascinating example of the way in which a sense of place can be created entirely through sounds is found in Paul Valéry's description of Paris in *Regards sur le monde actuel* (1988). Valéry explores through language the textures and spatial distances that sounds create, and these distances are replicated in filmic terms in Davies's use of sound to deepen and extend the off-screen space.
6 A parallel may be drawn here with the opening sequences of Jean-Luc Godard's autobiographical *JLG/JLG* (France, 1996). In this case, we are inside a flat, and, as the camera focuses on a small black and white photograph of Godard as a child, we hear the voices of children at play. In Godard's film, these voices will never 'materialise', will remain situated in the spaces of memory and the imagination. The films of both Davies and Godard contrast strikingly with more traditional approaches to autobiography (for example John Boorman's *Hope and Glory*, UK, 1987) where the opening sequences clearly indicate both the period setting and the protagonist of the film.
7 Only two occasions disturb the neat presence as absence dialectic: the first is a memory of Christmas, which will be dealt with in greater detail as part of this book's treatment of music in Davies's films; the second is a scene in which the children secretly observe the father as he grooms a horse. As he does so, he sings and whistles. These two occasions, which constitute the only moments of tenderness shown by the father, are also marked as significant by being the only two when his presence involves music.

8 In fact, in the screenplay of *Still Lives*, Davies does have the family tableau posing for the photographer, as they leave the church after Tony and Rose's wedding. We are told that 'they all smile' for the photographer, although, immediately afterwards, the mother's face 'crumples into tears' (p. 131). However, this scene does not appear in the film itself. Davies does make use of the device of group wedding photograph in *The House of Mirth*, as an economical way of encapsulating the wedding ceremony.

9 Godard includes a similar shot, making very much the same link between the relationship of phallus and money in his film *Vivre sa vie/My Life to Live* (France, 1962), in a scene in which Nana, the heroine, forced to become a prostitute, has to wait as the client reaches into his trouser pocket for his money.

10 Sontag extends her analysis of the role played by photographs in family life, and comments that in most households 'not to take pictures of one's children, particularly when they are small, is a sign of parental indifference' (Sontag 1979: 8). Dangerous as such generalisations are, there is surely some significance in the fact that the only photograph in the house is of the father and his horse.

11 In his reading of this photograph in relation to Barthes's ideas of the *punctum* in photographs, Powrie refers to the animal in question as a pony. Given that my equestrian knowledge is limited, I am retaining the term which Davies himself uses in his screenplay and in conversation about the photograph: horse.

12 For an interesting discussion of similar distancing strategies in Hans-Jürgen Syberberg's controversial film *Hitler: A Film from Germany* (1977) see Koshar 1995: 159-61.

References

Barker, A. (1988), '*Distant Voices, Still Lives*', *Monthly Film Bulletin* 55/657, October, 294.
Barthes, R. (1977), *Image/Music/Text*, New York: The Noonday Press. Translated by Stephen Heath.
Barthes, R. (1984), *Camera Lucida: Reflections on Photography*, London: Fontana. Translated by Richard Howard.
Baxter, B. (1988), '*Distant Voices, Still Lives*', *Films and Filming* 400, January, 14-15.
Caughie, J. (1992), 'Halfway to paradise', *Sight and Sound* 2/1 (NS), May, 10-13.
Davies, T. (1992), *A Modest Pageant*, London: Faber and Faber.
Davies, T. (1993), *Hallelujah Now*, London: Penguin Books. Originally published 1984.
Dixon, W. W. (1994), '*The Long Day Closes*: an interview with Terence Davies', in Dixon (ed.), *Re-viewing British Cinema 1900-1992: Essays and Interviews*, Albany: State University of New York, pp. 249-59.
Eley, G. (1995), 'The family is a dangerous place: memory, gender, and the image of the working class', in Rosenstone, R. (ed.), *Revisioning History: Film and the Construction of a New Past*, Princeton: Princeton University Press, pp. 17-43.
Elsaesser, T. (1988), 'Games of Love and Death or an Englishman's Guide to the Galaxy', *Monthly Film Bulletin* 55/657, October, 290-3.
Everett, W. (1995), 'The autobiographical eye in European film', *Europa, An International Journal of Language, Art and Culture* 2/1, Spring, 3-10.
Everett, W. (1996), 'Timetravel in European film', in Everett, W. (ed.), *European Identity in Film*, Exeter: Intellect, pp. 103-11.
Falsetto, M. (1999), *Personal Visions: Conversations with Independent Film-makers*, London: Constable.

Finney, A. (1996), *The State of European Cinema: A New Dose of Reality*, London and New York: Cassell.
Floyd, N. (1988), 'A pebble in the pool & ships like magic', *Monthly Film Bulletin* 55/657, October, 295–6.
Gilmore, L. (2001), 'Trauma', in Jolly, M. (ed.), *Encyclopedia of Life Writing: Autobiographical and Biographical Forms*, vol. 2, London and Chicago: Fitzroy Dearborn Publishers, pp. 885–7.
Gusdorf, G. (1956), 'Conditions et limites de l'autobiographie', reprinted in Olney, J. (ed.) (1980), *Autobiography: Essays Critical and Theoretical*, Princeton: Princeton University Press, pp. 28–48.
Hattenstone, S. (2000), 'First steps in show business', *Guardian*, 6 October, Review, 2–4.
Higson, A. (1998), 'British cinema', in Hill, J. and Church Gibson, P. (eds), *The Oxford Guide to Film Studies*, Oxford: Oxford University Press, pp. 501–9.
Hill, J. (1999), *British Cinema in the 1980s*, Oxford: Clarendon Press.
Hinson, H. (1989), '*Distant Voices, Still Lives*', *Washington Post*, 1 September, 1.
Horne, P. (2000), 'Beauty's slow fade', *Sight and Sound* 10/10, October, 14–18.
Howe, D. (1989), '*Distant Voices, Still Lives*', *Washington Post*, 1 September.
Hunt, M. (1999), 'The poetry of the ordinary: Terence Davies and the social art film', *Screen* 40/1, Spring, 1–16.
Keighron, P. (1991), 'Condition critical', *Screen* 32/2, Summer, 209–19.
Kennedy, H. (1988), 'Familiar haunts: Terence Davies's *Distant Voices, Still Lives*, *Film Comment* 24/5, September–October, 13–18.
Koshar, R. (1995), '*Hitler: A Film from Germany*', in Rosenstone, R. (ed.) (1995), *Revisioning History: Film and the Construction of a New Past*, Princeton: Princeton University Press, pp. 155–73.
MacCabe, C. (1999), *The Eloquence of the Vulgar*, London: BFI.
Neale, S. (1981), 'Art cinema as institution', *Screen* 22/1, 11–39.
Orr, J. (1998), *Contemporary Cinema*, Edinburgh: Edinburgh University Press.
Petrie, D. (ed.) (1992), *Screening Europe: Image and Identity in Contemporary European Cinema*, London: BFI.
Powrie, P. (2000), 'The "family portrait": trauma and the *punctum* in *Distant Voices, Still Lives* (1988)', in Everett, W. (ed.), *The Seeing Century: Film, Vision, and Identity*, Amsterdam: Rodopi, pp. 20–35.
Sontag, S. (1979), *On Photography*, London: Penguin Books.
Sterritt, D. (1999), *The Films of Jean-Luc Godard: Seeing the Invisible*, Cambridge: Cambridge University Press.
Street, S. (1997), *British National Cinema*, London and New York: Routledge.
Valéry, P. (1988), *Regards sur le monde actuel*, Paris: Gallimard (Folio Essais).
Wagstaff, P. (2000), 'The dark side of Utopia: word, image, and memory in Georges Perec's *Récits d'Ellis Island: histoires d'errance et d'espoir*', in Everett, W. (ed.), *The Seeing Century: Film, Vision, and Identity*, Amsterdam: Rodopi, pp. 36–48.
Williams, C. (ed.) (1996), *Cinema: The Beginnings and the Future*, London: University of Westminster Press.
Williams, T. (1993), 'The masochistic fix. Gender oppression in the films of Terence Davies', in Friedman, L. (ed.), *British Cinema and Thatcherism*, London: UCL Press, pp. 237–54.
Wilson, E. (1999), *French Cinema since 1950: Personal Histories*, London: Duckworth.

1 'Stasis as drama': Eileen's wedding day, with the family posed around the photograph of the dead father. From left to right: Freda Dowie as the Mother, Dean Williams as Tony, Angela Walsh as Eileen, and Lorraine Ashbourne as Maisie, in *Distant Voices, Still Lives*.

2 The terrified children huddle under their cart as the air raid siren sounds in *Distant Voices, Still Lives*. From left to right: Sally Davies as Eileen, Susan Flanagan as Maisie, and Nathan Walsh as Tony.

3 Cinema as epiphany. Flanked by his mother (Marjorie Yates) and sister Helen (Ayse Owens), Bud (Davies's alter ego, played by Leigh McCormack) gazes in delight at the screen. In this screen-as-mirror shot, Davies's very identity is self-consciously articulated as filmic construct in *The Long Day Closes*.

4 Aunt Mae (Gena Rowlands) and the young David (Drake Bell) on one of their afternoon walks down Main Street in *The Neon Bible*. Aunt Mae is doing her Jean Harlow impersonation as she walks.

5 Object of the gaze: Lily Bart (Gillian Anderson) arrives at Grand Central Station in *The House of Mirth*.

6 The powerful sensuality of unspoken desire: Lily Bart (Gillian Anderson) and Lawrence Selden (Eric Stoltz) smoke a cigarette together in *The House of Mirth*.

Mapping the topographies of childhood: *The Long Day Closes* 4

> And the bird called, in response to
> the unheard music hidden in the shrubbery,
> And the unseen eyebeam crossed, for the roses
> Had the look of flowers that are looked at.
>
> ('Burnt Norton')

In *The Long Day Closes* (1992), Davies returns yet again to his childhood world, but this time the memories the film explores are directly his own, neither filtered through family stories as in *Distant Voices, Still Lives* nor projected into an imagined future as in the *Trilogy*. Instead, Davies clearly positions his own ten–eleven-year-old self, in the person of Bud (played by Leigh McCormack), at the very centre of the narrative. This is the third of Davies's memory narratives and, as such, the narrative structure is once again associative rather than chronological, memories flowing one into the next without explanation or causal logic. The memories can, however, be fitted within a loosely chronological framing, to the extent that *The Long Day Closes* traces approximately one year in Bud's life (1955–56), the year that marks his transition from child (reflected in the gentle atmosphere of his Catholic – and essentially feminine – primary school) to adolescent (expressed through his dawning sexuality, and his transition to secondary school).

In many ways, then, we find ourselves in very familiar territory. When we first see Bud, he is sitting half-way up the steep oilcloth-covered stairs of his house, the geographical layout of which (stairs to the left, directly opposite the front door, narrow hallway to the right, with door off to kitchen) provides powerful intertextual references to his earlier films. (Once you have seen *Distant Voices*, for example, the hallway in *The Long Day Closes* inevitably contains within its silent space the terrifying memory of the mother being beaten by the father, to the strains of 'Taking a Chance on Love'.) Within these familiar walls, we once again encounter the same family members: the mother sings in the kitchen, and brothers and sisters bustle about with their girlfriends and boyfriends, preoccupied with their own enticing and bewildering agendas. In addition to Bud's mother, this time the household consists of his brothers Kevin and John, and his sister Helen (Titch). And although the threat of violence presented by Davies's father has by now receded, its traumatic scars are still discernible in incidents such as Bud's nightmare, while the way the child is repeatedly framed by banisters, railings, windows and doors insistently reminds us that even in this warm, domestic space he experiences loneliness and isolation. The external topography of Bud's world is also quite familiar to us, for the house as space of containment is situated in the tight narrow area of Liverpool that we have already met in both the *Trilogy* and, if in less detail, in *Distant Voices, Still Lives*. Thus spaces created and explored by the film are clearly Davies's own, and are mapped and defined by his personal experiences. The boundary markers of Davies's space are clearly established: home, the locus of domesticity and sanctuary (even if its increasing fragility, already hinted at in *Distant Voices, Still Lives*, is now foregrounded through the child's fears of its violation); the dreaded secondary school with its high walls and forbidding iron gates, and its hostile and rigid interior; the church marked by mysterious and frightening doctrines and iconography, and – overwhelmingly in this film – the cinema, with whose images and openness Davies increasingly identifies. The world that exists within these limits is mapped by the narrow, terraced streets of Davies's Liverpool, and given depth and texture by pubs and singsongs, music and films, rain and deep shadows. And yet, despite its haunting familiarity, *The Long Day Closes* is startling in its originality, and overwhelmingly different from its all predecessors. Not only does the film reveal a significant new understanding of the nature of auto-biographical memory and identity construction, but its technical and formal innovations demonstrate a new awareness of the medium. In this film, more than ever, the director functions as composer, creating through shifting combinations of visual shapes and patterns, and with music, quotation and sound, a multilayered and densely referential visual and aural collage, a form of cinema which itself functions as music, and whose rigorously composed and richly textured images flow lyrically one into the other with both the simplicity and the extreme complexity of memories, or perhaps of time itself.

This chapter takes as its starting point the differences which set *The Long Day Closes* apart from *Distant Voices, Still Lives* and the *Trilogy*, using these to identify some of the ways in which the film contributes to our further understanding not only of Davies as a director but also of the nature of cinema both as component of (popular) culture and as an essential element in the articulation and creation of personal identity.

Critical reception

If, on the whole, *The Long Day Closes* received less attention than Davies's previous autobiographical works, and if it did not quite meet with the widespread enthusiasm that greeted *Distant Voices, Still Lives*, the primary reason would seem to reflect the combination of familiarity and difference that we noted above. At the time of its release, a good many critics were disconcerted to find that the film failed to live up to expectations they had based upon his earlier and more 'realistic' autobiographical accounts. In comparison with the 'complex emotional, social and familial landscape' of *Distant Voices, Still Lives*, for example, the world represented in *The Long Day Closes* was often judged 'affected', too heavily reliant upon its 're-presented and mediated nature' (Danks 1998). Its break with more traditional realism was thought to render its autobiographical account somehow less 'honest' than *Distant Voices, Still Lives* (Cavanagh 1995). In Britain, in particular, the film was quite widely described as nostalgic, self-indulgent and even trivial. For Caughie, writing in *Sight and Sound*, it was 'perversely narcissistic'; and he criticised in particular its 'self-absorption and knowing self-awareness' as well as its ironic detachment: 'the playful irony of the movie in-jokes and the aestheticisation of drabness seem to me to cast the shadow of cynical and detached reason over the whole film' (Caughie 1992: 11; 13). Radstone too appeared uncomfortable with the use of self-conscious quotation in the film, and, as part of her attempt to decide whether *The Long Day Closes* provides an example of nostalgia or history, she argues that it is nostalgic because it uses film clips not to create a discourse or to signify narrative as construct but to legitimise the filmic memories as 'historic'. Her conclusion states that 'a fleeting glance at the [narrative] of ... *The Long Day Closes* confirms [its] memories as nostalgia – nostalgia for a lost ideal of phallic masculinity and nostalgia in place of *Erfahrung* or memory as auratic experience' (Radstone 1995: 43).

Before we turn our attention to the film itself, therefore, it would be instructive to consider in slightly more detail the nature and the implications of these and similar comments. The key to Caughie's unease is revealed in the summary comparison he draws with the Bill Douglas *Trilogy*, and, although for this purpose it might have made more sense to compare it with Davies's own *Trilogy*, he instead situates *The Long Day Closes* as the third part of a second trilogy of which *Distant*

Voices and *Still Lives* form the first two elements. Whereas Douglas's *Trilogy* is 'rigorously autobiographical, at least to the extent that it is rooted in his own lived past', he claims, Davies sets out quite deliberately to create 'autobiographical fiction' (Caughie 1992: 11). Leaving aside for the moment both the fact that this comment reveals some confusion about the nature of autobiographical discourse which, as we have seen, is by definition part fiction, self-conscious and unstable, and the obvious fact that Davies's works too are deeply, even obsessively, 'rooted in his own lived past', what clearly remains in Caughie's comparison is the opposition between Bill Douglas's 'formal rigour' and Davies's 'aesthetic formalism'. In other words, by depicting his 'working-class memory' through 'a lens of aesthetics', Davies is seen to position his work irrevocably in the context of British art cinema, in an equation which sets in opposition an aesthetic, inauthentic, self-indulgent art film (formalism) and a gritty, realistic and authentic work in the tradition of British documentary (realism). And, furthermore, the apparent happiness, or at least the lack of overt suffering, in *The Long Day Closes* is automatically considered as further evidence of its lack of authenticity. Interestingly, Caughie's opinion has been fairly widely used by critics who make no attempt to question the terms of this equation. In the very short section devoted to Terence Davies in her study of British cinema, for example, Sarah Street quotes Caughie at length, and simply repeats that, by aestheticising the past, *The Long Day Closes* is less 'harsh' and therefore less authentic than the Douglas *Trilogy* (Street 1997: 184–5). The problematical nature of attempting a rigorous opposition between formalist and realist films has already been noted, as has Davies's understanding that the autobiographical imperative involves finding the dramatic, not the literal truth, through reworking the past at an aesthetic distance. Given that *The Long Day Closes* is a film which is concerned with the nature of time and the processes of remembering as much as with memories themselves, it draws attention to the role of cinema within these processes, and is therefore inevitably self-conscious. And while it is true that the period it deals with stands out in Davies's life as a time of intense joy which is both boundless and yet fragile and transient, nevertheless to accuse it of nostalgia or to imply that its intimations of happiness render it in some way inauthentic suggests a simplistic and partial reading. Far more than just an elegy for a lost paradise, *The Long Day Closes* provides an important insight into Davies's self-awareness, and in particular into his understanding of personal identity as (filmic) construct.

There is little point in rehearsing yet again the realist/formalist dichotomy, but it would seem from the above comments that Davies's film is being criticised because it is daring and innovative, and because it breaks a set of rules which are, in any case, imperfectly perceived, and have little to do with the generic characteristics of autobiography. Further proof of this last point is provided by Caughie's somewhat baffling remark that there seems no historical reason for setting 'The Long Day Closes in 1955–56, given that 'History, in the shape of Suez or Hungary or the break-up of the left, is almost totally absent' (Caughie 1992: 13). Thus, the lack of authenticity which is seen to result from the film's formal and aesthetic concerns, and its lack of (overt) suffering, is compounded by its failure to take issue with the historical events of the time. It must be said that such comments have led to widespread reaction in Davies's defence by those who recognise that the viewpoint of the remembering child is unlikely to reveal prescience of historical events, and that Caughie is here criticising the film for failing to achieve something it has no interest in doing (Hunt 1999; Williams 1996: 190–200). Moreover, it is clear that, far from being a random choice, the period covered by the film's narrative is vitally important to Davies because it contains both a new sense of security and happiness and a awareness of its fragility and of the loss of innocence that accompanies the development of his sexuality, the start of his adolescence. (Indeed, the onset of adolescence should be recognised as the most widely chosen period for the setting of autobiographical films in general.) And if the film does not include overt representations of the sort of brutality we find in the trilogies of either Douglas or Davies, or indeed in *Distant Voices, Still Lives*, nevertheless, one would need to be particularly unresponsive not to be aware of the suffering which colours the child's universe in this film. Far from being any less 'real' or 'authentic' than its predecessors, it attains perhaps a greater sense of reality or truth, a point recognised by Durgnat, for example, for whom 'Davies's double focus, on a vanished world and on subjectivity, far from diluting realism, only extends it' (Durgnat 1992). It is important now to identify and analyse some of the qualities which set this film apart, and which – as I suggested earlier – reveal new insight into the nature of memory and identity, and into the discourse of filmic autobiography. By way of approaching the innovative features of the film, I begin by examining some of the specific characteristics of this period in Davies's life that the film depicts.

Oedipal bliss

At the time that *The Long Day Closes* begins, Davies is ten and in his last year of primary school; during the narrative he will move into his first year at secondary school. Clearly, therefore, it is a period of major change and upheaval in his life. His father has been dead for some three years, and he and his family are beginning to recover from the fear and violence that had dominated their earlier existence. The scars are still there, of course, but they are hidden, less easy to spot. True, they do rise to the surface in incidents such as Bud's nightmare of being strangled, from which he awakes screaming 'It was a man. It was a *man*!', but for the most part they must be sensed, understood through minute indicators, just as in real life: in the mother's easy tears, in her children's protectiveness towards her and in the close-up gestures of affection and reassurance that pass between them. And, even in the happiest moments, deep fear still lurks in the shadows: in the quiet hallway where the children had earlier witnessed terrible scenes of their father's violence towards their mother; in the dark cellar, filled with memories of him relentlessly beating Maisie, and site of the only tears we ever see Bud shed; and in the child's own vulnerability and his desperate fear of rejection.

However, in contrast to the tension between the negative paternal and the positive maternal currents that structured *Distant Voices, Still Lives*, the period covered by *The Long Day Closes* is dominated by the positive: the maternal. The house is a feminine sanctuary, and, within its walls, the child can be with his mother without fear of punishment or displacement. To that extent, this is indeed a period of Oedipal bliss. The close and happy relationship between mother and son is repeatedly shown through the camera's framings of the two of them together, as well as in repeated images of the mother nurturing, protecting and caring for Bud. Predominant, however, amongst the many signifiers of their closeness is music, and as in *Distant Voices, Still Lives*, the adored mother figure in *The Long Day Closes* is tightly linked to music, particularly song. We shall, of course, be looking in detail at the role of music in all of Davies's films, but at this point it is worth drawing attention to its particular significance in relation to the pre-Oedipal, pre-linguistic state, and the formation of subjectivity. Since, as we now know, the infant hears before it sees, and recognises its mother's voice while still in the womb and long before it can identify her face, the association between music, particularly song, and the maternal is well established before birth, and the centrality of the auditory realm to the formation of subjectivity has been persuasively established (Rosalalo

1974 : 80). It would appear that the particular capacity of music to affect our emotions reflects this early association with the mother, hence its apparent promise to restore plenitude and the lost maternal object (Kristeva 1980: 286). It is within this relationship between music and anteriority, in particular, the close link between voice and self, or voice and mother, that the phenomenon of the use of popular song in Davies's work must be situated.

The suggestion that this period in Davies's life, characterised by his unlimited access to his mother's love, and by the songs and music with which he chooses to re-create it, is a time of Oedipal bliss finds justification in scenes such as Bud's nightmare, referred to above. When the child wakes, screaming, from the nightmare which, though its violence, is identified as masculine, and thus implicitly linked to memories of his father, as well as to fears inspired by his own dawning sexuality, his mother rushes to comfort him, and sits on his bed, cradling him in her arms. She is wearing her nightdress, and the camera, briefly focusing upon her bare arms and legs, provides a rare reflection of her as a sexual being.

Another key scene within such a reading occurs near the beginning of the film when the mother asks Bud to go up to the bedroom to fetch the net curtains so that she can wash them. Bud does so (hoping that in return she will give him some money to go to the cinema), but, instead of taking them down to her, he drops them from the bedroom window. The curtains float gently downwards, landing on the mother who is hanging out clothes in the garden, transforming her into a bride in a white veil, and, as she looks up at Bud, pretending to scold him, she smiles radiantly.

Processes of erosion

As I have already intimated, this period of bliss is only part of the story, and any reading that fails to see beyond it is flawed. Within the chronology of the narrative, it is Bud's transferral to secondary school that reasserts the harsh Law of the Father, and sets in train the various processes of erosion that will attack his happiness, his confidence, and his identity. However, in fact, such processes are already at work long before he changes schools, emerging particularly with the first stirrings of his homosexuality. Immediately after the net curtain incident, with its suggestion of maternal purity, Bud lifts his gaze from the garden, and looks out beyond its safe contained space to Smitten's Garage, where three young men are building a wall. They are stripped to the waist, and Bud stares at their muscular bodies with fascination, before being overcome with embarrassment when the man who has really caught his eye notices, and smiles and waves. Bud immediately slides out of view, beneath the window, and sits hunched, with his back to wall, away from the light, in a tellingly foetal position. Later, in the dramatic scene in the church in which Bud sees the hands of Jesus being nailed to the cross, the Christ figure is, in fact, the same builder he had stared at in that earlier scene. Sexuality is as mysterious to the child as are the various teachings of the Church, but is already clearly related to the concept of sin ('Jesus died for your sins'), while the relationship of religion, sexuality and sin within fantasies of sado-masochism is posited in close-up shots of nails piercing flesh.[1] In its own way, this scene is every bit as disturbing as the one in *Madonna and Child* where shots of the Stations of the Cross are accompanied by the telephone conversation in which Tucker desperately pleads to have his 'bollocks tattooed'. However, the violence and anger in *The Long Day Closes* are latent, and must be divined by the spectator in a more complex fashion.

The awareness that his desires must remain hidden, that he cannot discuss his sexuality with anyone, marks the beginning of Bud's loss of innocence as well as his increasing sense of alienation and difference. Such feelings are, of course, repeatedly explored in the film, in scenes such as the class session in the public swimming baths, where (as in the school medical examination) Bud's reluctance to reveal his body signifies his 'guilty' secret, his sense of being dirty and sinful. And along with a gradual realisation of his sexual difference comes a fear of isolation and rejection. Bud is inconsolable, for example, when his best friend goes off to the cinema with someone else, and bitterly hurt by his increasing exclusion from the (heterosexual) relationships and activities of his older siblings. In one scene, Bud is banished from the sitting room by his brother Kevin, who wants to be alone with Frances, his girlfriend. In another, Bud wistfully watches through the frosted pane in the closed door as John and Jean kiss. He is repeatedly left at home when his brothers and sister set off on their bikes for a picnic, or leave for a dance, chatting and laughing together. Bud is painfully aware that their lives are moving on and away, and that the secure happiness of his home is irrevocably fragmenting. That he cannot follow, and that nothing can last.

Acting as a potent metaphor for the various elements which attack the child's happiness, confidence and self-esteem is a lesson given by Mr Nicholls, Bud's/Davies's form master at secondary school, dealing with the processes of erosion. The fundamental importance of this scene is underlined by the time it is accorded, by the detailed attention we pay to its content and by repeated references to it elsewhere in the narrative. The camera watches intently as the children obediently copy the teacher's words into their exercise books; both his definition, 'Erosion is the cumulative effect of a great variety of processes ...' and the list of the five different types of erosion that he provides. The significance of this text to the processes of erosion we observe at work in the film is clearly underlined as we listen to his carefully enunciated words, and at the same time watch as he meticulously writes them on the board: '1. River Erosion; 2. Rain Erosion; 3. Glacial Erosion; 4. Wind Erosion; and 5. Marine Erosion'. The language is slow and repetitive, as much an incantation as a dictation, and the headings on the board are written with exaggerated neatness and care. Moreover, we focus closely on Bud as we hear the words, '... life also co-operates in the work of destruction'. Of course, this scene can be easily situated within the tradition of autobiographical films, and any number of equivalent examples may be cited. In particular, it seems to recall the classroom scene in Truffaut's *Les 400 coups / The 400 Blows* (France, 1959), in which a sadistic teacher similarly dictates and writes on the blackboard a long poem entitled 'The Hare'. But whereas much of the irony in Truffaut's version results from the total unsuitability of the poem for a class of inner-city adolescents, so that the viewer is able to add this observation to the wider framing of the school as sadistic and unjust, here Davies uses the lesson as an actual commentary upon the whole range of processes attacking or wearing away the innocence of his younger self. In both examples, therefore, the dual viewpoint of child and adult permits both memory and ironic comment upon that memory. And it is important that Davies has chosen to situate this 'commentary' within the locus of the school, perceived by him to be the centre of the forces attacking his younger self.

Time

Earlier in this chapter, I suggested that *The Long Day Closes* is a work about the nature of time, and it is clear that the child's awareness of the irrevocability of time provides a key to such concerns. It is essential not to see the film's exploration of memory as merely a nostalgic lament for a lost paradise, nor as an attempt, as it were, to freeze the past by creating a 'museum of collective traces', as Caughie suggests (Caughie 1992: 11). Instead, we are faced with a project altogether more daring and complex, which can be understood as an attempt to explore time itself. In *The Universe in a Nutshell*, Stephen Hawking introduces the notion of 'imaginary time'. He explains how, in Einstein's four-dimensional spacetime model, 'real time direction' is distinguished from the three spatial directions since, while time can increase or decrease within any of these, it must itself always move in linear fashion from past to future. Imaginary time, however, Hawking notes, is positioned at right angles to real time, and therefore behaves like a fourth spatial direction, offering infinitely richer possibilities than real time with its linear or circular trajectories (Hawking 2001: 59–63). It would appear that this imaginary time, that (at least some) physicists are now recognising, is a concept with which anyone working in film (or indeed in any form of narrative) will be familiar.[2] And this concept of the stitching together or stretching of times into a spatial dimension is, of course, particularly pertinent to autobiography, where not only is time linear (back from the present to the past, and, confusingly, simultaneously forward from the past to the future) and circular ('in my beginning is my end'), but above all a spatial concept which contains multiple, coexisting histories. Within such narratives, all distinctions between past and present dissolve, so that they operate in a 'no time', an imaginary time, a time outside time whose dimensions are indeed spatial. And that imaginary time is the dimension in which Davies situates his filmic analysis of the nature of time.

If, for example, we compare the opening shots of the *Trilogy*, or even *Distant Voices, Still Lives*, with those of *The Long Day Closes*, we are immediately aware that, for all its status as memory narrative, this film is attempting something different. As we have already seen, the *Trilogy* opens with a long static shot of the school, while *Distant Voices, Still Lives* begins by showing us Davies's childhood house in the rain, in a shot marked by the appearance of the mother, collecting the milk bottles from the step, and by the shipping forecast on the soundtrack. These films therefore begin by transporting us back to the locus of childhood memory (although, in fact, questions of viewpoint foregrounded by the self-conscious camera alert the spectator in both examples to the fact that the narrative time is not actually that simple). But the opening sequence in *The Long Day Closes* makes it immediately clear that something infinitely more complex is happening on this occasion.

The screen is itself divided diagonally from the top left to the bottom right. The right-hand triangle is black, and the credits, written in white, in an elegant and delicate script, appear and disappear in this space. The left-hand triangle is quite dramatically lit, from the top, and, against a rough background of what could be a painted brick wall, stands a low vase of flowers. The vase is curved, and metallic, and the light is reflected in its surface. The roses it contains are a delicate creamy yellow, full blooms with short stems. They are the focus of the light. The camera is static throughout the credit sequence, as the Boccherini Minuet in G (Opus 11, No. 5a, G275) is heard. 'This seems more like Greenaway territory than Terence Davies', Caughie comments suspiciously, and indeed, in a way, perhaps it does (Caughie 1992: 11). But, given that this is the start of Davies's autobiographical memories, this static composition must be integral to the process of remembering, and so it is important to unravel its meanings more carefully. As we have seen, the screen is clearly divided into light and dark sections. At its most obvious, perhaps, we might read this structure as a visual metaphor for day and night. Certainly such a reading is supported by the film's title, and by its ending, which is to do with dusk, with the coming of night. Moreover, like its predecessors, *The Long Day Closes* uses the symbolism of light and dark to articulate the various conflicts and differences that structure the child's identity and his relationship with the external world.

On the light side of the screen, we are shown a still-life composition of a bowl of roses, a reference that inevitably recalls the title of Davies's previous film. The stillness of the left half of the screen contrasts with the changing credits on the right, and it is certainly true that the film itself will be exploring these contradictory qualities of time: as irrevocable forward motion, as frozen or fixed moment. Of course, within its central temporal metaphor, the still-life painting is a genre which explicitly plays with and contrasts the relationship between form and reality. Like the painting, Davies is perhaps saying, the film image has everything and nothing to do with reality. The roses on screen are no more real than Magritte's pipe. They are roses whose temporal characteristics of fading and dying no longer hold sway now that they are 'captured' on film, and consequently they are roses that are positioned outside time. Entirely contained neither in the memories they serve to articulate, nor in Davies's present (where they would die), we must recognise them as a spatial configuration of an imaginary time which is that of the film itself. And, if they are roses outside time, they are also, crucially, 'flowers [with] the look of flowers that are looked at'. Like Eliot's *Four Quartets*, *The Long Day Closes* is about time and art and the role of art in time. The on-screen roses, like all the other images in the film, both represent the transience of time and yet escape it. Just like the roses in Eliot's poem, the film is here to be looked at, for it is by being looked at that it will achieve its life, its meaning, even its time. Thus, from the very beginning, Davies is foregrounding the status of the 'self' and of the memories the narrative will explore as filmic constructs.

If we consider the music in this sequence, similar patterns and concerns can be identified. Music, which is movement through time,

MAPPING THE TOPOGRAPHIES OF CHILDHOOD 97

uses strict measures in time, and this is illustrated by Davies's choice of a (Boccherini) minuet: a dance form characterised by its regular 3/4 rhythm. However, music is also situated outside time through the different memories and responses it engenders in each individual listener. Davies repeatedly explores these different attributes in the film: both its ability to create movement through time (for the rhythm of the songs and music that he uses motivate the narrative and establish the film's internal rhythms) and its power to transcend time, to unite past and present within the space of its melody. Indeed, the immediacy and potency of music in recalling past emotions and events renders it a key component of the autobiographical process. Of course, the form of a piece of music *is* its meaning, its irreducible reality, and this too reflects Davies's most passionate concern in his films. Moreover, this first piece of music also constitutes the first of many filmic references in *The Long Day Closes*, for it is heard in *The Magnificent Ambersons* (Orson Welles, USA, 1942), as well as in the last of the great Ealing Comedies, Alexander Mackendrick's *The Ladykillers* (UK, 1955), to which Davies will repeatedly allude. In *The Ladykillers*, the minuet is 'played' by the 'quartet' of crooks, and, just as this film functions as one of the triggers that transport Davies back to his childhood in *The Long Day Closes*, so too, in *The Ladykillers* itself, it is this minuet that sets Mrs Wilberforce on a journey of remembrance to her own childhood. Here we see Davies not only exploring the potential of music to recall the past but also paying subtle homage to earlier cinematic use of the same strategy.

The only movement in this first sequence is provided by the minuet and by the changing credits which detail the members of the cast. In its role as visual image on a black background, the delicate and meticulously formed italic script Davies chooses for the credits provides a visual signal of an earlier age, and yet another reference to the Ealing comedies of his childhood. Yet, even here, we cannot read these images as pure nostalgia, for just as *The Ladykillers* was both 'an apotheosis and a parody, mocking the studio's (and England's) fixation on age and tradition' (Kemp 1996: 371), so too the words themselves remind us of the essential artifice of the film, for they immediately suggest that the intimate memories it will explore are artificial constructs performed by actors. Being far closer to handwriting than print would be, Davies's chosen font has connotations of personal creativity and sincerity, as well as being unmistakably feminine in its grace and lightness. Nevertheless, it is not handwriting but print, so that it too is an artifice; a device.[3] Thus the film's blend of emotion and ironic distance is signalled clearly from the very beginning.

When the credits and music end, and the screen fades to black, we hear the Twentieth Century Fox theme and an extract from the soundtrack of *The Happiest Days of Your Life* (Frank Launder, UK, 1950) in which Margaret Rutherford announces (with heavy contextual irony): 'Tap, Gossage, I said "tap" – you're not introducing a film'. So the narrative too begins by drawing attention to its status as performance, just as the credits had done. In other words, from the opening seconds of the film, we are faced with questions about the nature of art and its relationship with 'reality', as Davies prepares us for his exploration of the nature of time, and the process of remembering.

As further indication of the fundamental place of music in *The Long Day Closes*, it is interesting to note that the title of the film refers to the song composed by Sir Arthur Sullivan ('The Long Day Closes'), and that this song, heard in its entirety, accompanies the darkening skies of the film's ending.[4] Within its metaphor of evening and nightfall, the song uses images of darkness and light that reflect Davies's narrative concerns, and provide a direct response to its opening credits. However, the film's concluding sequence is not one of closure, death and loss (although these possibilities are contained within it), but of transcendence and beginnings. The ending is tightly linked both to an earlier scene in which, shining his torch into the night sky, Bud grapples with the notion of infinity, and to the scene which immediately precedes this song, in which he explains to his friend Albie that the stars they are looking at are actually dead, and that their light originated centuries earlier 'when Jesus was alive', and still continues, although its source no longer exists. So the film ends, as it begins, as a self-conscious exploration of time, in all its paradox and complexity.

These complex themes that are introduced in the brief credits sequence, and are woven in shifting patterns and layers throughout the film's narrative, are immediately expanded and developed as the credits end and the film fades up from black to reveal a dark and derelict street, partly shrouded by heavy rain. This opening scene is depicted in a long static shot that obliges the spectator to engage creatively with its confusing signs. The street itself is strikingly artificial; not merely unrealistic, but blatantly so. Given its status as the establishing shot in an autobiographical account, a genre that critics are forever assessing in terms of its realism, the blatant artificiality of the set is disturbing. Of course, were the camera to start its slow forward track sooner, we might well accept the street merely as an unconvincing set, a failure to create the required and anticipated degree of visual authenticity. But since the shot is held for almost thirty seconds before any camera movement occurs, we are obliged to engage in a process of reassessment. And if the articulating I/eye is positing artificiality as reality, it is once again made clear that Davies is foregrounding his identity as construct.[5] Furthermore, any attempt to situate this street within a clear time scale is potentially even more confusing: is it the past? Obviously not, because the street is empty, dead, forgotten. The houses are in ruins, the street is cluttered with piles of rubble, and deep puddles have formed on its uneven surface. The most tempting reading would be to situate this scene as a reflection of the present; the street as it is now, its decay signalling the irrevocable passage of time. This hypothesis would prepare the way for a nostalgic transition to that past; a move from end to beginning, as it were. But the essential artificiality of the scene militates against any such reading. Moreover, while various objects, such as the gas lamps, function as traces, identifying the scene as the past, the fact that the lamps are actually functioning adds to our confusion, not least because this would not be the case were this street to be situated in the present. Since it can be fitted logically into neither the past nor the present, what we see must clearly be an example of imaginary time as spatial dimension. The street presents the fictional space of memory and imagination; the hybrid and multiple times and spaces of identity.

By confronting the spectator with temporal and spatial anomalies and contradictions, Davies draws attention to his preoccupation with time, and he continues to explore the topic through a whole range of tropes and devices as the opening sequence continues. As we have seen, the camera initially pauses on the desolate street, before slowly advancing part way along it, panning right, and moving into one of the ruined houses where it again comes to a halt, this time focusing on the broken staircase. A dissolve reveals the figure of a boy, Bud, sitting halfway up the stairs in the house now restored to its status as childhood home. In other words, we seem at last to have been transported back to a time which we can clearly identify as the past (whilst recognising, of course, that this 'past' in fact constitutes the narrative present). If this temporal transition might seem to have been brought about by the spatial movement of the camera, it is important to be aware that it is music (in this case, 'Stardust', one of the many popular songs that feature in the score) that performs as both the instigator and the real vehicle of that movement or change. Throughout the entire sequence (from the sounding of the Rank Organisation gong to the discovery of Bud on the stairs), we hear a recording of this popular song which clearly has significant personal connotations for Davies, since it instigates his autobiographical memories and transports him from adulthood to childhood.

The song is featured extra-diegetically, so that it is not contained by the narrative but is presented as part of the process of remembering. To some extent it functions as narrative voice-over; at least, it seems to have that authority.[6] However, as we have seen, Davies is not interested in providing an explicit indication of the status of the film we are watching. Instead, the complex nature of subjective memory is here approached through the tension between the desolate images and the romantic melody which leads him, and us, back to the past. 'Stardust' was extremely popular in Britain in the 1950s, and the version we hear in the film is the recording from the period by Nat King Cole. As such, it is still likely to be recognised by a proportion of the audience, for whom it will awaken a wide range of personal memories and responses, but, whilst it is part of the personal memories of the director/protagonist and possibly also those of the spectators, it is simultaneously used to reveal the essential artificiality or fiction of such memories. The voice of Nat King Cole is smooth and glamorous, by virtue of being American and therefore the product of an alien culture. As such, it is part of the explicit homage paid by *The Long Day Closes* to the magic of childhood, or rather, to those elements of it which were shaped by popular (American) culture. Moreover, at the very start of the sequence, even before we see the street, the camera pans down a brick wall and very briefly focuses on a tattered old poster advertising *The Robe* (Henry Koster, USA, 1953), the first Cinemascope film ever made, so that the notion of America and glamour have from the first been traced to the prime source of their mediation: cinema. While the dilapidated state of the poster situates the narrative in the past, our present historical awareness that *The Robe* was a film to which all Catholic schoolchildren in Britain would have been taken,[7] reveals further layers in Davies's memories, and contributes further indicators to our understanding of the context of his childhood. At the same time, the artificiality of the set, and the overtly cinematic quality of the rain, mark that childhood as partly fictional.

The song's lyrics, of course, contribute further layers of meaning to the sequence. Dealing with separation and distance, 'Stardust' self-consciously refers to itself as 'a song that will not die', and as 'the music of the years gone by'. Both song and film are simultaneously using and ironically evaluating the power of nostalgia and its role in shaping the past. Furthermore, the relationship between the song and the desolate images on screen is particularly disturbing, given the entirely ambiguous status of the images. Davies thus underlines the impossibility of establishing clear temporal or spatial boundaries in our memories. In visual terms, this is illustrated, for example, by the fact that the rain we see and hear (blatantly artificial 'Hollywood'-style rain) is falling both outside, in the street, and inside the house itself. And so this sequence, like the film, articulates the central concerns of autobiography: not the recreation of a static past but an exploration of the process of remembering; the dynamic negotiation of the complex temporalities and landscapes of memory.

It is not merely visual clues that we must look out for. Equally important here is the song's position within the soundtrack. We have already seen that the recording begins immediately after the extract from the soundtrack of *The Happiest Days of Your Life*; and, as the sequence ends, it cross-fades to an extract from the soundtrack of *The Ladykillers*. Thus the first spoken words of Davies's autobiographical film are in the form of a voice-over by Alec Guinness: 'Mrs Wilberforce? I understand that you have rooms to let?', the very line that heralds the start of the gang's nefarious activities in *The Ladykillers*.[8] In this way, American musicals and Ealing comedies, the two most enduring influences acknowledged by the adult Davies, provide a context or frame for his memories, and their significance in relation to his personal identity is unambiguously acknowledged as they are brought together in Bud's opening question: 'Mum, can I go to the pictures?'

It is easy to see why Davies's films should infuriate those who seek to categorise them as either realist or fantasy for, as the opening sequence implies, such distinctions are perceived by him as false. Consequently, *The Long Day Closes* repeatedly presents us with paradox and ambiguity, involving us, the spectators, directly within the narrative process. One particularly fascinating example of this is the film's representation of Christmas. Bud, as usual, sits alone on the stairs, as his mother and siblings sort out the decorations. Gradually, his expression changes from sadness to joy, and a series of cuts places him outside the dining room. Instead of the door opening, it appears to glide away like curtains parting before a film or theatre performance, to reveal the family seated at the table, as if on stage, and as they turn to smile at Bud and wish him happy Christmas they look directly to camera. Thus Davies deliberately sets up his memories as performance, or construct. Moreover, the scene he discovers is indeed fantasy; he appears to have walked into a Christmas card. His mother and sisters are wearing beautiful dresses, the table is laden, and here is a large and lavishly decorated Christmas tree (which has nothing to do with the 'reality' of the little artificial tree, stored all year in the attic, and lovingly brought out at Christmas). Confusingly, given that all the signs indicate Christmas, on the table stands a birthday cake, covered with brightly lit candles. But what is really amazing is that the dining room is simultaneously inside and outside: snowflakes drift down through the room, street lamps are lit and the interior wall appears to be the façade of the house. On one level, the scene is a highly romantic and nostalgic vision of the past, an effect which is increased by the intertextual references to American musicals such as *Holiday Inn* (Mark Sandrich, USA, 1942), and *Meet Me in St Louis* (Vincente Minnelli, USA, 1944). But the extreme self-consciousness of the scene-as-performance, and the fact that the family talks directly to camera, and thus to us, implicates us entirely in the narrative process, and requires us to consider actively the function of nostalgia in relation to memory. Much of the scene's potency comes from the way it condenses into a few brief minutes *all* the celebratory occasions of childhood: Christmas and birthdays, parties and presents, film and music are concentrated in one brief tableau. Thus contradictory times and spaces meet in a time outside time, an inner space which is both entirely impossible and yet absolutely true. (It is interesting to compare this scene with the silent and frozen family tableaux in *Distant Voices, Still Lives*, for the combination of movement and music here clearly illustrates that it is the making of film that enables Davies to overcome the traumas of the past.) This scene also contrasts strikingly with the depiction of Christmas in *Distant Voices, Still Lives*, where the initial promise of Christmas as time of joy for the children is brutally shattered by the father's violent outburst at the dining table.

Popular culture

Apart from the overall complexity of the project, perhaps the most innovative feature of *The Long Day Closes* is its recognition of the centrality of popular culture not only in the articulation of subjective identity but in its actual construction. However, while this feature clearly disconcerted a number of critics, its significance was often simply not understood. Instead, the 'artificiality' of the film was seen as a failure to achieve convincing realism, and its repeated homage to popular culture was interpreted as simple nostalgia; as an escape from reality. As we have seen, the film was even criticised for being altogether too happy, and it is certainly true that the bleakness and misery that marked Davies's earlier narratives are in many ways more muted, or at least less obvious, here, just as his anger is less violent. To some extent, this is an inevitable consequence of the period being recalled: with his father dead, Davies's home life offers a new sense of security, and, since his sexual awareness is only just beginning, there are still few signs of the rage so openly articulated by Tucker in the *Trilogy*. The child is, after all, only eleven. And although the young Bud is, in reality, as entirely trapped as was Tucker, unlike Tucker he has access to a form of escape through his love of popular culture, particularly the cinema. Indeed, the 'salvation' implicit in the *Trilogy*, since it would be by making a film about his existence that Davies would ultimately find release, is made much clearer in *The Long Day Closes* through its powerful homage to cinema. Davies of course has now found his salvation, as a film director, and along with the ability to re-create the world through film comes the recognition of the role that film has always played in forming his identity. Thus, while the film powerfully explores the child's sense of entrapment, also present from the beginning is the acknowledgement of the possibility of escape. It is important to take nothing for granted in a film by Davies, and so it is worth considering further the significance of a moment in the opening sequence, in which the camera pans down a brick wall, momentarily pausing on a poster for *The Robe*. Filling the screen entirely, the dark, wet bricks of the wall form a rigid boundary, an enclosure that predicts the constraints surrounding the child. However, even as the camera presents the wall as barrier or stasis, the dynamic soundtrack, with its multiple voices and filmic references, already indicates a space beyond, that the wall cannot entirely contain. This implicit suggestion of film as escape route is supported by the poster the camera discovers as it pans across the bricks, for this poster functions as a window or breach in the wall. Not only is the rich fantasy world of cinema acknowledged as a way of escaping the confines of everyday existence, but it also provides a way of articulating the subjective identity of Terence Davies. We are not dealing with nostalgia, or at least, not with nostalgia as an end, for, while it undoubtedly is an aspect of the songs we hear, and of some of the images we see, its function, just like the poster advertising *The Robe*, is to provide an opening; a self-conscious access to the inner topographies of the director.

Inner topographies

Davies's world is tightly constructed within the familiar landmarks of home, church, school and cinema. And if what differs here from the landscapes of the *Trilogy* and even *Distant Voices, Still Lives* is the increased prominence of the cinema itself, both as a space in its own right and in its ability to leak out into all the other areas, we must recognise that this fact radically changes our perceptions of the landscape.

Home, entirely shaped by the mother's presence, is a place of love, and music, a sanctuary despite its own vulnerability to the encroaching world. But it is, none the less, a place in which Bud's loneliness and difference are repeatedly depicted, and it still bears the scars of the family's traumatic past.

The church, at least through Bud's eyes, is an ambiguous and confusing place. To some extent it signifies security, reinforcing the relationship between mother and son since they go there together, but on the other hand it simultaneously represents a curtailment of freedom (for Bud is obliged to go to church instead of playing with his friend Albie). It certainly gives out confusing messages, and we see Bud repeatedly struggling to penetrate its rituals and myths. Whereas Davies's rage with Catholic doctrines is openly articulated in the *Trilogy*, here it is generally muted, for at this period he had still not rebelled against its rigidity and duplicity. Nevertheless, in the film's depiction of the church's dominating architecture, and in the violence of the scene where Bud imagines the crucifixion, we find both the child's perceptions and the adult's judgement.

The two different schools that are depicted can be seen to contrast feminine and masculine spaces, and the transition from the first to the second is itself a highly traumatic experience for Bud. The primary school is run by nuns, all of whom are depicted as gentle and caring. The rooms are small and filled with friendly clutter, and scenes in school frequently occur to the accompaniment of children singing. Secondary school, on the other hand, (just as in the *Trilogy*), is patriarchal, inflexible and threatening. Its bare walls, high windows and rigid classroom mappings signal its purpose as domination and control, and serve to emphasise both Bud's vulnerability and his difference. The new pupils are caned by their form master, merely to establish his power – 'You play ball with me, I'll play ball with you' – and, significantly, it is this same teacher who later gives the lesson on erosion. Moreover, the equation of power, masculinity and violence once again serves to establish the Law of the Father.

In a way, the cinema, the fourth space of childhood, is just another building, although of course it is a place of wonder and fantasy in which the children feel free. Unlike the other spaces that constitute Bud's world, it does not seek either to control or to dominate, and we are made aware of this fundamental difference in a number of ways. Our first view of the cinema occurs as Bud stands outside in the rain, waiting to find an adult willing to take him in to an A-rated screening. Two things are immediately apparent. First, all we see of the building is the doors, that is, its architecture is presented not as container but as entrance or exit, as opening or place of passage (as surely as the poster on the wall functioned as opening in the first sequence). Second, even though Bud is waiting in the torrential rain, there is no sense of unhappiness.

Indeed, the mood is much more that of *Singin' in the Rain* than of the persistent dampness of Liverpool, as if to underline the fact that what happens inside the cinema is so powerful that it leaks out into the environment, actually shaping Bud's reality. In this situation, Bud himself loses his customary timidity; he boldly asks passers-by to take him in, and, as he comes out at the end of the show, he is brave enough to tease one of the school bullies (which he would never dare to do within the hostile environment of playground or classroom).

If these four places define the limits of Bud's world, they also constitute its substance, for the spaces between them are rarely articulated. It is true that we see Bud's street, and watch him running along it, or out of it, just as we see his siblings leaving it for the wider world, but we never follow them. Usually the transition from one place to another is marked by a dissolve, which is motivated and often structured by music, as if the child's mind were constantly racing ahead, or looking back, or dreaming of escape. The effect is that Davies powerfully constructs the tightly contained, close-up world of childhood. And yet, because that world, like him, is created through and by film, its defences can be breached; it cannot entirely contain the child. One breathtaking sequence in particular, occurring some three-quarters of the way into the narrative, vividly illustrates this. Starting as Bud, solitary as usual, swings by his hands from the railing over the cellar steps, the sequence is structured as a continuous right to left track, with the camera looking vertically down at its subjects from a high crane. The trajectory of the shot follows Bud's street, then the projection beam through the smoke-filled cinema auditorium, then moves along the aisle of the church, reaching the altar just as the priest is celebrating Mass, then the classroom as the boys get up from their desks, about turn and file out, and finishes where it started, looking down at Bud in his street. What is so amazing about this single, continuous shot is that in it inner and outer spaces blend, barriers and differences dissolve, and the apparently discrete times and places of childhood form a single movement. The retrospective right to left track, of course, clearly indicates the process of remembering, while the vertical angle of the camera's viewpoint suggests the eye of the remembering adult looking back at the temporal and spatial construct of his childhood world. As a child, Davies/Bud was trapped within that world; as an adult, he is able to bring to his memories a sense of perspective and distance. Disparate times, spaces and viewpoints thus fuse through the movement of the camera, while the impossible logic of a shot which enables the camera to return to its starting point without changing direction both articulates and critiques the nature of the autobiographical process, the formation of subjective identity and the discourse of cinema created through the spatial and temporal movement of the camera.

While this sequence most perfectly sums up the landscape of childhood, it also reveals the innovative vision of the director. First of all, just as we saw in the opening sequence, the camera movement simultaneously constructs and deconstructs the relationship of time and space: past and present merge, and barriers between inside and outside disappear. Thus the child is both product of this world and yet never entirely contained by it; identity itself is posited as flux and change.

It is significant that, in relation to memory and to identity as process, the camera movement in this sequence is motivated and structured by music: a recording of Debbie Reynolds singing the title song 'Tammy', from the soundtrack of *Tammy and the Bachelor* (Joseph Pevney, USA, 1957) is heard throughout. The romantic melody and over-the-top lyrics ('I'd sing like a violin, if I were in your arms') contribute a powerful sense of nostalgia and loss, while the distancing vertical point of view of the camera reflects the ironic gaze of the remembering adult. Together music and camera create an imaginary, subjective time in which all of childhood is fused into a single 'long day'. The self is revealed as construct of the gaze: the self-consciousness of the landscape has 'the look of flowers that are looked at'.

One of the ways in which Davies manages to blur temporal and spatial boundaries so effectively is through the shifting relationship between sounds and images, for, if external and internal spaces are fused together by the camera's constant mobility, their essential permeability is highlighted by Davies's soundtrack. In the 'Tammy' sequence, for example, the recording of the song itself is overlaid with filmic quotations that leak out from and into all the spaces the camera simultaneously creates and explores. For instance, as the camera moves through the church, in addition to the romantic refrain of Tammy we hear not only the diegetic sounds of the altar bell and the congregation chanting their responses but at the same time an extract from the soundtrack of *Kind Hearts and Coronets* (Robert Hamer, UK, 1949). And as we watch the priest consecrating the host (film as transubstantiation?), we hear Alec Guinness's words: 'And in the pulpit, talking interminable nonsense, the Reverend Lord Henry Dascoyne. The Dascoynes certainly appear to have accorded with the tradition of the landed gentry and sent the fool of the family into the church.' This complex collage of conflicting times, spaces and realities allows the adult Davies to intervene in his own memories, to provide an ironic re-evaluation of these memories but also to acknowledge the extent to which both he and his remembered world are a filmic construct.

Identity

In his study of Italian cinema between 1986 and 1996, Pierre Sorlin (1996) suggests that it is the consumption of films (whether domestic or American) by successive generations in a given country that provides the key to the identity of its 'national' cinema. He thus replaces the traditional approach, based on the listing and analysis of domestic film production in relation to funding and distribution and in opposition to other cinemas, particularly Hollywood (see, for example, Hayward 1993; Higson 1995; Street 1997), with something less rigid and confrontational, explaining that four generations of cinemagoers have built up an enormous palimpsest of different sounds and images, domestic and other, which they use to organise their lives. What is intriguing about Sorlin's idea is its recognition, on a national scale, of something we have noted in relation to autobiographical films, namely that what matters to an identity is not so much the provenance of particular images as the manner in which they have been appropriated and re-used. As Sorlin points out:

> The evolution of community feelings is linked to the unstable, permanently moving relationship between the social organisation, the institutions, and the set of symbols (linguistic, visual and aural) which human beings use to make sense of the world that surrounds them. The process is itself determined by the existence or absence of a standardised, shared system of reference. The cinema was part of a cluster of tools which enabled the Italians to build a picture of themselves, both individually and as members of a group. (Sorlin 1996: 170)

Not only does this approach do away with rigid distinctions and oppositions between indigenous films and imports from Hollywood, but it also illustrates nicely the process which we can trace in *The Long Day Closes*, namely, the way in which the films that filled and delighted Davies's childhood not only provided the lens through which he would make sense of the world, but also have been assimilated by him to form part of his own identity. And through recognising this process of assimilation (which, in relation to *The Long Day Closes* we might approach as the opposite of erosion), we can attain a clearer understanding of what Smith, in her study of women's autobiography, refers to as 'the heteroglossic possibilities inherent in new ideologies of selfhood' (Smith 1987: 174–5).

With its innovative and intensely personal camera, its visual intelligence and its polyphonic and textured composition, *The Long Day Closes* is far more than 'just' another version of Davies's autobiography. As a complex and multilayered investigation of identity and memory which explores contemporary theories of time and space, the film reveals self-conscious modernist preoccupations with the processes and motivations of art, and psychological and sociological concerns with the creation of individual identity. And if *The Long Day Closes* was repeatedly criticised for failing to satisfy the spurious demands of social realism, this is because Davies is not concerned with notions of 'category' or 'genre'. Despite their shared references and common memories, his autobiographical films up to and including *The Long Day Closes* do not in any way seek to replicate each other. Instead each contributes afresh to a fluid and open-ended journey or process of exploration which constantly transgresses or blurs borders and distinctions of all kinds, whether between truth and fiction, past and present, inside and outside, or realism and formalism. Davies's fascination with quotation, modulation and collage in *The Long Day Closes* clearly situates this film within a postmodern context in which 'categories are not fixed once and for all. They are redistributed, reshaped and reinvented for each film' (Deleuze 1989: 185).

Notes

1 Even here, however, we can identify a filmic reference, since Davies traces this image of nails being driven into Christ's hands to a shot in *The Robe* (a poster for which features in the opening sequence of *The Long Day Closes*).
2 Particularly relevant, in this context, is Paul Ricoeur's concept of 'tiers temps' ('third time'), which relates to the interplay between the temporal dimension of narration and that of the narrated events (Ricoeur 1985).
3 It is interesting to contrast the adult and controlled script with which Davies introduces his autobiography with the deliberately childish examples of actual handwriting used by Moretti for the credits to *Caro diario/Dear Diary* (Italy, 1994) (despite his appearance within the film as an adult), and by Godard for the intertitles and captions in *JLG/JLG* (France, 1996).
4 The words of 'The Long Day Closes', published in 1902, were written by Henry Fothergill Chorley (1808–72), and set to music by Sullivan as one of a set of seven part-songs.
5 Recognition of the self as filmic construct is, of course, fundamental to autobiographical films in general, and to the awareness of other modernist directors such as Jean-Luc Godard, who acknowledges in an interview with Jonathan Cott that both his life and his own identity are a filmic construct (Cott 1988: 97).
6 Filmic autobiographies are frequently introduced by a voice-over by the director; one of the generic characteristics that relates to Lejeune's 'pacte autobiographique', whereby the author acknowledges the autobiographical status of the work. However, of course, there are more subtle but equally powerful ways of signifying authorial viewpoint. 'Diegesis' is the term used to refer to the entire fictional world of the film, to everything that is occurring on-screen. Thus diegetic music is music whose source is depicted on-screen (for example, a juke box or radio),

whereas extra- or non-diegetic sound or music has no such source. Examples of the latter would be voice-over or theme music.

7 Marketed as 'The miracle story of all time', *The Robe* tells the story of the various ways in which both the followers and the enemies of Jesus are affected by the robe handed down by him at his crucifixion.

8 As we have already seen, *The Ladykillers* is the last, and possibly the greatest, Ealing comedy. Mackendrick is reputed to have said 'To be frivolous about frivolous matters, that's merely boring. To be frivolous about something that's in some way deadly serious, that's true comedy', and it is interesting that this idea of laughing at painful memories is also one of the innovative features of *The Long Day Closes*.

References

Caughie, J. (1992), 'Halfway to paradise', *Sight and Sound* 2/1 (NS), May, 11–13.
Cavanagh, D. (1995), 'Terence Davies', *Empire* 77, November, 61.
Cott, J. (1988), 'Godard: born again filmmaker', in Sterritt, D. (ed.), *Jean-Luc Godard Interviews*, Jackson: University Press of Mississippi.
Danks, A. (1998), 'The art of memory: Terence Davies' *Distant Voices, Still Lives*', *Metro* 116, 53–4.
Deleuze, G. (1989), *Cinema 2: The Time Image*, London: Athlone Press. Translated by Hugh Tomlinson and Roberta Galeta.
Dixon, W. W. (1992), '*The Long Day Closes*: an interview with Terence Davies', *Cineaste* 19/2–3, December, 20–3.
Durgnat, R. (1992), '*The Long Day Closes*', *Sight and Sound* 2/2 (NS), June, 44.
Fuller, G. (2001), 'Summer's end', *Film Comment* 37/1, January/February, 54–9.
Hawking, S. (2001), *The Universe in a Nutshell*, London, New York, Toronto, Sydney and Auckland: Bantam Press.
Hayward, S. (1993), *French National Cinema*, London: Routledge.
Higson, A. (1995), *Waving the Flag: Constructing a National Cinema in Britain*, Oxford: Clarendon.
Hunt, M. (1999), 'The poetry of the ordinary: Terence Davies and the social art film', *Screen* 40/1, Spring, 1–16.
Kemp, P. (1996), 'Alexander Mackendrick', in Nowell-Smith, G. (ed.), *The Oxford History of World Cinema*, Oxford: Oxford University Press, p. 371.
Kristeva, J. (1980), *Desire in Language*, New York: Columbia University Press. Translated by Thomas Gora, Alice Jardine, and Leon S. Roudiez.
Radstone, S. (1995), 'Cinema/memory/history', *Screen* 36/1, Spring, 34–47.
Ricoeur, P. (1985), *Temps et récit*, Paris: Seuil.
Rosalato, G. (1974), 'La voix entre corps et langage', *Revue Français de Psychanalyse* 38, January, 75–94.
Smith, S. (1987), *A Poetics of Women's Autobiography: Marginality and the Fictions of Self-representation*, Bloomington: Indiana University Press.
Sorlin, P. (1996), *Italian National Cinema, 1986–1996*, London: Routledge.
Sterritt, D. (ed.) (1998), *Jean-Luc Godard Interviews*, Jackson: University Press of Mississippi.
Street, S. (1997), *British National Cinema*, London and New York: Routledge.
Williams, C. (ed.) (1996), *Cinema: The Beginnings and the Future*, London: University of Westminster Press.

Symphony for a new world? *The Neon Bible* 5

> *Erhebung* without motion, concentration
> Without elimination, both a new world
> And the old made explicit, understood
> In the completion of its partial ecstasy,
> The resolution of its partial horror.
>
> ('Burnt Norton')

With the completion of *The Long Day Closes*, Davies claimed that his autobiographical 'phase' had reached its natural conclusion, and that he was now ready to attempt something entirely different. Amongst the considerable speculation as to just what sort of film might result there was even talk of 'a contemporary "thriller" set in New York', although one suspected that Davies was perhaps being ironic here (Dixon 1994: 249). Whilst the move away from autobiography to fiction is common in both literature and film, and acknowledging that Davies's earlier films had, despite their autobiographical framing, explored time, memory and cinema in radically different ways, nevertheless their intensely personal discourse made it difficult to predict where Davies would go next. That he should choose to move into adaptation is not surprising given his profound love of literature, and that he should adapt the text himself seems inevitable given his passion for writing, and the controlling vision that characterises his extraordinarily detailed shooting scripts. Even the text he chose, *The Neon Bible*, a short first novel written in the early 1950s by the then very young John Kennedy Toole, seems, with hindsight, scarcely surprising although, without doubt, it would have been less easy to predict

The novel is set in the American Bible Belt in the Deep South in the 1930s and 1940s, and tells of the experiences of a quiet, introverted boy (David) who, following the death of his father in the Second World War, is brought up by his mother and his exotic Aunt Mae, a professional singer. In terms of Davies's personal film-making journey, on the one hand this film represents a significant change of direction, entailing not only a move away from his personal autobiographical material but also a shift of continent (in relation to the setting and the cultural and historical context of the narrative, but also to the process of filming, which constituted Davies's first (and so far, unique) experience of working in the United States). However, on the other hand, the territory in which he finds himself in *The Neon Bible* is less alien than might at first appear. True, the setting is remote from the narrow terraces of postwar Liverpool, Catholic ritual has been replaced by evangelical fervour and pubs have given way to drug stores but, despite all this, the central theme of the novel is entrapment, and its predominant concern is with time and memory (reflected in its form as well as its content, since the story itself is structured as an extended flashback). Moreover, the story is related by its young protagonist as a first-person memory narrative, and the background and experiences it explores are strikingly similar to those which had characterised Davies's own childhood. Paternal brutality, religious intolerance, bullying by teachers and other children, loneliness and the awkwardness of developing sexuality are the novel's tightly interwoven themes. Even music is accorded a vital role, to the extent of being foregrounded through the character of David's Aunt Mae. And the cinema (which David frequently visits with his aunt and his mother despite its condemnation by the local pastor as immoral and corrupting) is shown to provide his only means of escape from the claustrophobic atmosphere of the small town. It is thus evident that *The Neon Bible* occupies a transitional position within Davies's work, for in it we can identify both the continuation of technical and formal concerns that had emerged in his earlier films and clear indications of the changes that will lead on to his subsequent film, an adaptation of Edith Wharton's *The House of Mirth*. Davies willingly acknowledges the transitional status of *The Neon Bible* in various interviews about the film, saying, for example, 'I think it was a transitional work because it came mostly from the book and yet was a bit autobiographical too. Because it was about the nature of time and memory, it was close to my heart, but a lot of people said it was just more autobiography, but poorly disguised' (Fuller 2001: 55).

This last comment about the response to the film as thinly disguised personal autobiography reveals no little bitterness on Davies's part since, while allowing that the film was to some extent flawed, he nevertheless believes this particular criticism to be unjust. It is interesting that, whereas critics had found the self-conscious irony and quotation in *The Long Day Closes* too radically different from their expectations of the film as a further chapter in Davies's autobiography, they would then criticise *The Neon Bible* for not being different enough. Having speculated about the sort of fictional work Davies might produce, they were frustrated that the film appeared, yet again, to be dealing with his own childhood memories, 'unconvincingly' transposed to the Deep South. Jonathan Coe, quoted in *Sight and Sound*, exemplifies this fairly widespread reaction: 'Those of us who were on the whole relieved to hear that Davies had finally got his family history out of his system might, it seems, have been jumping the gun actually, *The Neon Bible* could almost be another slice of Davies's autobiography, relocated to America's deep South and provided with a tragic denouement' (Horne 2000: 14). To make matters worse, *The Neon Bible* was summarily dismissed by critics at Cannes, and it still remains relatively unexplored, despite its importance as the transitional work that enables us to trace Davies's progression from autobiography to fictional adaptation.

Moreover, it is just as dangerous to condemn *The Neon Bible* for being too predictable as it had been to condemn *The Long Day Closes* for being too different, since both these reactions are based upon preconceptions rather than on any consideration of the films on their own terms. For example, many of the comments about the 'sameness' of the narrative content of *The Neon Bible* are unfair given that the incidents it portrays can be directly sourced within the novel Davies had faithfully adapted (so that it is his choice of text, rather than his film, that might more fairly be criticised in these terms). To clarify this notion, it is important to consider *The Neon Bible* in relation to the processes of adaptation since this will provide valuable insight into Davies's aims and specific concerns in the film.

However, before we do so, it is interesting to note that as well as being criticised for its content, *The Neon Bible* was accused of being stylistically repetitive. This is a somewhat puzzling comment given that the film is certainly no less inventive or technically innovative than its predecessors. It is true that the film is immediately recognisable as the work of Terence Davies, marked as it is by its fluid camerawork, its audacious tracking shots and deliberate framings, its musical structures and slow rhythms. But given that such formal and stylistic features constitute to some extent the defining characteristics of Davies's work, it is hardly surprising that they should feature in *The Neon Bible*. (We could easily compile a list of such characteristics for any number of directors, not least Bergman, Ozu or Antonioni, all of whom have been seen as part of the context in which Davies's own work should be approached.) And the fact that such features exist in *The Neon Bible* in no way indicates stasis, or – and this is surely a necessary corollary of Davies's belief in the inseparability of form and content – a failure to adapt the film's stylistic composition to its meaning. Furthermore, in

The Neon Bible Davies is actually extending his formal range considerably with, for example, the increasingly daring choreography of his camera, as well as taking issue with new questions such as the fractured and mirrored doubling fundamental to the narrative. And it is important to recognise the many strengths of *The Neon Bible*: its dramatic narrative development and emotional power, the convincing performances given by the actors (particularly Gena Rowlands's portrayal of Aunt Mae) and the stunning photography and camerawork. It had long been an ambition of Davies to work in Cinemascope, and it is especially exciting to see someone famous for the intimacy of his camera exploring the epic potential of this format. Scenes which stand out in particular include the townsfolk flocking down the street to the religious revival meeting, or the single white sheet flapping on the washing line to the accompaniment of the theme tune from *Gone With the Wind*. Above all, therefore, it is essential to recognise the film's complex and innovative nature.

The novel

Since this is Davies's first work of adaptation, and since it constitutes his first move away from the directly personal, it is interesting to map his creative response to *The Neon Bible* in order to establish whether he is, in fact, merely using the novel as a frame on which to display once again his own autobiographical experiences, or whether, on the contrary, he is using these experiences as a lens through which to achieve a clearer understanding of the text. This chapter therefore begins with a brief examination of the novel.

The Neon Bible was written by John Kennedy Toole when he was still only a teenager, although it was not published until 1989, twenty years after his suicide (the most likely cause of which was his repeated failure to get his work published). It is, in many ways, quite clearly the work of a young writer with a tendency to overexplain and a taste for the melodramatic, and it lacks both the confidence and the verve of Toole's second – and only other – novel, the far better known *A Confederacy of Dunces*. Written a decade later, although similarly unpublished until after his death, *A Confederacy of Dunces* was awarded the Pulitzer Prize upon its publication in 1981, and went on to achieve bestseller status, quickly establishing the international reputation of its author.

Whereas *A Confederacy of Dunces* provides a broad, fast-moving and satirical portrait of New Orleans, John Kennedy Toole's home town, the chosen setting for *The Neon Bible* reflects a very brief visit to rural

Mississippi that he and a school friend made sometime in 1952. The novel paints a detailed, intimate and reflective picture of the claustrophobic existence of its young protagonist in a small town relentlessly oppressed by prejudice and religious bigotry. For David, one of the few glimmers of light in an otherwise drab existence is provided by the arrival of his exotic Aunt Mae, who quickly becomes his only childhood friend and companion. David's family is poor, and increasingly marginalised by the town, particularly once his father is sacked for union activities, as is no longer able to afford the church dues. Nor does the arrival of the unconventional Aunt Mae help the situation; she is seen as too brash and too confident, and her clothes and general appearance meet with universal disapproval. Even worse, she comes from outside the valley, undoubtedly the most heinous of all crimes. The family is marginalised physically as well as socially, exiled to a tumbledown shack on the hillside overlooking the town and forced to eke out a precarious living on its barren soil. Under these pressures, David's father becomes frustrated and violent, his mother's mental instability increases and the child who watches as his father beats her unconscious is himself subject to ruthless bullying by other children and by his class teacher. When America is drawn into the Second World War, David's father enlists and is sent to fight in Italy, where he is later killed. Upon the news of his death, David's mother has a complete breakdown, and after Aunt Mae's sudden decision to move to Nashville, David is left alone to cope with her illness and death. In a desperate attempt to protect her body from the clutches of the preacher who arrives (not knowing of her death) to transport her to a lunatic asylum (part of the town's determination to rid itself of 'difference' of any type), David shoots him, and then leaves on the next train.

Despite the melodramatic conclusion to the story, it is not difficult to understand why it might have attracted Davies. Clearly, many of David's experiences are ones he would find familiar, a fact that would give him a particularly vivid insight into the motivations and concerns of the child. Moreover the child's essential solitude and his quiet and submissive observation of the world around him seem to provide a close reflection of the character of Davies himself as a child, particularly as portrayed in *The Long Day Closes*. In other words, Davies's reading of the novel would inevitably have been sympathetic, and his interpretation based on an imaginative and emotional identification. Moreover, the tragic history surrounding the book's young author, and the fact that it was almost entirely due to his indomitable mother that Toole's work did eventually achieve the recognition it deserved, would inevitably have further intrigued Terence Davies. However, it is clear that as much as anything he was fascinated by the formal structure of the novel, by its concern with time and memory and by its painstaking portrayal of what Davies has, in another context, characterised as 'the poetry of the ordinary'. The first-person narrative creates David's limited viewpoint, and the world we see is observed entirely through his eyes, inevitably reflecting his partial and limited understanding of the events he witnesses. The tiny details which enable the reader to bring his or her own understanding and experiences to bear on the text thus serve to imbue David's words with deeper layers of meaning and a wider viewpoint, and this notion of multiple viewpoint, being a key feature autobiographical discourse, is something Davies understands profoundly.

The narrative of the novel is constructed as an extended flashback. It opens intriguingly as the (as yet unnamed) narrator sits on the train: 'This is the first time I've been on a train. I've sat in this seat here for about two or three hours now. I can't see what's passing by. It's dark now, but when the train left, the sun was just beginning to set, and I could see the red and brown leaves and the tanning grass all along the hillside' (p. 3).[1] Three paragraphs later, a reference to his own toy train serves as a trigger which transports us directly back to his early childhood, 'But I had a train of my own. It was a toy one I got for Christmas when I was three' (p. 4), and we then move, with David, through other salient memories which are unleashed by that of the toy train. At the end of the first chapter, we return to the present 'So here I am riding on this train', as past and present fuse within the rhythm of the journey: 'The clicking on the rails is getting faster, and I can see the trees crossing the moon quick now. The years before I went to school passed by just about as quick as those trees are passing by the moon' (p. 19). From this point, the narrative explores David's memories until the very short final chapter in which, still on the train, just as dawn is breaking, David brings us back to the present, describing the journey he has made through the night, and the countryside through which the train is currently passing. The entirely open-ended conclusion (David has no idea where the train is taking him, or what he will do when he gets there) offers a direct answer to the dark sightlessness of the book's opening, 'The sun's up full now over the short trees, and I can see the sky's the same clear blue that it was yesterday in the valley' (p. 162). Thus the novel self-consciously explores the circularity of time ('In my end is my beginning'), just as Davies had done in his autobiographical films and, in so doing, it plays with images of darkness and light, with night and morning, with motion and stasis just as he had done.

Life in this small town, symbolically situated within a steep-sided narrow valley that marks the boundaries of David's world as surely as the terraced streets of Liverpool contained that of the young Davies, is inflexibly ruled by prejudice and bigotry. It is a place in which everyone knows everyone else's business, and no form of difference is tolerated:

> If you were different from anybody in town, you had to get out. That's why everybody was so much alike. The way they talked, what they did, what they liked, what they hated ... They used to tell us in school to think for yourself, but you couldn't do that in the town. You had to think what your father thought all his life, and that was what everybody thought. (p. 138)

The weak and vulnerable, just like those who are in some way different, are ostracised by this implacable society. Dancing, singing (unless hymns), literature and, of course, film are all condemned as sinful, as the work of the devil. And the predominant concern of the preacher and his followers is the need to protect, at any cost, the 'purity' of the valley's blood, whether from people of colour (p. 138) or from 'contamination' by outsiders of any sort, especially those 'heathens' from Europe, a concern whose irony in the postwar context of the story provokes a powerful response in the reader (p. 95). Indeed, after the war, a society is organised by the church with the sole purpose of '[keeping] the valley blood pure and Christian and free from the heathen blood that might ruin it and bring damnation to the valley' (p. 95). Culture of any sort is viewed with suspicion, and whereas in his last year at school David is introduced to classical music and poetry (he quotes Longfellow's 'The Day Is Done' as 'the only beautiful thing I ever heard') (p. 101), such interests are scorned by the community at large, and the poetry written by his English teacher, Mr Farney, is dismissed as trash when it is published in the local paper.[2]

Like Tucker, in Davies's *Trilogy*, David seems hopelessly trapped within this world. When his father is killed and his mother has a breakdown, he is forced to leave school to work in the local drugstore to support his family, so that he does not even have the possibility escaping to high school and university, as his classmates do. And this situation, which so closely echoes Davies's own experience, would be bound to excite his sympathy. Throughout his childhood David dreams of escape, and this is repeatedly symbolised in the novel by his toy train and the imaginary landscape he constructs for it in an empty upstairs room. A taste of the possibility of freedom is given by Aunt Mae, with her album of photographs and newspaper cuttings, and her exotic tales of faraway and unimaginable people and places, and it is of course significant that she is the only adult who actually plays with David. It is also through Aunt Mae that David discovers the cinema, which increasingly provides him with a form of escape as he grows older. With the onset of war, visits to the cinema become part of the town's way of life, despite the disapproval of the Church:

> With nothing much for anyone to do with their fathers and husbands and boyfriends gone, the movies were where everyone went ... They had a lot of Technicolor movies playing that Mother and I and Aunt Mae liked. In town we got the movies about a month after they played in the capital, and the bill was changed three times a week. We saw lots of black-and-white movies too, but Bette Davis seemed to be in every one of them ... They had Rita Hayworth too, but she was always in Technicolor, and her hair was the reddest I ever saw. We saw Betty Grable in this movie about Coney Island. It looked like a wonderful place, and Aunt Mae told me she had been there and that it was down on the gulf. (p. 57)

Through cinema, therefore, the worlds of small town Mississippi and postwar Liverpool collide and merge.

Another important element in the novel is its depiction of the ways in which the social dynamic of the town changes when the men are away at war, becoming more tolerant and good-natured, and this of course is another observation that reflects Davies's own experiences. Not only does going to the cinema become increasingly popular at this period, but the grip of the Church is weakened, and even Aunt Mae is accepted and respected by the community. She is made a supervisor at the war plant which has been rapidly constructed in the valley (it is a propeller factory, in a significant continuation of the myth of escape), and one night she organises a party at the plant for the women and children of the town. There is a band, the women dance and joke together, drink beer and applaud Mae's singing in one of the rare moments of happiness provided by the novel. However, this respite is temporary for after the war such activities are quickly curtailed, and even the increase in pregnancies that marks the return of the menfolk is frowned upon as further proof that they have been contaminated by the promiscuous world outside the valley. In addition to trips to the cinema and the occasion of Aunt Mae's party, the only other event which provides David with any escape from routine is the visit to the town of the Revivalist preacher Bobbie Lee Taylor; Toole devotes nineteen pages to this event, which he describes with remarkable detail (pp. 57–75). From this lengthy description emerges his anger with religious hypocrisy and intolerance; an indictment which closely mirrors the treatment of the Church in Davies's earlier work

The first point to emerge from the above description is the number of similarities between *The Neon Bible* and Davies's own childhood experiences as articulated in his autobiographical films. This observation is of fundamental importance in revealing that the widely criticised overlap between this film and his earlier works does not result from Davies attempting to impose his vision upon that of John Kennedy Toole, any more than it indicates his limitations as a director, but instead reveals the film to be a faithful adaptation of the novel itself. Indeed, Davies's film does not substantially alter any of the original narrative, retaining both its chronology and its form. Any critical evaluation of his film must recognise this, and, instead of pointing out that the story too closely resembles his own, should rather consider ways in which Davies interprets and adapts the novel, looking in particular at his ability to move from literary and linguistic structures to the image-based mobility of film.

Questions of adaptation

The process of adaptation is, of course, highly complex, involving far more than just the simple retelling of a story in a different medium. An often neglected reason for this is that the events occurring in the narrative must be recognised as little more than mileposts within the novel's overall development, whereas its 'meaning' is a complex blend of form and content. Since Davies is particularly sensitive to this aspect, we would expect to find that his adaptation is as much a response to the form and style of the novel as to its narrative content.

Before evaluating the success or failure of any adaptation, it is essential to be aware of the fundamental differences between literature and film, given that the process is one of movement from the essential linearity of linguistic structures to the simultaneity and immediacy of visual images, characterised by constant movement and by the multiplicity of signifiers which include not only visual symbols and colours, framings and camera movement but also performance, dialogue, music and a whole range of other sounds both diegetic and non-diegetic. (For example, on occasion in Davies's *The Neon Bible*, not only do we watch events occurring on screen while listening to dialogue, voice-over and/ or music, but we also hear the sound of the train on which David is sitting, so that different times and spaces are simultaneously brought together in a way that no written text could quite achieve.) In film, even a single shot is perceived as part of a shifting composition of light, camera angles and movement, involving characters and images, and that sense of movement and change is fundamental to any discussion of the medium. Davies is a particularly interesting director in this context, first because his own autobiographical films both articulate and self-consciously explore the multilayered potential of film, and foreground his conviction that form and content are inseparable, but also because his talents as writer and scriptwriter and his love of literature and poetry have made him particularly sensitive to the differences between the two forms of expression. Whilst retaining the general structure and the main events of the novel, and introducing only minimal changes in its overall chronology, Davies uses the text sparingly and with great clarity of focus. Of course, as with any adaptation, he is able to omit the lengthy descriptive passages since he can recreate the scene directly for us, but even so he ruthlessly reduces both the dialogue and the number of narrative events that the novel charts. That is not to say that he changes or limits the story or the dialogue which, indeed, is remarkably faithful to the original. He retains David's first-person narration as a voice-over, while clearly recognising the 'literary' flavour of this device. In his *Anatomy of Film*, Bernard Dick scornfully characterises voice-over as an overused device which provides 'an easy solution for unimaginative filmmakers', and we shall see in the next chapter that Davies rejects this device in his adaptation of Edith Wharton's *The House of Mirth* (Dick 1990: 21–2). However, in this case, it is the self-conscious intimacy of David's voice, and the slight sense of artificiality it introduces, that provide the thread linking the film's mobile and unmarked shifts through time and space. And as these complex temporal and spatial shifts reveal with overwhelming clarity, the voice-over in this film is being used not to replace more complex and inventive filming techniques, but alongside them, as part of the film's complex layering.

The film also retains both the major events which form the plot of the novel, and the order in which they occur: the arrival of Aunt Mae; the scene in which David is bullied by Bruce; the seeds incident which leads to the first abuse of the mother; the Revivalist meeting; the father's departure for war; the women's party in the factory; the news of the father's death; David's graduation; his first date; the departure of Aunt Mae; and David's shooting of the preacher. The narrative development of the film therefore closely reflects that of the novel. Davies does subvert the novel's linear chronology to some extent, using the camera's ability to fuse different times and spaces in order to recreate the particular intimacy of the novel, the world within David's head, and ensuring that we experience the external world entirely on David's terms. I commented earlier that Davies retains the novel's basic flashback structure (whereby the narrative is framed by David's train journey), but this too he subverts somewhat, returning more frequently to David in the train, or allowing the sound of the train to intrude over the 'past' events we are watching. And of course, the perceived 'present' of all film images allows him to recreate the temporal shifts of memory more directly and with greater 'realism' than the discrete tense shifts of language permit. Within this basic flashback structure, therefore, the film's chronology is more fluid than that of the novel, and it provides far less explanation, and almost none of the temporal or spatial signposting of the book. One exception to this is the inclusion of a recording of Roosevelt's famous address to the nation, 'A Day that will Live in Infamy', which recounts the events of Pearl Harbor, and marks the start of America's involvement in the war. This addition, which contrasts quite strikingly with the novel's throwaway comment that 'the war had been on for quite a while now when Poppa got his notice of the draft' (p. 55), does perhaps identify Davies's gaze as that of an outsider who needs to clarify national experiences that are not his own. To this extent, its function may be compared with a number of the songs that Davies includes in the film since they too are redolent of period and place. (This aspect will be studied at greater length in Chapter 7.) However, Davies's re-creation of small-town America in the 1930s and 1940s, his awareness of American artistic and musical traditions and his exploration of the social and political structures of the town all reveal convincingly that the experiences he shares with his protagonist are being used not as an end but as a means; as a way of understanding intellectually as well as emotionally the new universe his film explores. What the film seems therefore to achieve is something part way between the memory narratives of his earlier films and the linearity of Toole's novel.

I have already commented that the 'present' tense of the train intervenes at several points within the past-as-present tense of the story, and suggested that this temporal mobility creates an intimate sense of actually being inside David's head. One clear illustration of this concerns the burning of books. In the novel, this scene springs from David's recollection of his sadistic and cruel primary school teacher, Mrs Watkins. He recalls that her husband was a deacon in the church, and that he was well known in the neighbourhood for his campaigns against 'coloured people' and 'dirty' literature, such as *Gone With the Wind*. This book, in particular, was targeted by him because the fact that it was going to be made into a film was proof enough of its corruption. In the novel, we are told that 'a group met in front of the library in black masks and went in and took *Gone With the Wind* off the shelf and burned it on the sidewalk' (p. 25). In the film, Davies portrays this incident on two separate occasions: initially, David sees the event almost in passing, and neither he nor we are given any explanation. Moreover, in the relevant scene, Davies brings together the two prejudices Toole describes, by dressing the men who are burning the books in the white robes of the Ku Klux Klan. The event then recurs in voice-over as David sits on the train much later in the film, when we hear his younger self asking 'What are they doing?', and the reply that he is given, 'they are burning the books'. By splitting the event over time in this way, Davies clearly replicates the processes of memory and comprehension; only as a teenager is David able to understand the significance of the event he witnessed as a small child. But we could go further, for, if we consider this event as a secondary framing device, it serves to stress further the extreme bigotry of the town, and obliges us to situate David's action in killing the preacher within that context. It also sets up the opposition between prejudice and culture as a strong underlying dynamic in the film. For Davies, of course, the attack on freedom of expression illustrated by the book-burning incident is made even worse by its specific relationship with cinema, and this perhaps goes some of the way to accounting for the role he accords *Gone With the Wind* throughout his film.

Clearly the shift from personal memory to narrative fiction serves to introduce into Davies's work an awareness of a world beyond the purely domestic. The interior of the house in *The Neon Bible* is not the spatial focus of the film in the way it was in his autobiographical works, since that role is accorded to the town itself consequently the predominance of interior shots and studio-based filming seen in his earlier work is here replaced by location shooting, and wider exterior vistas. Moreover, for all the passive introversion of its protagonist, *The Neon Bible* does impose on Davies a more conventional dramatic narrative structure than is found in his autobiographical works, and for the first time his film includes intrigue and confrontation, melodrama and murder. The film also signals a move away from the theme of homosexuality, whilst the substitution of the vibrant and complex Aunt Mae for the mother figure who dominates his personal memory narratives frees Davies somewhat from those particular emotional ties, and enables him to embark upon a more distanced exploration of a female character, an experience which will prove essential for his following project, *The House of Mirth*. It is interesting to note, however, that both the mother and the colourful and glamorous Aunt Mae are essentially portrayed as victims of a male-dominated society in ways that have been made familiar in Davies's earlier films. David's mother is abused physically by her husband, and mentally by external social pressures. Aunt Mae reveals that beneath the glamour that she portrays, she is just 'a used up piece of goods', an object of the male gaze, to be repeatedly used and abused by men. And, of course, Lily Bart in *The House of Mirth* is also very much a victim of an equally pitiless patriarchal community.

While the deliberate and stylised framings, the reflective and mobile camera, and the slow rhythms of *The Neon Bible* make it immediately recognisable as Davies's work, they exist only as ways of exploring filmically the situations represented in the novel. And despite these 'recognisable' features, the film remains fundamentally innovative, in both technical and formal terms. Although the foregrounded music, self-conscious quotation and complex layerings of diegetic and non-diegetic sound which are so central to *The Long Day Closes* do have a role to play here, nevertheless it is clear that differences of approach are more significant than the apparent similarities. For example, in *The Neon Bible*, while music is still used to create passageways or openings between different times and spaces, and to trigger and shape memory as much as to articulate mood, nevertheless it is perhaps less important overall than visual composition and camera movement. When I interviewed Davies, in February 2001, I suggested that moments of greater detachment, or freedom, in his work were inevitably signified by a more mobile camera, an idea that he accepted, and this theory is borne out by the extreme mobility of the camerawork in this his first fictional film (see Chapter 8). However, this is not a mere stylistic tic, for, as we have repeatedly commented, form and content are conceived by Davies as inseparable. I shall therefore explore how the framings, camera and editing which are at the very heart of Davies's adaptation, should be recognised as part of the process of recreating in visual terms the world that John Kenney Toole fashions from language.

It is clear that one of the reasons why Davies was so excited at the prospect of making this film was that it enabled him to work in Cinemascope, not only because for the first time he had a budget that made this possible but also because it seemed to him the only way of articulating the American myths and dreams that underlie the narrative, or more specifically the Hollywood representations of those American myths and dreams. And if the occasional epic dimension that the film provides might seem to be at odds with a first-person and essentially intimate view of the world offered by Toole, nevertheless this element plays a key role within Davies's adaptation.

Entrapment

The central dynamic of *The Neon Bible* is created by the opposing themes of entrapment and escape. On the one hand, we have the imploding pull of the town, characterised by prejudice and mental rigidity, on the other the longing to break free, to escape. Weaker characters, such as David's mother, conform or are destroyed, while the more resilient, such as Aunt Mae, escape as soon as they are able. It is significant that, when

David's father is forced by the war to remain in Italy, his letters to his family reveal the extent to which he has changed. The mere experience of distancing himself from the valley has enabled him to grow as a person, has given him a wider perspective and new understanding of the world. 'The sun wasn't prettier anywhere else, he said, than it was in Italy. It was the brightest and yellowest he ever saw, much brighter than in the valley in the middle of summer' (p. 85). David, for his part, is entirely trapped by his family circumstances within the town and his longing to escape, like his dreams of freedom, fills his fantasies: 'I wished I could fly and follow those birds and be two hundred feet above the hills and see into the next valley where I'd never been' (p. 51).

The film sets up this sense of entrapment from the title sequence, in which we see a pattern of four bibles, overlaid with four crosses, and outlined in neon lights, forming a square, and then gradually moving closer and closer together to create ever tighter and more complex boxes or divisions until, finally, they overlap in a single image. John Kennedy Toole's mother recollects that it was her son's fascination with an image of a bible depicted in neon lights on a church that he once glimpsed as he drove along a highway that provided the inspiration for this novel, and thus Davies's title sequence powerfully unites this reference with a powerful indication of the claustrophobic rigidity of the world that the film will explore. The image also situates the Church as being at the centre of this constructed world, while the neon lights convey a sense of tackiness that will be further enhanced in the film's depiction of Bobbie Lee Taylor's great Revivalist meeting.

From the first, the young David is tightly framed on screen in ways that clearly foreground his entrapment. He is repeatedly placed within windows or doors, and whether in confrontational shots with his father, on occasions when he is being bullied or when securely flanked by his mother and aunt, David is still equally trapped. Indeed, shots such as the one in the Revivalist meeting, where the camera focuses directly on David seated between his aunt and mother, make it clear that he is trapped by love and family responsibilities just as much as by external pressures. And while it is obvious that David needs these two women, so too they, at different times, need him just as badly. For example, it is with David, rather than with her husband, that David's mother chooses to sleep after the bullying incident (in further reference to the Oedipal myth, of course), just as, later in the film, it is Aunt Mae who asks him to sleep next to her, to hold at bay the demons and fears that haunt her. Initially, the reasons why David is unable to leave town as he so longs to do are that, with his father dead, it is he who must support the two women, and later because, when his aunt decides to leave, he must take care of his ill mother.

Escape

Within this narrow entrapment, a number of visual devices provide metaphors of escape. The small town is entirely hemmed in by the steep sides of the narrow valley, and its confined geographical locus is reflected in the narrow minds of its inhabitants. Thus the image of the train which frames the narrative and acts repeatedly as a trigger from present to past, and past to present, both on its own and through its relationship with David's treasured toy train, provides a potent symbol within the story since its mobility symbolises freedom and escape from the stasis of the town and valley.

We have already commented that the book opens with David's first ever ride on a train, as he tells us that it is night, and that he is cold, and then describes the scene as the guard walks along between the carriage seats, turning off the lights. The opening of the film, however, emphasises the significance of the train itself with a series of mythologising shots which set it up as an object of power and mystery. The very first shot provides a close-up of the wheels of the engine, which function here as signifiers not only of change, motion and circularity but also, through their complex geometry of spokes and circles half obscured by clouds of steam, of the complexity of David's situation. This is a hauntingly beautiful image which immediately captures the interest of the spectator, and it is one which later will be reflected and developed in the opening shots of *The House of Mirth*. The restricted tonal range of blues and greys, and the muted and sad music (*Perfida*, composed by Alberto Dominguez, and performed by Glenn Miller, a piece which will again be heard in the closing sequence of the film), together create a powerful mood of melancholy and uncertainty.

Strikingly, when we first see the wheels, they are motionless, defying their normal indexical connotation, and, as the film develops, we will gradually understand this as a comment upon the ultimate hopelessness of David's attempt to escape. As we focus on these wheels, they begin to turn, building up momentum as the train moves from right to left across the screen, in what we therefore read as a retrospective journey.[3] The camera then pans slowly upwards, still in close-up, denying us any wider context, until we see a close up of David, on the right of the screen, framed by the window. Thus the compartment window forms a screen within a screen, a *mise-en-abyme* that both reveals Davies as a self-conscious director and presents David as a fictive construct. Surrounded by a wide black framing, the shot clearly indicates a restricted and enclosed locus which, like the static wheels in the opening shot, contrasts strikingly with the usual perception of train as escape or change.

It is fascinating in this context to consider the French critic Roland Barthes's description of train travel as stasis within movement. Trains (like cinema) restructure space and time by constructing a subject (passenger/spectator) who is simultaneously still and in motion. In his essay on the experience of eating in the dining car of a moving train, Barthes draws attention to the fact that it is because the passenger in a moving train is paradoxically static and yet at the same time moving that she or he has the impression that it is the countryside that is flying past the train, the countryside that is actually moving past the window rather than the other way about. Barthes refers to this phenomenon as 'transported immobility', and this is precisely the reaction we have as we look at David (Barthes 1993: 790–2). The train may well be transporting him through space, but we can see that mentally he remains static, looking inwards and backwards, utterly absorbed in his thoughts, still trapped in his past. And indeed, as both the framing and the retrospective right to left movement of the train clearly indicate, this is in fact a journey through time and memory as much as, or more than, it is a journey through space. The image is resolutely multilayered and complex in its composition. For what it shows, more precisely, is not simply David's profile framed within the inner screen of the train window but also his image repeated in a reflection in the window on the other side of the carriage. Whilst the double image reflects his inner turmoil and confusion, his fragmented identity, the three-dimensional space created by the two images captures him within a four-sided box as inner and outer spaces merge entirely.

The only sound is the engine as David turns to look at us directly, making us complicit in his self-conscious journey. A cut to a point-of-view shot of the guard advancing through the carriage, switching out the lights, is followed by a third-person shot of David in close-up, this time from inside the carriage. We then return once again to a profile shot, but now he is facing right rather than left, so that we read a forward-moving journey, and as this happens we hear more cheerful music. Gradually, the camera moves closer to his profile, which slowly disappears left, as if he is being left behind by the moving train. A fade to black then leads to an audacious shot. We appear to be looking in through the train window once again, and once again this window forms an inner screen within the screen, but what we see now is David as a small child in the centre of the frame, as his voice-over remembers 'People came to see us that Christmas'. The apparent forward impetus of the train thus in fact resituates the past as present as Davies subverts both time and space and simultaneously confuses notions of inside and outside, subjective and objective viewpoints. For while the voice-over prepares us to see the teenage David remembering his younger self, instead it is that younger self who gazes directly out at us from the train window. (We are back in that 'third' time, or 'imaginary' time discussed in relation to *The Long Day Closes*, but it is now given a clear dimension.) Four minutes have elapsed since the beginning before we hear David's voice-over and the first spoken words of the film, and already we are aware that the journey we appear to be witnessing is as subjective as is the space it crosses. The film then cuts to a truly astonishing inner/ outer shot in which the screen itself is divided vertically into two distinct halves. On the left side, we see balcony railings with snowflakes falling from the dark sky, while gleaming icicles hang from down from the top of the screen in a fantastic Christmas card scene. On the right-hand section of the screen David, as a small child, squats on the floor inside the house, absorbed in playing with his toy train. As we watch the snowflakes, his teenage voice is heard, saying, 'There was no snow. No not that year.' Thus, the shot presents both internal and external states simultaneously, while what we see and hear are in direct conflict, and in the tensions and spaces that result we start to read the layers of times and memories that crowd into the single image. This is condensed and powerful filming, and it conveys the emotions and time shifts of memory with a spare delicacy that the book fails to achieve, and at the same time reveals the potential of the visual image for creating complex multiple meanings.

It is thus possible to explore the film as a meeting of the creative sensibilities of two very different 'authors' – John Kennedy Toole and Terence Davies – and to appreciate the ways in which Davies's film, like any critical reading, is both a reflection and a creation, a simultaneous movement into and out of the original novel. We began this chapter by looking at some of the similarities which linked the fictional experiences of David and the actual experiences of Davies, as a way both of approaching Davies's possible reasons for making this film and of assessing the validity of the suggestion that his film was quite simply a version of his Liverpool childhood transported to the Deep South. That such comments are unjustified is apparent as soon as the film is examined in any detail, for its original and innovative techniques create powerfully, in filmic terms, the atmosphere, concerns and meanings of the text. However, there is one particular feature through which we can clearly analyse the film as an expression of Davies's own directorial concerns, as *auteur* rather that adaptor, and this key aspect, which relates in particular to the self-reflexivity of the film, has been almost entirely ignored in existing critical accounts.

It is at this point essential to return to Davies's concerns in *The Long*

Day Closes. In the previous chapter, we noted how, in the last of his autobiographical works, identity is posited as a construct, and is centred within Davies's personal relationship with cinema. Film, we saw, both shaped and coloured Davies's childhood, providing him with a tool for exploring the world outside the narrow topography of his own Liverpool street, but also leaking out into his world, his everyday reality, and in so doing transforming (and thus offering escape from) even the greyest of Liverpool rain, and the bleakest of streets or walls, and ultimately shaping his own identity. I suggest that in *The Neon Bible* we can discover a number of ways in which Davies is continuing to explore and develop these ideas. And it is perhaps this aspect above all else that highlights the film's originality, as well as pinpointing its transitional function. The concluding section to this chapter will therefore look at the role played by film itself as mediator and vision in *The Neon Bible*.

Film and text

As we have repeatedly seen, the cinema is in fact accorded an important position within Toole's novel, not least through its role in allowing his young protagonist to escape from reality for a while. However, the cinema ultimately provides neither salvation nor epiphany for David any more than it does for John Kennedy Toole. Obviously, this constitutes a major difference between his experiences and those of Terence Davies, and this key difference emerges clearly in Davies's adaptation which self-consciously reveals itself as a construct of other films; in other words, the world in which we view David is in fact a world which has been mediated through the lens of Hollywood, through the American musicals and epics that filled and coloured Davies's childhood.

Let us begin with a brief consideration of the nature and frequency of references to cinema that occur in the novel. We have already noted that going to the cinema is portrayed as an important form of escape for David. Moreover, it is significant that for him, just as for Davies, the cinema is established as a specifically female space. Initially, David discovers the cinema through his Saturday outings with Aunt Mae (p. 57), but later, during the war, these outings also include his mother. At this period, when the men were away at war, 'the movies were where everyone went' (p. 57), despite the preacher's repeated warnings that the cinema is a corrupt and corrupting place (pp. 25, 57). In this way, the cinema itself is constructed as an oppositional place, an alternative to the harsh Law of the Father as well as the narrow bigotry of religion. (In this, its affinities with Davies's autobiographical films are made clear.)

The third female figure related to David's experiences of cinema is his first girlfriend, Jo Lynne, with whom he goes to see a film on their first date. In fact it is possible to chart David's growth and development through his relationship with the movies which he initially sees as an extension of the games he plays with his aunt. A year or so later, it is because he understands the titles and credits on screen that David realises that he can read (p. 27). And finally it is the cinema that provides the setting for his first sexual experiences: 'The white light from the screen was shining on her lips, and they were wet, and I wondered why. She kept looking at the movie. I looked from her face down to where her arm was touching mine' (p. 126). Just as David sees Jo Lynne through his awareness of cinematic portrayals of female beauty, so too both his notion of romantic love and his belief in the classic Hollywood happy ending are constructs of the cinema: 'She didn't know what I thought when I saw the moon on her face, or when my arm touched hers in the movie, or even when I heard her walk into the drugstore ... She didn't know she was the only thing I ever wanted to have that I thought I'd get' (p. 133). In passing, it is worth noting that for David, too, woman is perceived in this instance as object, even more precisely as the object of his gaze. However, of course, it is not only Jo Lynne that lets David down; ironically all three of these women will later abandon him, so that neither they nor the cinema with which they appear so closely linked will provide him with salvation. But in the meantime, the movies do offer a source of escape, love, enjoyment and education, even if reality never quite lives up to its filmic version. Through David's observations, we also learn a good deal of general information about who goes to the cinema, how the programmes are organised and above all what stars and films are watched. We learn that while he, his mother and Aunt Mae enjoy the black and white movies (all of which, in David's opinion, seem to star Bette Davis), it is above all the Technicolor films that capture their attention, while their favourite stars are Jean Harlow, Rita Hayworth, Bette Davis and Betty Grable.

So cinema is accorded an important role in the novel, and Davies, of course, reflects all these and other filmic references in his film; however he goes much further because he uses his memories of the Hollywood films of his childhood to give sense and shape to the world his film explores. And in this context, it is the references in the novel to *Gone With the Wind* that are the particular focus of his attention.

Gone With the Wind

Gone With the Wind, the first and only novel by Margaret Mitchell, had been published in 1936, and awarded the Pulitzer Prize in 1937. Set in the South during and after the Civil War it was an immediate (and lasting) success, selling more than 1.5 million copies by the time the film version was released in 1939. In *The Neon Bible*, of course, we are given an indication of the highly controversial subject matter of the novel (which included rape, drunkenness and adultery), particularly through the incident in which a number of copies are taken from the library shelves and burned. However, we are also made aware that, in the eyes of the men responsible, the ultimate proof of the novel's moral debauchery is the fact that it is also made into a film.

The film itself does not feature in Toole's novel, or indeed directly in Davies's film. However, I would argue that, despite this, it does in fact play a major role in the film, providing a dominant subtext that emerges through musical and stylistic quotation, and exerting a key influence over Davies's depiction of both place and events. It is as though he were using his knowledge of that film as a means of visualising the world he seeks to represent in *The Neon Bible*. Before exploring the significance of this idea, it is perhaps worth making a few brief observations about the film version of *Gone With the Wind*, a star-studded romantic and melodramatic epic depicting the suffering and changes which the Civil War imposed on the traditional way of life in the Deep South. The film had an enormous budget, and was released in a blaze of publicity at its gala première in Atlanta on 15 December 1939, quickly achieving what we would now describe as blockbuster status. It was shot in three-strip Technicolor, and characterised by its dramatic and emotive use of colour, its sweeping photography and its powerful romantic score composed by Max Steiner. *Gone With the Wind* was the first colour film to win an Oscar, and in fact received some thirteen nominations and eight Academy Awards including Best Picture, Best Director, Best Actress and Best Film Editing, as well as being awarded two honorary plaques, one of which was for its use of colour 'for the enhancement of dramatic mood'. The screen credits tell us that it was directed by Victor Fleming, although four other directors also contributed (Sam Wood, William Cameron Menzies, George Cukor, Reeves Eason). The narrative itself covers about twelve years in the life of its heroine, Scarlett O'Hara, stretching from the start of the American Civil War, shortly after the election of Abraham Lincoln, and continuing into the Reconstruction period, and it places her various romantic and sexual encounters against a backdrop of historical events such as Sherman's march on Atlanta.

The film opens with a foreword which describes this world as a lost dream, a golden age, and thus accords a mythical status to the Old South: 'There was a land of Cavaliers and Cotton Fields called the Old South. Here in this pretty world Gallantry took its last bow. Here was the last ever to be seen of Knights and their Ladies Fair, of Master and Slave. Look for it only in books, for it is no more than a dream remembered, a Civilization gone with the wind'. Presenting a Southern viewpoint, the film is uncritical of issues such as slavery or class, and its depictions of servants and slaves are two-dimensional stereotypes, and often figures of fun.

In any consideration of the enormous success of the film, as well as the mythical status it would acquire within the popular culture and consciousness of the United States, the time of its release must be recognised as significant. War had been declared in Europe just a few months earlier, and the film's themes of conflict and survival acquired an added poignancy as a result. Not only would Scarlett O'Hara's opening complaint about the disruption war brings seem particularly relevant, but the depiction of the resulting upheaval might equally have helped to prepare Americans for their eventual involvement in the conflict.

The qualities of the film likely to have particularly impressed British audiences in the years of postwar austerity would of course have been its lavish spectacle, epic dimensions, glorious colour, romantic theme and powerful music. '*Gone With The Wind* complemented the flamboyant picture temples of the inter-war years and satisfied a public need for mass-consumer baroque' notes Rhode in his work on the history of cinema (Rhode 1976: 358). And it is true that the very 'baroqueness' of the exotic and unfathomable world it portrayed would have had considerable impact. It is scarcely surprising, therefore, that it should have provided Davies with a range of images of life in the Southern States that would inevitably have been triggered by his reading of *The Neon Bible*, nor that these images would subsequently inform his own film, as part of a whole range of different cultural, historical and geographical references. However, what is particularly interesting in this context is perhaps less the direct references (such as musical quotation) than the extent to which *Gone With The Wind* provides the mediating lens through which *The Neon Bible* is projected.

Davies had for a long time wanted to make a film in Cinemascope and, like David in *The Neon Bible*, was a great admirer of Technicolor, in particular of the notion of colour as an expressive tool. We have already seen the obsessive attention he paid to obtaining just the right colours in his autobiographical works, seeing this, in particular, as a way of accessing a lost past. It is therefore not surprising that, in creating his version of a small town in the Deep South in the 1930s and 1940s, he should have desired to re-create the colours with which *Gone With the Wind* had mythologised that region, and which would therefore have become part of the experience of people living in the South at the time in which *The Neon Bible* is set. From the cold blues and greys of the train to the brilliant sunrise that marks the end of David's journey, or the orange flames of the torches outside the marquee, the colours are marked by their strong clarity and emotive power. Similarly, the spatial freedom accorded by the Cinemascope format offered Davies the possibility of using epic proportions in his exploration of the tight intimacy of David's world. Two key illustration of this approach are the depiction of the Revivalist meeting and the long take of a white sheet flapping on a washing line, and it is helpful to consider each of these in greater detail.

We have already noted that Toole devotes an entire chapter to the Revivalist meeting, thus clearly signalling its importance in his eyes. Davies re-creates its importance, not by making it particularly lengthy but rather by making it larger than life; in other words, by depicting it in epic terms. The camera first follows and then rises above and behind the crowds as they walk down Main Street heading for the marquee in which the meeting is to take place, in a movement which almost directly quotes the crane shot in the railroad depot in *Gone With the Wind*, in which the camera similarly pulls back and up to reveal Scarlett O'Hara walking amongst thousands of wounded Confederate soldiers.[4] This is an effective and reflective shot in *The Neon Bible*, and the camera draws us, with the crowd, towards the marquee. In a dramatic and powerful shot, we see the huge tent, lit from outside by flaming torches, but also brilliantly illuminated from inside, so that the colours and spectacle inevitably recall the Atlanta fire sequence in *Gone With the Wind*, a point to which we will shortly return.

The scene with the flapping sheet, which is similarly depicted in epic terms, follows directly upon the scene dealing with the return of the soldiers from the war, with its emotional mixture of joy and grief, powerfully captured in Davies's travelling shot of the line of coffins, each draped with a flag, and inevitably recalling cultural memories of the wounded and dying soldiers in *Gone With the Wind*. Thus, although it might seem unlikely that a scene of washing flapping on a line could ever be a powerfully moving shot, let alone one suitable for epic treatment, nevertheless the context in which it is placed, along with the crescendo of Tara's theme from *Gone With the Wind*, enables it to perform in just such a way. And there are a number of other such epic moments that can be identified in *The Neon Bible*.

What are we to make of them? What do such scenes contribute to the narrative meaning and, more importantly, what do they tell us about the nature of Davies's filming? It is worth beginning this examination by noting that, for all its vast panoramas and sweeping vistas, the Southern world portrayed in *Gone With the Wind* shares much of the claustrophobic and prejudiced self-absorption depicted in *The Neon Bible*, and that this emerges through its treatment of non-whites, of 'white trash', and indeed of women in general (as mere commodities to be bought and sold). Moreover, comments such as that made to Scarlett by her (Irish) father near the beginning of the film – 'Well, what difference does it make who you marry – *so long as he's a Southerner and thinks like you?*' (my italics) – are echoed strikingly by David in *The Neon Bible*: 'You had to think what your father thought all his life, and that was what everybody thought' (p. 138), and by the town's obsession with protecting 'the purity of the valley's blood' (p. 138). In this way, *Gone With the Wind* can function as an extended metaphor, expanding the audience's understanding of the issues being explored. But it is important to look deeper, and essential to remember that the world Davies creates on screen is in fact a depiction of David's inner world. Given that we, the spectators, are required to share his narrow viewpoint, how then can Davies's use of epic features be understood?

This question is most easily approached in terms of the importance to David of the event he is recalling. Thus, for example, the evening on which he goes to listen to Bobbie Lee Taylor with his aunt and his mother (who, by then, was already something of a recluse, rarely leaving the house) is an occasion that would have assumed epic proportions in his memory. It was almost unknown for them to venture out at night, and this is almost the only time in which they are made to feel part of the whole town, rather than being marginalised, isolated on its edge. It is therefore hardly surprising that everything about that event should be larger than life. And for all its apparent exaggeration, the earlier reference to the burning of Atlanta in relation to the torch-lit marquee can thus be seen as an indication of the amazement David feels at this dramatic sight, while later, perhaps, the external image of the marquee might have become confused in his mind with the message of sin and hellfire that is meted out within. (Particularly since this memory is recalled as he is leaving the town after having murdered the preacher.) Similar comments apply also to the other scene of epic proportions noted above, namely the arrival of the coffins. On one level, by directly sourcing this event in *Gone With the Wind* Davies is able to situate the experiences of the Second World War within the context of the mythology surrounding the American Civil War, and thus to increase the multitextuality of his film. On another level, it is possible to see in these scenes the representation of the enormity of the experience for David. His first encounter with death is also the death of his father, an event that will alter his life for ever. Moreover, the horror of the occasion will inevitably assume new dimensions as he remembers it in the context of his mother's recent death, and of the murder he has committed.

References to *Gone With the Wind* thus serve to add new dimensions, new layers of meaning to the narrative of *The Neon Bible*, just as the 'period' songs and quotations from other films included in Davies's autobiographical films served to access and articulate different layers of memory and experience. He is thus implicitly reminding us that we cannot understand or represent identity or reality without recourse to earlier representations. But he goes much further than this by self-consciously drawing our attention to the cinema as the prime source of such representations. If we return briefly to the Revivalist meeting, for example, we are immediately aware that the scene of the crowds making their way towards the marquee, or seated inside, fanning themselves rhythmically with their hymn sheets, are 'exaggeratedly' epic also because Davies does not want us to be able to accept them as naturalistic in any way. On the contrary, he wants to draw our attention to them as cinematic construct. Even the opening shot in this sequence, where the camera pans slowly down past the banner which advertises the event, gives the impression of a curtain being raised and frames the scene as spectacle. And later, inside the marquee, as David, his aunt and his mother listen to the service, they are seated, facing the camera, immediately above the entrance, in a shot which is very reminiscent of the way that Bud sits in the balcony of the cinema in *The Long Day Closes*, while the camera focuses on his face as the light of the moving images flicker across it.

This self-conscious representation of memory as spectacle, and as spectacle mediated through film, particularly *Gone With the Wind*, is most clearly articulated in the scene to which I have already referred, in which the camera focuses on a sheet hanging from a washing line, gradually moving in closer until the sheet fills the screen entirely with what appears to be another screen and Tara's theme from *Gone With the Wind* swells to a climax. The sheets are being washed, the novel tells us, in preparation for the return of the menfolk from the war, and, as this scene immediately follows the shot of the line of coffins, it therefore carries with it the knowledge of the loss and suffering caused by war. By linking this with the dramatic images of death and suffering in *Gone With the Wind*, and drawing our attention to the method he is using by obliging us to stare at a blank screen, not only does Davies ensure that visual and other images must be created in our heads, but he also foregrounds the nature of film as construct, and its power in shaping our memory, our identity and indeed our reality. Moreover, the shot itself offers a particularly daring combination of visual simplicity (the screen is, to all intents, blank) and extreme referential complexity.

The final reference in this chapter is to the huge moon (another of the 'mythical' characteristics of the Deep South that we find in various filmic representations) that recurs like a refrain throughout *The Neon Bible*. David reaches up towards this moon at various stages in his memories, signifying his longing for escape. While the way in which it is photographed is stunningly beautiful, the moon is somehow too large, too dramatic to be naturalistic, and the futility of David's attempts to reach it, emphasised by the panes of glass that separate them, as well as by the vast distances, signify the moon as ideal, as desire to escape and be free. On one occasion, which extends this sense of artificiality to its extremes, as David reaches up he slowly morphs from childhood to adolescence. The intervening years are thus all condensed into this single shot, again foregrounding the power of film to subvert time and space, and to create its own reality. It is also significant that this particular scene is accompanied by the noise of the train, again expressing David's desire to escape, but this time placing it firmly within its filmic context.

Thus a film which, as we saw at the beginning of the chapter, was widely criticised for failing to be sufficiently different from its predecessors, reveals itself to be startlingly innovative and complex. And the images, criticised for being stilted and stylised, illustrate Davies's self-conscious awareness of film as construct, and his desire to involve the spectator critically within the creative process. As such, *The Neon Bible* repositions literary adaptation as an open-ended and multiple process as well as revealing ways in which Terence Davies challenges and redefines the notion of filmic narration in relation to postmodern constructs of identity.

Notes

1 This and all subsequent page references to *The Neon Bible* are to the 1989 Grove Press edition listed in the references to this chapter.
2 It is surely significant for Davies that this glimpse of the rich cultural world beyond the confines of the valley is given to David by his teacher Mr Farney, who is the only gay character, as well as the only intellectual, that we meet in the book. It is also worth noting that the title of Longfellow's 'The Day Is Done', significant by virtue of Longfellow's iconic literary status in the States, as well as for what it reveals about the nature of David himself, also resonates closely with the title of Davies's previous film, *The Long Day Closes*, and the eponymous anthem whose verses close that film.

3 It seems to me not entirely unreasonable to see in this opening sequence a playful reference to the opening of *Gone With the Wind*. Reputedly the biggest credits ever made, the letters of the title of that film appear, one at a time, each filling the screen, and slowly tracing a retrospective movement from right to left. To help the illusion, little lines drawn from the right hand side of each letter further suggest their movement.

4 This particular scene, which is indeed extremely impressive in its overwhelming portrayal of the sheer scale of the death and suffering involved, is famous in the mythology of *Gone With the Wind* for having necessitated the involvement of over two thousand live extras and dummies.

References

Barthes, R. (1993), *Oeuvres complètes*, vol. 1, Paris: Editions du Seuil. Translated by Richard Howard (1984) as 'Dining car', in *The Eiffel Tower and Other Mythologies*, New York: Hill & Wang.
Dick, B. (1990), *Anatomy of A Film*, second edition, London: St Martin's Press.
Dixon, W. W. (ed.) (1994), 'The Long Day Closes: an interview with Terence Davies', in *Re-Viewing British Cinema 1900–1992: Essays and Interviews*, New York: State University of New York Press, pp. 249–59.
Fuller, G. (2001), 'Summer's end', *Film Comment* 37/1, January/February, 54–9.
Horne, P. (2000), 'Beauty's slow fade', *Sight and Sound* 10/10, October, 14–18.
Rhode, E. (1976), *A History of the Cinema from its Origins to 1970*, Harmondsworth and New York: Penguin.
Toole, J. K. (1980), *A Confederacy of Dunces*, London and New York: Penguin.
Toole, J. K. (1989), *The Neon Bible*, New York: Grove Press.
Wharton, E. (1995), *The House of Mirth*, New York: Simon & Schuster. First published in 1905.

'A tapestry of small things': *The House of Mirth* 6

> The detail of the pattern is movement,
> As in the figure of the ten stairs.
> Desire itself is movement
> Not in itself desirable;
> Love is itself unmoving,
> Only the cause and end of movement,
> Timeless, and undesiring
> Except in the aspect of time
> Caught in the form of limitation
> Between un-being and being.
>
> ('Burnt Norton')

In contrast to the largely apathetic response that greeted *The Neon Bible*, the release in autumn 2000 of *The House of Mirth* met with almost unanimous acclaim. The film was variously described as a 'triumph' (Johnston 2000: 5) and an 'unpredictable, unformulaic success' (Horne 2000: 15). As an adaptation it was 'glorious' (Fuller 2001: 54), if 'sometimes harrowing' (Jackson 2000: 54), characterised by its 'intelligent fidelity' (French 2000: 7) and its 'intelligent beauty' (Jackson 2000: 54). It received a host of Oscar nominations including Best Actress, Best Film, Best Director, won a number of important international awards and inspired countless articles and reviews across the world. Davies was invited to give lectures and interviews in Britain, Europe, Canada and the United States. On a visit to New York for the film's gala opening, he was accompanied by Simon Hattenstone who, reporting the experience in a long and detailed feature in the *Guardian*, described how American journalists, stunned by the film, hung on Davies's every word, and how Davies handled the media attention imperturbably, and with his usual blend of humour and modesty (Hattenstone 2000: 2–4). Could this be the breakthrough that would, at long last, give Terence Davies the recognition he deserves?

The decision to adapt and direct *The House of Mirth* was bold in the extreme. It is one thing to adapt a short and relatively unknown novel such as *The Neon Bible*, but quite another, of course, to tackle a book which is considered a literary classic and therefore accorded a quasi-mythical status within a nation's cultural heritage, particularly if that heritage is not one's own. That, however, was precisely the task facing Davies when he decided to film Edith Wharton's 1905 novel. Inevitably, the risks and problems relating to adaptation which we touched upon in the last chapter are magnified when a book is considered to be a classic, and the director has the often thankless task of attempting to steer a path between such potential hazards as servile fidelity, on the one hand, and insufficient regard for the original, on the other; or between the requisite concern with period authenticity and the easy temptations of heritage cinema whilst, at the same time, deftly skirting around existing adaptations of the same novel or of other novels by the same author. And, most importantly, the director must remain true to *his or her* vision, *his or her* interpretation, for above all the film must be able to stand on its own. After all, the finished product, the film itself, is *not* a pale reflection of a literary text, and yet, despite our recognition that what we require from great film-makers is 'a show of independence', works that are 'sufficient in themselves', nevertheless the majority of critics and reviewers will still tend to evaluate such films in terms of their fidelity to the original (Taubin 2001: 62). In other words, as McFarlane has so often pointed out, discussion of adaptations continues to be 'bedevilled by the fidelity issue' (McFarlane 1996: 8).[1]

This chapter begins with a short introduction to both Edith Wharton and her first novel, and will provide a very brief description of its main features before examining Davies's reasons for choosing to adapt this work. This act of choosing is, of course, of fundamental importance for it already provides us with some understanding not only of the aims and ideas underlying the interpretation but also of the film that Davies has created; the film of which he is, without any doubt, the *auteur*. And given that Martin Scorsese had directed a generally popular version of Wharton's *The Age of Innocence* in 1993, and that comparisons between the two films were an almost inevitable component of the film's reception, we shall also look at this and other films that formed part of Davies's own cultural baggage in making his film. However, the main focus of this chapter will, of course, be the film itself, and the ways in which it articulates the fictional world it reflects, but also the ways in which it further develops and clarifies Davies's own directorial skills and interests. In other words, the chapter asks just how *The House of Mirth* relates to Davies's earlier films, and what new insight it provides into Terence Davies, the director.

Edith Wharton

Despite the risk of appearing to support exactly the reverential approach to the source text that I reject, nevertheless in this instance it is useful to start with a brief look at Edith Wharton not least because it is her position as someone who is simultaneously a part of, and yet marginalised by, the society that she describes in *The House of Mirth* that gives the novel its particular ironic distance and its multiple viewpoints, as well as suggesting one of the possible reasons why Davies was immediately attracted to her work. Edith Wharton was born into the rigidly structured and wealthy upper-class New York society in 1862. An intelligent and gifted child, she began making up stories when she was still very young and as an adolescent wrote both poetry and fiction. Wharton was never sent to school but, as befitted a young girl of her class, was taught at home by a governess, secretly supplementing the narrow education that was deemed suitable for her by devouring all the books in her father's library. She married young and attempted with increasing frustration to fit into the prescribed role of society hostess. That a woman in her situation should be a professional writer was simply not tolerated at that time, and the resulting stresses and pressures meant that Wharton did not publish her first book until she was in her midthirties.[2] Intellectually frustrated and emotionally suffocated by these social constraints, she suffered from bouts of depression which she seems to have controlled by escaping every year to France and Italy, and it was these trips, and the sudden freedom they offered, that inspired her to write a number of volumes of short stories and articles about gardens, architecture and art. Eventually she left her husband and moved to France, where she spent the rest of her life. In 1908 she began a lasting affair with Morton Fuller, a journalist on the London *Times*, and she quickly blossomed in the stimulating intellectual and artistic atmosphere of Paris, becoming part of a circle that included, for example, Paul Bourget, Jean Cocteau and André Gide. She formed a close friendship with Henry James, and with various expatriate artists such as Walter Guy and Ralph Curtis. Wharton developed into an extraordinarily prolific writer, producing, from 1902 onwards, an average of one book each year. During the First World War she played an active role in the Allied cause, particularly through her relief work with refugees, but also reporting from the front for American publications, and exerting considerable pressure on the American government to join the war. Her later years were spent in France, moving between Hyères, in the south, and a small village just north of Paris. In 1921 *The Age of Innocence* was awarded the Pulitzer Prize, and two years later Wharton was given an honorary degree from Yale. She died in France in 1937.

Despite their widely divergent social backgrounds, therefore, Wharton and Davies certainly share the experience of feeling both trapped and, at the same time, marginalised by the respective societies in which they grew up, and particularly by the rigid gender stereotyping these social contexts imposed. Both found physical escape the necessary prerequisite of creativity, and for both of them, of course, it was art that ultimately provided salvation. What Davies's autobiographical works share with Wharton's novels (specifically, in this case, *The House of Mirth*) is thus that combination of close familiarity and ironic distance, of hopeless entrapment and a longing to escape, and Davies thus could empathise with Wharton's experiences and her work and feel 'at home' in his filmic exploration of her fictional universe.[3]

The novel

The House of Mirth was published in 1905 when Wharton was forty-three. She had not written much fiction up until then, although she had published volumes of short stories and a historical 'romantic chronicle'. The title of her first novel is taken from Ecclesiastes 7, 4 – 'The heart of the wise is in the house of mourning; but the heart of fools is in the house of mirth' – and the basic material for the narrative is provided by the New York upper-class society in which she had grown up, and whose weaknesses and foibles she ruthlessly exposes: materialism; hypocrisy; superficiality; prejudice. A quick glance at the historical context affords some insight into the culture and society that the novel depicts. The turn of the century was a period of high immigration in the United States, and labour was therefore plentiful and cheap, hence the abundance of servants employed by rich New York society. Money, which could purchase new luxuries such as cars and yachts, suddenly opened up exciting possibilities of travel for such people. But, at the same time, the climate was marked by an uneasy awareness that society was changing irrevocably as the 'old' wealth was giving way to the 'new', and it is clear from her novel that Wharton herself was antagonistic towards such changes, and critical of the new breed of self-made and successful businessmen. That she was a creature of her time and upbringing is revealed also in her anti-Semitic prejudice (shown in her disparaging portrayal of Sim Rosedale, the self-made Jewish businessman who becomes one of Lily's suitors), and her somewhat condescending treatment of the working class, two elements of the novel that Davies elected to omit.

Davies was quite widely criticised for not making references to Rosedale's Jewishness. Writing in *Cineaste*, for example, Nochimson claims that 'Davies recalls the worst of classical Hollywood by repressing the word "Jew" from the dialog and attempting to substitute dated codes'. Her criticism is that contemporary audiences will not read such codes, and thus will not recognise ethnicity as an issue within the film, and that this is a basic flaw in Davies's adaptation (Nochimson 2001: 42). However, the claim that Davies was attempting to hide the issue behind outdated codes appears itself to be fundamentally flawed. It is rather the case that, in his reading of the novel, it is the social implications of the marginalisation of Rosedale as a self-made man attempting to buy his way into society that are the important ones. For Davies, the marked anti-Semitism of the text, like its condescending treatment of the poor, reveals a good deal about Wharton's own prejudices and those of the age, but contributes nothing to the narrative dynamic. On those terms, he was not prepared to replicate the prejudice: 'I found the anti-Semitism the most dispiriting thing about Wharton's work, in her later novels, as well. I deleted it. I simply could not bring myself to write it or to direct an actor to do it' (Constanzo Cahir 2001: 169). In practice, Davies not only rejects the book's anti-Semitic tone but perhaps actually compensates for it on a subtextual level through two of his musical sources: Morton Feldman's *Rothko Chapel*, with its quotation of traditional Hebrew melodies, and Alexander Volkoviski Tamir's 'Shtiler Shtiler', a wartime Estonian Resistance song. (This notion will be more fully developed in the next chapter.)

Briefly, the novel is set in the upper echelons of New York society during the opening years of the twentieth century, and it charts the experiences of Lily Bart, a beautiful orphan who, although penniless is, nevertheless, socially well connected. Supported by her wealthy aunt, Lily more or less makes a career out of being a house guest in the homes of her fashionable friends, where she is tolerated because of her beauty and charm and in the expectation that she will inherit her aunt's fortune. However, when we first encounter her, Lily is twenty-nine, and the need to secure her future by finding a rich husband is pressing. She nearly succeeds on a number of occasions, but generally does something at the last minute to spoil her chances, such as when she forgoes an arrangement to go to church with the wealthy but boring Percy Gryce, in order to spend time alone with Lawrence Selden. Although she is strongly attracted to Selden he is not rich enough to be considered a suitable husband, while other wealthier suitors, such as Rosedale, are rejected for lacking the necessary breeding and social standing. When Lily is falsely accused of having an affair with the husband of one of her 'friends', she is socially ostracised and her chances of finding a rich husband are ruined. Disinherited by her aunt, she is forced to work as a milliner, and, when this job too fails, she falls deeper and deeper into poverty and despair. The novel concludes with her death from an overdose of chloral. The irony is that Lily could have saved herself had she chosen to exploit certain compromising letters that had by chance come into her possession. However, she cannot bring herself to do this, largely because of the repercussions such an act might have for Selden. She could also have had her debts cancelled by Gus Trenor or settled on her behalf by Rosedale had she agreed to become a kept woman but this, too, her strong inner morality would never contemplate.

Wharton's novels are of course famous for their detail, their sharp sense of irony, their stinging satire and strong morality. Her characters are vividly drawn, but, while secondary characters may often be two-dimensional, her heroines in particular, such as Lily Bart in *The House of Mirth* and Ellen Olenska in *The Age of Innocence*, have a complexity and vulnerability that makes them entirely believable. They are frequently portrayed as the victims of a pitiless patriarchal society governed by rigid conventions of respectability and appearance, and entrapment and constriction emerge as key themes in her writing.

Davies's reasons for choosing this novel

Davies first became interested by the idea of filming *The House of Mirth* some fifteen years before actually doing so, when he heard on the radio a reading of the letters which had been written by Edith Wharton to Henry James.[4] Fascinated by these, he embarked upon her novels and her autobiography and, as he explains in a number of interviews and articles about the film, what attracted him in particular to *The House of Mirth* was its overwhelming modernity. In its total obsession with money and appearance, Davies insists, the world depicted in the novel offers a clear reflection of our own. 'It's about what do you look like and how much money have you got. And what is modern society about? Nothing's changed except for the frocks that are worn ... That's why the book is very modern, it's about surfaces. It's the perfect example of that line from *The Importance of Being Earnest*: "We live in an age of surfaces." We did then and we do now' (Stone 2001: 1). Tellingly, Davies relates this world to what he sees as its contemporary cinematic equivalent – Hollywood – and finds it to be just as sinister and cruel. Lily, of course, is entirely trapped within this hermetically sealed world, in a way that inevitably recalls the situations of Davies's earlier characters, including his autobiographical self, as it does that of Edith Wharton. Any such parallels are further enhanced by the way in which, within this narrow setting, Wharton uses Lily Bart to explore the extent to which individual identity is shaped and strengthened by adversity, for Lily does grow and develop, and the story is ultimately about her journey to self-awareness or clear-sightedness as much as her social decline. Davies's adaptation therefore reflects the contemporary relevance of the book and its key themes. He is interested in using film not as a means of replicating the novel as a historical artefact but rather as a way of exploring the insights it can offer into contemporary life and identities.

So once again we find the themes that dominate Davies's earlier films: entrapment, exploitation, social exclusion and cruelty, as well as the individual's overwhelming desire to escape, to be free. *The House of Mirth* also reflects something of the male/female dialectic central to Davies's own experience and to his films: Lily Bart's vulnerability, her suffering and eventual downfall can all be understood as the direct outcome of the dictates of a patriarchal society. This is because Lily, like all the other women in the book, is essentially a commodity to be purchased or rejected by men, and both her social status and her ultimate fate are thus dependent upon them. Wharton underlines these ideas right from the opening chapter of the book when, in her conversation with Lawrence Selden, Lily explores the difference between their respective situations and comments 'What a miserable thing it is to be a woman' (p. 22).[5] For his part, watching Lily as she measures the tea into the pot, Selden presciently notes that 'She was so evidently the victim of the civilization which had produced her, that the links of her bracelet seemed like manacles chaining her to her fate' (p. 23). From the first, therefore, Lily is presented as a victim in a society that prizes appearance and money above all else. However, like the mother figure in Davies's autobiographical accounts, Lily is also a fighter, and it is therefore not surprising that Davies would have been attracted to her character. And indeed, if he sees *The House of Mirth* as 'a great modern tragedy', Lily Bart herself is conceived as 'a great tragic heroine' (see Chapter 8). Moreover, and certainly in Davies's reading of the text, it is Lily's fierce and uncompromising morality which ultimately proves her undoing; she can never quite play by 'the rules of the game', to refer to Renoir's earlier filmic observation of social hypocrisy and its victims (*La Règle du jeu/The Rules of the Game*, France 1939).[6] It is her innate sense of morality and innocence that prevents her from actually agreeing to marry for money, rather than love, as it would also prevent her from subsequently indulging in what Davies has called the 'peccadillos' considered normal within that society's hypocritical moral rules. She is thus doomed not by her misdemeanours but by her innocence and her fundamental morality.

Davies was, of course, just as fascinated by the book's linguistic resonances, the rhythms and nuances of its language, as by its moral dilemmas and narrative conflicts. Lily Bart, like the world of which she is a part, is a linguistic creation; both her weaknesses and her strengths are a construct of Wharton's vivid prose and powerful dialogue. And so it is this formal aspect as much as the narrative itself that Davies needed to address in his filmic interpretation of the novel: the nature of Lily and her world as fictional construct, and the tones and rhythms of the text that create her. Furthermore, the fact that the novel is about the power of the (male) gaze, and the objectification of those it looks at, makes it perhaps particularly suited to Davies's self-conscious film-making.

A key reason for his determination to make this film was that, as Davies read the novel for the first time, he knew immediately where the camera should be placed, and what it should be doing. In other words, he was able to visualise the text as film at once, so that, as he explains in a brief interview included on the DVD version of *The House of Mirth*, he never for a moment doubted his ability to make this film (Davies 2001).

Davies on adaptation

'The text tells you everything and you try to keep in mind its tone, which is important, and the look and the feel of it. But it's got to be cinema as well', comments Davies, acknowledging the dichotomy at the heart of adaptation: the need to remain true to the original text but also to break free of it in order to create something which is cinema (Davies 2001). And as we have seen, in the process of understanding the original text, its formal construct (its 'look' and 'feel') is of equal or greater importance than the narrative events it traces. What Davies also realises is that it is even more essential to look 'between the lines of the text'; to read beyond and between the words; to respond creatively to the silences and intervals that lie at its heart. The rare ability to read between the lines of the text, I suggest, is exactly the quality that sets Davies's adaptations apart from so many others, and creates their particular and powerful resonance. For in Davies's opinion, one of the greatest fascinations of film is its unique ability to explore or create meanings which are not shown or stated. As he explains in his commentary on the film, the intense close-up focus on Lily's face, particularly her eyes, powerfully illustrates the way in which cinema achieves this (Davies 2001).

Stressing the central importance of what is *not* said, the gaps and the silences between words and images, does not of course decrease that of the language that creates them. Davies's first response to a text is to its language, for it is the way in which it is written that will ultimately dictate the underlying pace and rhythms of his adaptation. Preparing to compose his screenplays thus inevitably involves a detailed analysis of the original written text, both its narrative structure and dynamic and, in particular, the cadences, sounds and rhythms of its language. In *The House of Mirth*, while Davies retains Wharton's own words for much of the dialogue, there are a number of occasions on which he is obliged to compose his own, and it is obviously a matter of honour that such additions should be indistinguishable from the original. We have commented upon the extraordinary detail of his screenplays, and the way that they reveal that every camera move, every gesture and vocal inflection has been visualised by him well before shooting begins. Nevertheless, Davies insists that, like the original text itself, the screenplay is only the blueprint, the starting point in what he refers to as the 'long, constant, organic process' of making a film (Davies 2001). He believes that on set the director must be receptive to the changes and additions that the actors themselves may contribute, and be prepared to modify the text if necessary. Thus, at all levels, the making of a film emerges as a long and complex journey; an open-ended process of exchange and reassessment.

Even once the filming is complete, this process continues through the editing, presenting director and editor with the need to make vital decisions about where to cut, for it is these decisions that will establish the film's form, its internal rhythms, and therefore its meanings. 'Do you cut before she drops her eyes and before the doors open or vice versa? Both of these things mean different things and that's when you begin to discover the subtext – that's when the subtext really emerges. That's when the film begins to sing, if indeed it does sing' (Davies 2001). For Davies, the 'music' of the film, therefore, is part of what he calls its 'subtext', created both through and between its images and sounds, and this idea reinforces yet again his belief in the inseparability of form and content. Davies's films are as self-contained as music, hence their extraordinary emotional power.

However self-evident such considerations may initially seem in evaluating a filmic adaptation, it is also worth remembering the constraints and practical problems facing the director as the result of inadequate funding. Overcoming such problems requires an originality and inventiveness based upon a fundamental understanding of the nature of the medium and of its difference from the literary text that inspired it. Davies decided, for example, to film *The House of Mirth* in Glasgow rather than New York as this was by far the cheaper option. The locations in which he recreated 1905 New York included the Kelvingrove Art Gallery and Museum, the Glasgow City Chambers, and the Theatre Royal (which was used for the New York Metropolitan Opera House interiors). Whilst not authentic (a point that seemed to worry a number of American reviewers), the locations nevertheless appear entirely credible in terms of the film: 'if like me you believe that what you don't see is just as important as what you do see, then we're in New York in 1905', Davies comments (Davies 2001). However, the need to use Glasgow instead of New York gave rise to a number of problems. One example was the filming of the Van Osburgh wedding for which, as Davies explains, the script required an Episcopal church. Unfortunately, such churches are not to be found in Scotland, and, since there was no money to build the necessarily complex set, Davies was suddenly faced with the need to find a solution, and he did so with typical imagination and flair. 'So what is the easiest way to tell you about a wedding? What do all weddings have in common? They have photographs. Well in those days the image in the camera was upside down. So you see them upside down ... "I now pronounce you man and wife", and they're the right way up. It's witty, it's succinct. And it's cheap' (Davies 2001). Thus by including a single frame showing an inverted image of a bride and groom, a device that could not have worked in another medium, Davies both creates an entire wedding in the spectator's imagination and enables his narrative to move directly to the reception in a coherent and convincing manner. This is only one of a host of instances where lack of money required radical and innovative solutions. Others include the carriage ride that Lily has with Gus Trenor. Davies wanted to have a carriage passing through the streets of New York but this would have been impossibly expensive. Instead, the scene was shot against a black backcloth, in an interior set of a carriage, with lights continually going past, and it is these changing lights that powerfully suggest movement and create a sense of dislocation or alienation. We therefore see the light and shade chasing across Lily's face as she persuades Gus Trenor to help solve her financial problems. However, while talking, she frequently drops her head, further obscuring her face so that we cannot be certain of her motives or her emotions but must continually imagine or deduce them for ourselves. Davies thus successfully draws the spectator into the storytelling process.

Lack of adequate funding also accounts, for example, for the fact that the engine dramatically belching out steam in the film's opening scene is a construct of plaster and wood, while a number of sweeping vistas, including the coast of the south of France and the view of the

Mediterranean from the yacht, are, in reality, computer-generated images. None of this matters, of course, to the extent that we recognise film as a fictional construct and accept that the 'authenticity' of locations and artefacts is far less important than their contribution to the film's meanings. However, as the above examples clearly demonstrate, inventiveness and flexibility are constantly called for in transferring script to film, and what matters above all in the process is that the resulting shots are both imaginative and specifically filmic in their conception, and that they directly contribute to the integrity of the director's vision.

The House of Mirth as filmic construct

As is so often the case with Davies, the starting point for understanding this film is his awareness of the fictionality or artificiality of the universe he simultaneously creates and explores. *The House of Mirth* is a film which, above all, is about the gaze, the nature of sight (both physical and metaphorical) and the complex power struggle between looker and looked-at, and this is true as much of the filmic gaze, that of the camera and spectator, as the narrative (male) gaze which, in both book and film, seeks to objectify and thus to control Lily. In this film, as in his autobiographies, therefore, Davies foregrounds the multiplicity of gazes, not only through close-up observations of characters' faces and eyes and repeated play with mirrors and windows, but also in the self-conscious manner in which it interrogates its own status as film. It is this transition from literary text to self-conscious, self-reflexive film through the gaze of the camera that constitutes the film's fascination, and in this section we shall consider some of the elements that lead to this ultimate transition.

It is significant that Davies eschews the use of voice-over in *The House of Mirth*, not least because it would be hard to justify the sense of control that it would impose, given that voice-over almost always assumes a position of authority and encourages the viewer to accept its version of events. In literary adaptations, the device is often seen as a tempting and rather easy way of retaining the authority of the narrator or author, and indeed Martin Scorsese uses this device with some success in *The Age of Innocence* as his way of allowing Wharton's words to be heard. Davies, however, recognising *The House of Mirth* as a novel about looking, about viewpoint, finds it essential to retain the interplay of fluid and unstable gazes that lie at the book's core, and he therefore refuses the 'easy' solution of voice-over.[7] Instead of using a narrator to articulate Wharton's language, he allows her voice to emerge through the dialogue and rhythms of the film. In the novel, much of what we learn about Lily comes from other people's descriptions of and reactions to her, and these tell us more about the speakers than about Lily, particularly since such observations are often partial and flawed. Thus the reader must gradually construct a response to Lily based upon an independent and creative reading of the text. Davies's film works in a similar way, for in it the viewpoint shifts constantly from first to third person, and frequently we cannot identify who is looking, particularly since we are denied the guidance of an omniscient narrator. Moreover, within the film's acknowledged status as construct, it is the camera that performs the role of narrator and, since it acknowledges this function openly, it obliges the spectator to be the creator of images. The film thus reflects upon the nature of the gaze, and uses devices such as mirrors, veils, curtains and eyes themselves to draw attention to the need to look not only at the images but between and behind them as well: 'That's what I love about cinema. It always reveals what goes on behind the eyes. It's the only medium that does that. It's just wonderful. So much goes on without being said' (Davies 2001). It seems to me that it is precisely this awareness that makes Davies's adaptation much sparser and more delicate than Scorsese's, which seeks to tell and to show everything through its dense surplus of images.

We have already noticed, in relation to Davies's earlier films, that though important, locations are valued less for their 'realism' than their conflation of exterior and interior spaces within a 'memory realism', or psychological realism that is composed of interwoven times, places and viewpoints. In other words, Davies uses settings or objects never merely for the sake of it, or simply because they are, or appear to be, authentic period artefacts, but only as an articulation of the fundamental meanings of the film. This approach gives his work an essential focus that is often lacking in literary adaptations, certainly in period adaptations of literary classics. It is this rigorous focus that immediately sets this film apart from the more traditional heritage adaptations that dominate British cinema, a point recognised by critics such as Romney, for whom *The House of Mirth* feels altogether 'un-British' in its rejection of what he calls the 'comforts of heritage cinema', and the 'touristic distractions of costume drama' (Romney 2000). In his opinion, Davies's directing is characterised by its 'matter-of-fact austerity', and this judgement appears to be justified, certainly if compared with Scorsese's somewhat lush and filled-in camerawork, surfeit of period detail, authoritative voice-over and relentless romantic background music. 'Austerity', however, is a particularly interesting word to use in this context, given the frequency with which Davies himself has in the past been accused of 'self-indulgence'. In Davies's methodology, there is no justification for paying excessive attention to detail unless in so doing the camera replicates the gaze or thoughts of (one of) the characters, or unless it is in some other way contributing a new dimension to the film's deeper meanings. Whereas Scorsese claims that the visual detail in his film reflects Edith Wharton's own descriptions, in *The House of Mirth* it is precisely Lily's indifference to such details that repeatedly frustrates her aunt who, requesting graphic accounts of what was eaten, how it was served and what was worn on specific social occasions, is annoyed by Lily's inability to provide her with such information (p. 160). Lily does *not* pay attention to such details because they form part of her everyday experience, and are thus so mundane as to be taken for granted. Davies sees no point in gratuitous detail unless germane to the meaning of the scene. We could cite the intense attention he pays to the silence inside Aunt Peniston's drawing room, for example, which foregrounds the smallest sounds of a clock ticking or a floorboard creaking, because it is central to the intense claustrophobia that Lily is experiencing. Similarly, when Lily – and we – do notice objects or furniture, it is because she is suddenly reminded that she has no space of her own, but must always exist according to the rules and habits of those whose space she inhabits.

It is the precise focus of Davies's reading that enables him to forge a clear path through the novel's often repetitive narrative descriptions and its plethora of characters and social events. Davies's Lily is a character who is destroyed less by her lack of money than by her own strict inner morality and her inability to compromise. What Lily deplores in herself as the failure to do the right thing at the right moment is understood by Davies as her ultimate unwillingness to prostitute herself. She will not marry without love, in a society in which such behaviour is the norm; she does not use the powerful weapon she possesses to clear her name and to wreak revenge on the woman who has harmed her, because she will not countenance hurting Selden; she will settle her debts even if in so doing she brings about her own destruction.[8]

This reading of Lily's character thus shapes Davies's adaptation. He retains the novel's basic narrative shape, along with its language and rhythms, but conflates a number of occasions and characters so as to ensure coherence and to increase the dramatic power of the narrative. In the film, for example, Grace Stepney, who inherits the money Lily had hoped for, is combined with the character of Gerty Farish, who is in love with Lawrence Selden. 'Separately, the characters are not interesting,' Davies believes. 'Together they're much more interesting because it makes Grace much more vicious. She's not just refusing to help Lily out of moral rectitude and Christian charity in which there's no love. It's out of sexual jealousy and that's much more interesting. It's all the more dramatic because she's not consciously aware of it, although she knows it to be true' (Davies 2001). Although this move attracted criticism from a number of critics for whom the original text is sacrosanct (see, for example, Nochimson 2001: 41), in dramatic terms it is clear that the film gains in intensity as a consequence.

Language

I have already referred to the fact that Davies's adaptation strives for close fidelity to the language of the novel. The original dialogue (shortened, of course, in accordance with the principles outlined above) is, wherever possible, precisely replicated in the film, and any additions to it have been scrupulously written to echo Wharton's own style. The language is used not only to express the characters' thoughts and comments but also to establish the rhythms and musicality of the film and, like music, it serves to determine the pace of the action and the gestures and movements of the characters themselves. Davies refuses to simplify the language in any way, and never uses visual illustration for the sake of replacing or clarifying complex dialogue. Instead he deliberately draws our attention to the beauty and complexity of its textures, foregrounding it with a static or slow-moving camera, and affording the words the space and time they need. The result has sometimes been criticised for its 'artificiality', but again we need to remember that Davies is not remotely interested in naturalism or realism; he *is* interested in the nature of art and its truth, and in the complex processes of construction.

One striking example of the foregrounding of language occurs in the second scene of the film, in which Lily and Lawrence Selden take tea in his flat. Preceded only by their chance encounter at Grand Central Station, the scene is daringly long and slow and as part of the establishing sequence of a film is therefore quite surprising. There is almost no action, apart from the tea being poured or Lily wandering across the room to look at Selden's collection of first editions, and there is a total absence of background street sounds or indeed of music to provide us with any wider context. Thus, nothing distracts our attention from the words themselves. The effect on the characters of this total isolation from the outside world is to enable them to talk with a degree of perception and frankness that would not be permitted in the social circles in which they normally meet. Unusually then, for the opening of a film, it is the slow, deliberate conversation that matters, serving to introduce both the characters and the themes that the narrative will develop, and the spectators must use their ears and their intelligence as much as their eyes.

The original version of this scene was in fact considerably longer, and contained far more of the book's dialogue. Davies was forced to cut it precisely because, it was argued, it was too dense and too long for an opening scene. The imposed cuts resulted in the loss of a number of key elements of the dialogue, not least Lily's request that Lawrence should be her friend (a comment that is reflected at the end of the film, when she again visits him and asks for his friendship), and Davies's opinion that the scene is infinitely weaker because of the cuts appears justified. The original version was more densely layered and subtle, and offered more time for the 'ebb and flow' of their words, Davies comments on the DVD. That he was obliged to cut it nevertheless is a telling indication of the sorts of pressures imposed by the commercial exigencies of a larger-budget film.

Of course, we are not dealing with a film that is preoccupied with the language of the text to the detriment of its own filmic identity, and, for all the lack of action or visual impact in this scene, what we see is nevertheless fundamental to our overall understanding. For this reason, from the first, we need to consider the setting, the composition of visual space, in terms of the characters that are being introduced to us. As we have seen, the flat in which Lily and Selden talk is entirely isolated from the outside world, and we have already noted the absence of street noises. But it is isolated visually as well, for the windows are shrouded in thick lace curtains through which a muted light filters, but which permit no outside vistas. Nor does Lily want to be perceived by the outside world, of course, for, in risking having tea in Selden's flat, she has already broken one of the rules concerning the appropriate behaviour of an unmarried woman, and thus her reputation is at stake. The conversation we hear is about Lily's position as a woman for whom a suitable marriage is the only possible way of ensuring any satisfactory living standard. Ever since the death of her father, the novel tells us, Lily has been brought up to believe that her face is her fortune, and that she must use her beauty to find a rich husband, and this imperative entirely governs her behaviour: what she may and may not do. In social terms, Lily has no space of her own, no identity in her own right, and she enviously contrasts her situation with that of Selden who, despite not being rich, can nevertheless lead an independent life because he is a man. 'You see, there's the difference – a girl must [marry], a man, if he chooses', Lily reflects. The camera moves little, and, as befits Lily's constrained situation, its focus on her is in intense close-up. Even when

Lily moves over to the window she remains contained by the interior, for there is no wider view; indeed, as we have seen, far from offering freedom or escape, the outside world is the very cause of her entrapment. Despite its visual restraint, however, the scene communicates a powerful sensuality, particularly at the moment when Lily and Selden smoke a cigarette together and, for a few seconds, gaze at each other intensely. The unstated, unacknowledged sexual desire with which the moment is charged immediately establishes a powerful subtext: Lily's unacknowledged feelings for Selden and the repugnance inspired by the game she is obliged to play, and which she actually describes as 'business' in acknowledgement of her status as object to be bought and sold.

The importance of the visual is established even earlier, in the opening scene, as Lily and Selden meet at Grand Central Station. The temptation here must surely have been to provide local colour and to create the bustling crowds of the busy station. But Davies does not do this at all. Instead he isolates the characters, so that we are at first aware only of the breathtaking beauty of Lily's silhouette gradually emerging from the clouds of white steam. Her isolation, like the grace of her form, highlights her essential femininity (a key feature in the narrative, of course), while the initial impossibility of making out her features also prepares us for society's refusal to view women as individuals in their own right. Within seconds, however, she and Selden exchange glances and it is as if the rest of the world had ceased to exist. The intense focus of the characters' gazes, like their slow and deliberate speech and movement, is erotically charged, and draws us immediately into their story, while the artificiality of their movements already prepares us for the complexity and self-consciousness of the film itself.

Space and time

I have discussed at length the way in which in all of Davies's work filmic space is conceived as a combination of internal and external realities and perceptions, and thus must be read as a multilayered component of the film's meaning. I have also suggested that one of the fascinations of *The House of Mirth* is its extreme self-awareness, its concern with its own filmic identity rather than, for example, subscribing to the 'fetishistic' approach to adaptation in which the film is conceived as a 'presentation' of the original (Taubin 2001: 62). It seems to me that Davies's approach is nowhere more tellingly illustrated than in the sequence with which he marks the transition from Part 1 to Part 2 of the novel. Here we see at their most brilliant both his skill at reading between the lines of the original text and his extraordinary ability to transform his ideas into the language of cinema, highlighting the medium's innate spatio-temporal qualities, and thus visualising and creating meaning through form, texture and movement. It is therefore essential to look at this sequence in some detail.

The novel itself is divided into two books: the first opens with Lily's arrival and chance meeting with Lawrence Selden at Grand Central Station, and ends as Selden fails to turn up to have tea with her at her aunt's house (p. 257). By this point in the narrative, Lily's future is already very uncertain, given her urgent need to repay Gus Trenor, and her aunt's adamant refusal to settle her debts. The doorbell rings, but, instead of Selden arriving, a servant brings Lily a telegram from Bertha Dorset: 'Sailing unexpectedly tomorrow. Will you join us on a cruise in Mediterranean?' Book 2 opens with Selden standing on the steps of the Casino in Monte Carlo, as he takes in 'the whole outspread effect of light and leisure' (p. 261), and ends with him kneeling beside Lily's body, 'draining their last moment to its lees' (p. 461). Davies's film retains a similar two-part structure but whereas Wharton's transition from Book 1 to Book 2 might suggest a simple jump cut from New York to Monte Carlo, reflecting the abrupt shift in time and space, instead Davies creates an entire transition sequence, lasting some three minutes. At one level, the sequence provides an extremely beautiful flow of images and music which is both abstract and lyrical, but at the same time it accesses whole layers of meanings that articulate the unworded, hidden, innermost experiences of Lily.

As the first notes of 'Soave sia il vento', the trio from Mozart's *Così fan tutte* are heard, the camera begins a series of slow left-to-right pans across a vast drawing room in which all the furniture has been shrouded in dust sheets. Photographs still standing on the mantelpiece add to the atmosphere of a room outside time, a preserved and deserted space from which all life has vanished.[9] In a series of lap dissolves the constantly mobile camera deconstructs space and time as it transports us, very slowly, first forwards towards the window, and then backwards and out, looking back so that we see the window as an inner frame positioned centrally within the frame of the screen, gradually receding and growing smaller. Interior and exterior spaces are woven together as we slowly move away from the prim and upright façade of the house. The dust sheets have now been replaced by sheets of rain, partly shrouding our vision, as the camera moves onwards past tall trees, dripping with rain, past the high and forbidding walls that surround the garden, and across the sodden lawns to the stream. It then skims low across its surface, splattered and fragmented by the heavy raindrops. Moving more swiftly now, but still retaining its vertical close-up focus, the camera pans forward across the surface of the water, as its texture gradually changes, becoming brighter and smoother, and then starting to sparkle in the increasingly intense sunlight. Still from above, we then see an extreme close up of the bow of a boat cutting through water as the glittering waves move outwards and away from it. The camera, still moving, tilts steeply upwards across water to show the coast of Monte Carlo in brilliant sunshine. As the Mozart trio draws to its close, we dissolve to Lawrence standing on the shore as a voice enquires: 'What brings you to Monte Carlo?'

It would be tempting, but unwise, to suggest that this sequence, which is stunningly beautiful in its blend of light, texture, movement and music, is an example of a director not fulfilling his duty to the original text. After all, as we have seen, Wharton offers no exploration of the transition from Book 1 to Book 2. Such criticism could, of course, be answered by a close reading of the text itself. For example, the extraordinary sense of desolation and loneliness created by the sight of the shrouded furniture at the start of the sequence may well be picking up upon an earlier comment by Edith Wharton: 'Mrs. Peniston had kept her imagination shrouded, like the drawing-room furniture' (p. 181). Similarly, the movement from darkness to light, from entrapment and rigidity to freedom and openness suggested by the move away from enclosing architecture to the vastness of sea and sky, can be seen to reflect Selden's emotions, for Wharton tells us that 'as he took in the whole outspread effect of light and leisure, he felt a moment of revulsion from the last months of his life' (p. 261). In these terms, the transition from 'surroundings made for the discipline of the senses' (p. 261), where 'the ugliness of things rasped the eye as the gritty wind ground into the skin' (p. 262), to the light, colour and exuberance of Monte Carlo, described by Davies as 'just full with sensualty and implied sex', reflects Lawrence's experiences and desires (Constanzo Cahir 2001: 169).

However, the sequence needs to be read in still more complex and subtle ways, particularly in its dissolving of space and time, of outer and inner worlds. For, if our focus throughout the film is predominantly upon the character of Lily, here, without actually showing her or having recourse to dialogue or voice-over, Davies succeeds in moving us deep inside her mind. In the book, of course, the drawing room is not closed and shrouded with dustsheets, and Lily is not alone in the house. But in the bleakness of the room we see on the screen, we read Lily's loneliness and despair. And the move from confinement and hopelessness into light and space echoes her hopes, briefly seeming to offer escape, even salvation. By using water and light as his central metaphor, and combining these with a mobile camera and with music, Davies powerfully expresses Lily's dreams and longings.

The irony is, of course, that while Selden is able to make the transition to light, space and freedom (as did Wharton herself), Lily will remain trapped. The sense of hope that the journey inspires will quickly be crushed. And as Selden stands in the sun, gazing out at the vastness of sea and sky, Lily remains inside the confines of the yacht (itself the object of the gazes of those on shore, including Selden). And although the yacht itself is the facilitator of movement and change, Lily's place in it is entirely prescribed by the whims of her hosts. This is clearly shown as the camera returns to the interior of the boat and we see Ned Silverton reading a Verlaine sonnet ('Mon rêve familier') to Bertha Dorset, before moving on to Lily, seated in the corner and framed by the vertical and horizontal bars that surround the deck, quietly reading and dozing. She is trapped in a situation which she does not understand, and from which, as Carry Fisher warns Lawrence Selden, there is no escape. As Carry points out, Lily is simply too naive to play society at its own game and so is doomed by the pitiless strategies of self-protection devised by the predatory Bertha Dorset.

This transition sequence therefore serves to move the narrative on, guiding the spectator through its temporal and spatial shifts, but more importantly it also explores the spaces behind the words or images, and it does this in such a way as to enable us not only to reach a deeper understanding of Lily's inner feelings and her precarious situation but also to become aware of the specific power of cinema to articulate all this.

Texts and contexts: film

If the film provides a perceptive exploration of the character of Lily Bart and of Wharton's novel as a whole, it thus also provides a self-conscious exploration of the nature of film. And, as we have already seen in relation to *The Neon Bible* and *The Long Day Closes*, Davies's films repeatedly articulate their own identity by referring to other films (alongside a whole range of other cultural references). This section considers some of the works that have played a key part in shaping *The House of Mirth*, and will examine their significance to the overall construction of the film.

The extent to which Davies's earlier films reflect, quote and self-consciously play with the films that particularly influenced his childhood and adolescence has already been noted. Such films provide a lens through which he examines his personal memories but which also serves to shape his own images of different places and times. Given the essential self-consciousness of *The House of Mirth*, it is not surprising that Davies's awareness of other films should therefore have played an important part in the way he chooses to interpret Edith Wharton's fictional world.

Among the many filmic influences he acknowledges, the one to which he repeatedly refers in this context is *Letter From an Unknown Woman* (Max Ophuls, USA, 1948). This film, which fascinates Davies because of its powerful story of doomed love, its lyrical camerawork and its richly lit and textured *mise-en-scène*, acquires a particular resonance in relation to *The House of Mirth* through its atmospheric re-creation of turn-of-the-century Vienna. The screenplay, written by Howard Koch (who also scripted *Casablanca*), was based on a fairly weak short story by Stefan Zweig, and the film recounts the story of a young woman's doomed love for a self-obsessed concert pianist who seduces and abandons her, leaving her pregnant, and who later does not even remember her. The subject matter, therefore, is in many ways similar to *The House of Mirth*, and, like Lily Bart, its heroine Lisa Berndl is a victim of a patriarchal society. The film is structured as a series of flashbacks triggered by Lisa's voice reading the letter she writes as she is dying, and the hopeless circularity of its plot is emphasised by the letter's opening sentence: 'By the time you read this I shall be dead.' While *Letter From an Unknown Woman* was not commercially successful on its release, it subsequently acquired the status of classic, and it is significant that Scorsese too cites this film as an important influence on the making of *The Age of Innocence* (Vincendeau 2001: 71). For Davies, *Letter From an Unknown Woman* served as nothing less than a 'template', and undoubtedly its atmospheric shots, for example the opening sequence showing a horse-drawn carriage moving along wet cobbled streets gleaming in the gaslight, or the sumptuous and intricate interiors of the houses and cafés, may well have influenced the composition of a number of his own New York shots. Interestingly, he describes *Letter From an Unknown Woman* as 'a kind of opera', undoubtedly relating its structure and its emotional power to that of music, as well as acknowledging the essential theatricality of its composition. And, as we shall see in the next chapter, it is also possible that the decision to use a trio from Mozart's opera *Così fan tutte* for his transition sequence constitutes a form of homage to Ophuls. Almost certainly the beautiful crane shot of the crowd climbing up the opera steps in *The House of Mirth* makes a number of visual references to the sequence where Lisa and her husband go to the opera in *Letter From an Unknown Woman*, and it is just possible that the fact that the opera we hear in this sequence, Mozart's *Magic Flute*, might have contributed in some way to Davies's choice of *Così fan tutte*. Even the presentation of the various characters in their opera house boxes suggests a number of parallels, and certainly Davies's wish to include a panning shot of the whole opulent interior (thwarted by the lack of funds) reflected his love of just such a shot in *Letter From an Unknown Woman*.

Other films which are also acknowledged by Davies as reference points include *All that Heaven Allows* (Douglas Sirk, USA, 1955), *Magnificent Obsession* (Douglas Sirk, USA, 1954), *The Little Foxes* (William Wyler, USA, 1941) and *Love Is a Many-Splendored Thing* (Henry King, USA, 1955). Like *Letter From an Unknown Woman*, all these films can be classified as melodrama, or more specifically as a particular type of melodrama known (somewhat condescendingly) as 'weepies' or 'women's movies'. 'Absolute crap, but there's a great gusto about them. There's something about the vulnerability of a woman in that era', muses Terence Davies (Horne 2000: 17). While such films constituted an important component of Hollywood production in the 1940s and 1950s, when Davies watched them as a young child, the genre did not receive any serious critical attention until the 1970s, and until then such films were generally considered trite and insignificant, a judgement which may even seem excusable in the light of their typical story lines. All the above films, for example, focus upon the doomed love affairs of their heroines: between a middle-class widow and her younger gardener in *All that Heaven Allows*; a widow and the man who (unknown to her) was responsible for her husband's death in *Magnificent Obsession*; and a Eurasian female doctor and an American journalist in *Love Is a Many Splendored Thing*. But if the genre is indeed without significance, and if such films are merely trite, we must ask ourselves why they should appeal to Davies, and why he should repeatedly highlight their significance in relation to his adaptation of *The House of Mirth*.

That Davies feels respect and affection for *Letter From an Unknown Woman* is clear from the many references he makes to it in *The House of Mirth*. But he also admires, for example, Douglas Sirk's expressionist approach to colour in *All that Heaven Allows*, an approach which he may even reflect in *The House of Mirth*, in the way that the tonal range and intensity of the colours becomes increasingly restricted as the story develops until, in the final credits sequence (a freeze frame of Lily's body), all colour gradually leeches away until she appears as insubstantial as ashes, or perhaps as the steam through which she emerges in the film's opening shots. Moreover, many of the tight framings and complex settings with which Davies creates the claustrophobic middle-class world of Lily Bart may equally reflect some of the stock devices of melodrama. It is obviously important to look in more detail at the significance of this genre.

Melodrama

Thomas Elsaesser was probably the first critic to study melodrama seriously when, in an article first published in 1972, he identified it as a genre which in fact provided a serious reflection of contemporary social change and whose development was inextricably bound up with that of the rising middle class (Elsaesser 1987: 2–15). His work was followed closely by that of other critics, notably Peter Brooks (1976), and Geoffrey Nowell-Smith (1987), whose Marxist and psychoanalytical analyses of the secular world of melodrama, fundamentally driven by capitalist desire for material accumulation, led to its wider assessment as an expression of modernity that approached key issues of social crisis within the essentially enclosed and private context of family life (Singer 1995). Significantly, Douglas Sirk, who, on emigrating to the United States, was obliged to concentrate exclusively on women's melodrama films, found that within this 'insignificant' format he actually had considerable freedom to deal with contentious social issues, a point discussed by Elsaesser, who, describing Sirk's films as 'sophisticated family melodramas', notes the way that their ironic and baroque *mise-en-scène* provided the means of 'undermining the conformist ideologies of Eisenhower's 1950s' America' (Gledhill 2000: 224). It is certainly the case that, within their rather predictable plots, Sirk's films provide a perceptive and powerful indictment of the mores of contemporary American society and the American dream, particularly through their depiction of the despair of individual lives governed by middle-class respectability, intolerance and materialism. As critics began to appreciate this fact more fully, melodrama came increasingly to be recognised as an ideologically subversive genre, a popular form whose elaborate *mise-en-scène* and its 'aesthetics of the domestic' could indeed articulate the deeper truths of human existence. By the middle of the 1970s, melodrama had become the focus of feminist critics, attracted in particular by the films' insistently feminine perspectives, and their articulation of (repressed) female desire (Mulvey 1977–78; Doane 1984; Williams 1998).

Essentially, melodrama focuses on the central character as victim; this character is inevitably a woman, and her perspective is privileged throughout. Concerned with emotions rather than action, the films tend to have a circular structure with frequent recourse to flashback (Cook 1985: 80). The sense of claustrophobia this circularity induces is further enhanced by the genre's highly stylised *mise-en-scène* which essentially functions to provide an outer symbolisation of inner emotions (Elsaesser 1987: 59), whilst also serving to circumvent the strict censorship and morality codes that predominated until the 1960s (Elsaesser 1987: 53).

In other words, in the very style or form of the film we read deeper meaning of female subjectivity and repressed desire. At the same time, the genre functions ideologically to repress such (forbidden) female desire, and the narratives reveal that the woman must either be recuperated as reproducer or nurturer or be finally destroyed. The tears associated with the genre are caused by the ultimate impossibility of the fulfilment of female desire (Hayward 1996: 210), in a narrative in which dream fantasy comes to stand in for reality (Fischer 1989: 101). The films therefore reproduce fantasies of female masochism (Doane 1984: 80). Lucy Fischer, in a fascinating examination of *Letter From an Unknown Woman*, posits this film as a telling example of masochistic fantasy functioning not as a vehicle for sexuality but as a replacement for it (1989: 101).

Even this brief account reveals that the genre is complex and significant, and that it is indeed pertinent both to Davies's analysis of the text of *The House of Mirth* and to his film. Indeed, it would not seem unreasonable to consider Wharton's text itself as bearing many of the hallmarks of melodrama. Furthermore, however, we might also assess the extent to which Davies's film could be classified as melodrama. As we have seen, he inherits a narrative which, in its form and its subject matter, and of course its underlying criticism of contemporary society, already to a large extent sets itself up as melodrama. That Davies recognises this fact is clear in his choice of filmic reference points. And it is true that he uses much of the genre's classic iconography in his own exploration of female desire as something to be articulated between the words and images, something which cannot be addressed directly. However, what prevents his film from itself becoming melodrama, and sites it instead firmly within the postmodern, is its knowing and self-conscious references to the genre, and its ironic recognition of its theatricality. Moreover, the essential sparseness of Davies's vision (as opposed, for example, to the more straightforwardly melodramatic detail of Scorsese's *mise-en-scène*), its tight focus and control hold at bay the very excesses which Wharton's narrative suggests. When Davies quotes, he does so knowingly, and all the time, as we have seen, his camera and his techniques keep the spectator at a distance, insistently reminding her or him of the film's identity as film. We are not allowed to wallow emotionally in Lily's story, for we are constantly being required to assess, understand and evaluate it for ourselves.

And as part of his filmic borrowings and quotations a number of very different films must therefore also be taken into account. One important example that Davies also acknowledges as a key point of reference is Billy Wilder's *Some Like It Hot* (USA, 1959), or more specifically the shot in that film of Marilyn Monroe walking along the platform through the steam. Again, this example is interesting in a number of ways – first of all, of course, because in that example Marilyn Monroe is being acknowledged by Wilder as an icon of femininity. 'Jello on springs' is how Jerry (Jack Lemmon) describes her, as he and Joe (Tony Curtis), respectively disguised as Daphne and Josephine, watch in awe as she passes. And indeed it is true that the silhouette we see of Lily in the opening shots of *The House of Mirth*, for all the differences of costume and period, similarly articulates the essence of femininity. Moreover, my earlier suggestion, that the fact that Lily appears in silhouette, so that we cannot at first see her face, foregrounds her position as mere object of our (and Selden's) gaze, might equally apply to Marilyn Monroe, both as Sugar Kane (who is here the object of our gaze and that of the two male protagonists) and as a star whose life was destroyed by the exploitative gaze of the public. These and other references to film that Davies makes in *The House of Mirth* are included to further our awareness of the film's meanings, but also to remind us of its filmic status.

Art

Paintings and photographs play a key part in Davies's films, particularly in relation to his fascination with light and texture. In *The House of Mirth*, the turn-of-the-century interiors with their opulent fabrics and rich colours offered him the chance to experiment with chiaroscuro, the delicate balance of light and shade, in ways which were in no small degree inspired by Dutch interiors. In particular, Davies refers to the work of Vermeer, whose small, detailed domestic interiors are notable for their innovative use of light and perspective. Many of Davies's interior shots, perhaps above all those which occur in Aunt Peniston's house, make use of daylight filtering through a curtained window to create perspectives and textures that strikingly bring together the rich stillness of Vermeer's canvases, and the claustrophobic silence of Lily's world. However, beneath this key element of Davies's fascination with Vermeer, we can discover a number of other, equally important reasons why it this particular painter that he refers to in relation to this film.

First, the subject matter, with its detailed portrayal of the closed, interior world of domesticity, is particularly suited both to Wharton's novel and of course to the genre of filmic melodrama that we have been considering. But the form too is important, for, as Newton suggests, in creating 'those elusive shades of gesture and behaviour in everything that is implied by the world domesticity', the formal balance of Vermeer's paintings is so perfect, so 'finely adjusted', that 'a fly settling on one of his canvases would produce an intolerable disturbance in its balance of hushed, golden tones' (Newton 1964: 194). While 'hushed golden tones' acts as a strikingly apt description of Davies's interiors, so too this rather strange comment forcibly recalls MacCabe's suggestion that altering the tiniest element of the shortest of scenes in Davies's script of *Distant Voices, Still Lives* would have enormous repercussions for the entire film (MacCabe 1999: 15). In the work of both Vermeer and Davies, we may conclude, it is essential to recognise that form *is* meaning. And given the work done by Elsaesser and others on the formal significance of *mise-en-scène* in articulating the essential meanings of melodrama, we can achieve an even deeper appreciation of Davies's avowed influences or artistic references. Finally, if we return briefly to the essential self-consciousness of Davies's use of such references in his work, it is worth noting not only Vermeer's apparent aloofness or distance from the domestic trivialities that are his subject matter (Newton 1964: 194) and suggest him as quiet and intelligent observer of his world, but also that the titles of his two most famous paintings are the *Allegory of Painting* (c. 1665, Vienna), and *Woman Reading a Letter* (c. 1662, Amsterdam), both of which appear particularly apt in the context of Davies's film.

The artist whose role in *The House of Mirth* has been most widely quoted is the American John Singer Sargent. It would seem that Davies used Sargent's society portraits very much as a guide to the period, much as, in filmic terms, he used *Letter From an Unknown Woman*. It has been widely reported, for instance, that in casting the film he chose Gillian Anderson not because of her fame and popularity (never having previously heard of her, and never having seen *The X Files*) but because he was immediately struck by her beauty: 'I was trying to find someone who looked like she might have stepped out from one of John Singer Sargent's portraits, and there she was' (Johnston 2000: 5). John Singer Sargent was a fashionable portrait painter at the turn of the century, whose work was in great demand by upper-class society on both sides of the Atlantic, and his canvases, with their dramatic use of light and shadow, and their detailed recreation of the sumptuous gowns, rich velvet drapes and fine furnishings of the period have certainly influenced Davies's own *mise-en-scène*. Updike suggests that the beauty of the details in Sargent's society portraits is so striking that it threatens to overwhelm 'the intelligent intensity with which their faces are rendered' (Updike 1989: 48), but it seems to me rather that, as in the women's pictures we looked at earlier, Sargent is foregrounding the very fact that the identity of his subjects, particularly his female subjects, is largely read through their possessions and finery, an idea that would echo

Davies's comments about the period as one which is obsessed with surface and appearance. Nevertheless, as in our response to Lily, we never doubt the existence of their subjective identities, not least because these women seem supremely aware of their status as objects of our gaze. They stare out of the canvas directly at us, making us complicit in the acts of looking and being looked at and, like Davies's films, the paintings thus foreground the strategies of their own composition.[10] There is a further direct reference to painting in the film through the depiction of Lily as 'Summer' by Watteau. This too raises a number of interesting issues, as we shall see in the next chapter.

Music

In many ways, Davies's use of music in *The House of Mirth* differs fundamentally from his other films. The most immediately striking of these is the fact that it is used far more sparingly, in terms of both the time it occupies on the soundtrack and its range and variety. The fact that we do not hear any popular songs constitutes a further major change, clearly indicating the move away from autobiographical discourse but also reflecting the complete irrelevance of popular culture to the world portrayed in *The House of Mirth*. The six different works that Davies includes are almost entirely classical, and range in period from the early eighteenth century to the 1970s.

While it is easy to understand the preponderance of the baroque, and of essentially intimate and small-scale musical forms in this film, what makes Davies's score so fascinating is its extreme precision and focus and its overall complexity. By 'focus' I mean that the music never functions simply to explain or clarify the narrative or to manipulate the spectator emotionally. Indeed, at moments which express most fully the passions and desires of the characters, the soundtrack is often silent, either reflecting the tight emotional restraint that they experience, or serving to focus attention on other modes of expression in the scene. For example, when Davies wants us to experience Lily's feelings of claustrophobia, he foregrounds the silence and sense of stasis within a room. '*The House of Mirth* radically cuts our ration of music so we become acutely aware of ticking clocks, closing doors, the lighting of cigarettes: we are closer to the intense, hushed, charged sound world of Bresson, Rohmer, late Kieslowski or of Ingmar Bergman's harrowing *Cries and Whispers* (1972)', notes Horne in relation to the tight focus and control of Davies's film (Horne 2000: 16). When music is included, therefore, it is used much as Vermeer (or Davies) might use light: to highlight detail, to create depths and texture, to suggest layers of meaning that cannot be shown directly. If Davies's approach thus differs fundamentally from that governing classical narrative, not least melodrama, where non-diegetic music swells and diminishes with the emotional tides, it also differs radically from other literary adaptations of the time, and exemplified, for instance, by Elmer Bernstein's lush and romantic score for *The Age of Innocence*. Davies does not use a specially composed score to support the narrative; he does not have recourse to a leitmotif or theme tune, in fact music is rarely repeated (we do on three occasions hear excerpts from the slow movement of the Marcello Oboe Concerto in D minor; however, as we shall see, subtle changes in performance assume key importance in our understanding of this piece). Rather than performing the traditional 'silent' role, therefore, Davies's film music requires us to listen with minute attention, and to respond creatively to its form, its textures and its multiple references. To that extent, music functions as a central and key signifier in *The House of Mirth*.

The function of music in *The House of Mirth* will receive more sustained attention in the next chapter. However, it is important at this stage to provide a few indications of the subtle and fascinating complexities of the film's score. In Davies's films, as has already been seen, music is never used merely as background or mood creator, even on the rare occasions when it does accompany moments of passion or tenderness. For example, in the scene in which Lily and Selden kiss for the first time, it is the case that we hear, as non-diegetic music, the excerpt from Marcello Oboe Concerto that also accompanied the film's opening shots. Thus we begin to associate this piece of music with Lily herself. Davies's choice of baroque music is important not only because its delicate control and balance so perfectly express that of the period he is dealing with, but also because its intricate structure reflects the character of Lily herself: complex, apparently delicate and fragile, and yet with a great inner strength. Davies has already established a visual metaphor through the film's association of Lily with lace and lacy patterns, of course, and this key metaphor is further extended through its association with Marcello's music. For example, during the opening credits of the film, this is the music we listen to as we watch the intricate patterns on the screen that grow increasingly more complex and elaborate before our eyes. These patterns are immediately reflected by Lily's veil as she emerges through the steam at the train station, and then appear again on the curtains of the windows that frame her in Selden's flat. At the end of the film too, when Lawrence raises the blind in Lily's bedroom, he seizes the lace curtain, and holds it tightly in his hand, before turning to look at her body as we hear Marcello's music for the third and final time. What links these elements therefore? If the beautiful patterns in lace with their apparent fragility but underlying strength are actually created by the gaps between the threads, then equally, we might maintain, the structures of the music are also a function of its hidden rhythms and the intervals between its notes. The character of Lily too, Davies is suggesting, must be understood by our creative response to just such gaps and silences.

We have already noted the largely unacknowledged feelings of passion and desire that mark the scene in which Lily and Selden kiss for the first time. Although a less original director might, at such a moment, have provided romantic music to enhance our emotional involvement, Davies repeats the Marcello that was heard when Lily and Selden first met. However, instead of the same recording of this music, what we hear is a version that has been transposed to F# minor and is performed not by an oboe but by a string quartet. While the change is subtle, nevertheless its effect is to make the textures and tone more delicate, less obvious than in the original version. This, along with the fact that the excerpt ends with an imperfect, unresolved cadence, warns us that their relationship too is unresolved, open-ended. This detailed understanding of music, and its intricate role as signifier, is a fundamental characteristic of all Davies's work.

The role of music, of course, is intimately and intricately related to that of all the other signifiers that we have been considering, and each of the pieces we hear is used to create references and to add further layers of meaning. Thus, for example, the 'simple, delicate, fragile sounds' of Morton Feldman's *Rothko Chapel: Why Patterns?*, which we hear in the milliners' sequence, articulate something of the fragility of Lily at this moment (Griffiths 1990: 172), while the composition itself, a tribute to the American artist Mark Rothko, and originally written for performance in the Rothko Chapel a year after its opening, aims to reflect the architectural form of the chapel, as well as the paintings by Rothko that it contained. Feldman's scores are strikingly visual, and his music is essentially conceived as a spatial construct, shaped by chance and time, something which would seem particularly significant to Davies's work. And, finally, *Rothko Chapel: Why Patterns?* contains references to Stravinsky's funeral service in New York, as well as to Jewish traditional music (which Davies may well have included as part of his reaction against the anti-Semitic comments in Wharton's novel).

In addition to the above works, three different pieces from Mozart's comic opera *Così fan tutte* are heard, so that the work is inevitably foregrounded as a dominant theme. The significance of this and other pieces will be discussed in greater detail in the next chapter, but again it is important to recognise that Davies's choice of a Mozart opera is almost certainly influenced by *Letter From an Unknown Woman*, while his choice of *Così fan tutte* reflects both his desire to use the beautiful 'Soave sia il vento' for his transition sequence and his playful exploration of the opera's plot which also deals with women as object and potential victims of the male gaze.

Conclusion

If this chapter began by considering Davies's *The House of Mirth* in terms of its status as literary adaptation, while pointing out the requirement that any adaptation should both reflect and yet break free of the text which lies at its source, the above analysis reveals the extent to which Davies's film succeeds. It also illustrates the complex and multi-layered nature of his directing, including the richness and diversity of his references which the spectator gradually discovers with each new viewing. However, a film must also be able to communicate successfully at a single viewing, must interest and intrigue the spectators at once, and must in some way reveal not only its narrative truths but also its relevance to their world and their understanding. There is little doubt that Davies achieves this. The spectator is involved emotionally in the events portrayed on screen, and the film's intelligent restraint can only heighten the savagery of its tragic climax. At the same time, its fundamental self-awareness, its refusal to provide clear-cut answers or unambiguous conclusions and the richness, variety and complexity of its references all require an active and creative response that ensure that the spectator will continue to reflect upon its characters and the issues it raises long after the performance has ended.

Notes

1 Many of the arguments relating to the problems caused by the tendency to view adaptations merely as filmed reflections of novels were succinctly dealt with by Brian McFarlane in a keynote address at the Millennium Film Conference held at the University of Bath in July 1999, and reproduced in McFarlane (2000).
2 Her first published book was a work of non-fiction, written in collaboration with Ogden Codman, and entitled *The Decoration of Houses* (1897). It is interesting that the social observations and eye for detail which this book reveals remain characteristics of her later fiction.
3 Significantly, the protagonist in each of their first works (Lily Bart in *The House of Mirth*, and Tucker in the *Trilogy*) is not able to escape the constraints imposed by a prejudiced society, and both are ultimately doomed. Other similarities between

the experiences of Davies and Wharton can be traced by referring to her autobiography, *A Backward Glance*, published in 1934.
4 In fact, Henry James had a great influence over Wharton, advising her about her writing, and suggesting settings and themes. Wharton acknowledges her debt to him in *The Writing of Fiction* (1925).
5 This and references are to the Scribner Paperback edition of *The House of Mirth*, published by Simon & Schuster (1995).
6 *La Règle du jeu / The Rules of the Game*, one of the best known examples of poetic realism, is also widely considered to be one of the masterpieces of French cinema. The film offers a vivid exploration, and condemnation, of a class-ridden society in decline, and a number of parallels could be drawn between the world it explores and that of Wharton's *The House of Mirth*.
7 The question of narrative voice-over is crucial in adaptation. It is often seen as an essentially literary device which is included in an adaptation to increase its 'fidelity' to the original text. With regard to Scorsese's *The Age of Innocence*, the device of using shots of handwritten text as underlying image during the credits, along with the sustained voice-over commentary throughout the film, suggests an overwhelming concern with just such fidelity. In his *Anatomy of Film*, Bernard Dick presents voice-over as 'one of the most abused techniques in film', an essentially 'easy' solution for unimaginative film-makers (Dick 1990: 21–2). In *The Encyclopedia of Novels into Film*, however, Tibbetts and Welsh argue that Scorsese's use of voice-over not only conveys the novelist's voice but also serves to reconstruct the social atmosphere of New York at that time (Tibbetts and Welsh 1998: xvii).
8 In fact, the scene in which Lily, in despair, takes the letters to the Dorset's house in a futile attempt at blackmail has been invented by Davies in order to clarify the drama and to intensify the tragedy. 'In tragedy, it's always the small things. For me it felt right that she has the letters and then she goes there, and – a seemingly small thing – they're out. They're not there. There is something extraordinarily moving in that, for, had she gone the day before, they would have been home (Constanzo Cahir 2001: 170).
9 The mood created in the opening scenes of this sequence recalls something of the sense of death and decay found in the cellar in *The Long Day Closes* when, as the camera pans round the thick cobwebs hanging from the dusty, black walls, we hear Martita Hunt's voice-over from *Great Expectations* describing her ancient and crumbling wedding cake as symbol of decay, loss and despair (David Lean, UK, 1946).
10 Interestingly, it was Sargent who painted what is now regarded as the definitive portrait of Henry James his friend and admirer.

References

Brooks, P. (1976), *The melodramatic imagination. Balzac, Henry James, melodrama, and the mode of excess*, New Haven and London: Yale University Press.
Constanzo Cahir, L. (2001), '*The House of Mirth*: an interview with director Terence Davies and producer Olivia Stewart', *Literature/Film Quarterly*, 29/3, 166–71.
Cook, P. (1985), *The Cinema Book*, London: BFI.
Davies (2001), Commentary on the film by the director included as one of the 'Special Features' on the DVD recording of *The House of Mirth*, London: Granada Film Limited and FilmFour Limited.
Dick, B. (1990), *Anatomy of Film*, second edition, London: St Martin's Press.
Doane, M.A. (1984), 'The women's film: possession and address', in Doane, M. A.,

Mellencamp, P. and Williams, L. (eds), *Re-vision: Essays in Feminist Film Criticism*, Frederick, MD: The American Film Institute and University Publishers of America.

Elsaesser, T. (1987), 'Tales of Sound and Fury: observations on the family melodrama', in Gledhill, C. (ed.), *Home Is Where the Heart Is: Studies in Melodrama and the Woman's Film*, London: BFI, pp. 43–69. First published in 1972 in *Monogram* 4.

Fischer, L. (1989), *Shot/Countershot: Film Tradition and Women's Cinema*, Princeton: Princeton University Press, and London: BFI/Macmillan.

French, P. (2000), 'Daylight snobbery', *Observer Review*, 15 October, 7.

Fuller, G. (2001), 'Summer's end', *Film Comment* 37/1, January/February, 54–9.

Gledhill, C. (2000), 'Rethinking genre', in Gledhill, C. and Williams, L., *Reinventing Film Studies*, London and New York: Arnold, pp. 221–43.

Griffiths, P. (1990), *Modern Music: A Concise History from Debussy to Boulez*, London: Thames and Hudson.

Hattenstone, S. (2000), 'First steps in show business', *Guardian*, 6 October, Review, 2–4.

Hayward, S. (1996), *Key concepts in Cinema Studies*, London and New York: Routledge.

Horne, P. (2000), 'Beauty's slow fade', *Sight and Sound* 10/10, October, 14–18.

Jackson, K. (2000),'*The House of Mirth*', *Sight and Sound* 10/11, November, 53–4.

Johnston, T. (2000), 'Even my therapist hates my father now', *Independent*, 1 October, 5.

MacCabe, C. (1999), *The Eloquence of the Vulgar*, London: BFI.

McFarlane, B. (1996), *Novel to Film: An Introduction to the Theory of Adaptation*, Oxford: Clarendon Press.

McFarlane, B. (2000), 'It wasn't like that in the book', *Literature/Film Quarterly* 28/3, 163–9.

Mulvey, L. (1977/78), 'Notes on Sirk and melodrama', *Movie* 25. Reprinted in Mulvey, L. (1989), *Visual and Other Pleasures*, London: Macmillan.

Newton, E. (1964), *European Painting and Sculpture*, London: Penguin Books.

Nochimson, M. (2001) '*The House of Mirth*', *Cineaste* 19/2, 41–3.

Nowell-Smith, G. (1987), 'Minnelli and melodrama', in Gledhill, C. (ed.), *Home is Where the Heart Is: Studies in Melodrama and Women's Film*, London: BFI. First published in *Screen* 18/2, Summer 1977.

Romney, J. (2000),' British filmmaker Terence Davies's adaptation of Edith Wharton's *The House of Mirth*', *Film Comment*, May/June. Reproduced at http://gauk.net.

Singer, B. (1995), 'Modernity, hyper-stimulus, and the rise of popular sensationalism', in Charnley, L. and Schwartz, V. R. (eds), *Cinema and the invention of modern life*, Berkeley: University of California Press, pp. 72–99.

Stone, J. (2001), 'Old obsessions remain', interview with Terence Davies published on the official Gillian Anderson Web Site at: http://gaws.ao.net/hom/print/oaklandtribune.html

Taubin, A. (2001), '*The Age of Innocence*: dread and desire', in Vincendeau, G. (ed.), *Film/Literature/Heritage*, London: BFI, pp. 61–5.

Tibbetts, J. C. and Welsh, J. M. (1998), *The Encyclopedia of Novels into Films*, New York: Facts on File.

Updike, J. (1989), *Just Looking: Essays on Art*, London: André Deutsch and Penguin.

Vincendeau, G. (ed.) (2001), *Film/Literature/Heritage. A Sight and Sound Reader*, London: BFI.

Wharton, E. (1995), *The House of Mirth*, New York: Simon & Schuster. First published in 1905.

Williams, L. (1998), 'Melodrama revised', in Browne, N. (ed.), *Refiguring American Film Genres: Theory and History*, Berkeley: University of California Press, pp. 42–88.

Music and time: a new dimension 7

> Words move, music moves
> Only in time; but that which is only living
> Can only die. Words, after speech, reach
> Into the silence. Only by the form, the pattern,
> Can words or music reach
> The stillness
>
> ('Burnt Norton')

Throughout this book, I have made repeated references to the central role played by music in Davies's films, and have suggested not only that the way in which he uses music on the soundtrack is innovative and exciting but also that his conception of the nature of film, clearly reflected in the methods that characterise his directing, is of a medium whose affinities are closest of all to music. In fact, so fundamental is music to Terence Davies's life and work that no study devoted to him would be complete without detailed consideration of its significance.

This chapter begins by briefly considering Davies's passion for music, before going on to explore how this passion is reflected in his work. It will look at the ways in which Davies uses music in his films concentrating, in the first section, on his autobiographical works, where it will focus in particular on the role played by popular songs within the process of mapping and articulating the self. This section will also examine briefly the relationship between music and memory, and will identify ways in which Davies uses popular songs in order to recreate a remembered past but also, simultaneously, to interrogate and deconstruct that past. And it will also touch upon the traditional roles accorded to music in classical (Hollywood) narratives as a means of pinpointing his fundamental originality.

In the light of our examination of the role of music within Davies's autobiographical works, it will be particularly interesting to consider what changes occur as he moves into the fictional narratives of *The Neon*

Bible and *The House of Mirth*, and this will be the aim of the following section. Given that, as we have seen, *The Neon Bible* is an essentially transitional work in which Davies explores memories and identities that are not his own, but with which, nevertheless, he feels a strong affinity, then we might expect the function of music to occupy a similarly transitional position. Following on from this, the focus will be upon the function of music in Davies's most recent film, *The House of Mirth*. Here we shall see that, whilst it is true that music is used far more sparingly and in many ways quite differently from in his previous films, nevertheless its role is no less vital and innovative.

By way of conclusion, and in order to assess how the focus upon music can further our understanding of Davies's films, we shall consider the basis for, and implications of, his idea that film itself functions in ways which are very close to music.

Davies and music

Terence Davies's deep love of music is reflected as much in the many interviews he has given as in his films and writings. In a lengthy interview which I had with Davies in February 2001 (an edited version of which appears in the next chapter), music was a recurring theme throughout. In the first period of the discussion, which was not recorded, Davies talked at length about poetry, art and film, but most of all about music: the powerful and beautifully structured symphonies of Shostakovich (especially numbers five and ten), and the controlled intensity of his string quartets; the music of Bruckner, Britten, Sibelius and Bach; the relative merits of particular singers, instrumentalists and conductors; and the precise performances and recordings that he had chosen for particular films were in turn discussed, with tireless passion. By his own admission, Davies could not survive without music, and it therefore follows that he would never be content to accord it a secondary or subsidiary role in his work.

It is immediately striking that, when Davies is explaining or commenting upon his own films, he tends to use musical analogies. Thus, describing *The Neon Bible* as a work which is essentially 'transitional' but nevertheless vital, since without it he would never have been able to make *The House of Mirth*, he further qualifies its transitional status as 'my equivalent of the Shostakovich Fourth Symphony and the Sibelius Fourth Symphony, both of which are transitional works' (see Chapter 8). And as we have already seen, in identifying the strength or weakness of a particular scene, he evaluates it in terms of its rhythms and beats.

MUSIC AND TIME 169

He repeatedly makes reference to the symphonies of Bruckner and Sibelius as his model or 'template' in his own work, and when advising students about directing suggests that it is the works of these composers that they should study, rather than existing screenplays, if they want to learn how to create an 'emotional structure'. He recalls with intense passion the first time he himself ever listened to Bruckner's Seventh and Eighth Symphonies (on 78 rpm recordings that he had borrowed from his local public library), and the first time he went to a performance of the Sibelius Fifth Symphony that was 'so electrifying' that 'I don't think I came down for about three weeks' (see Chapter 8). And whereas Davies claims that he now watches very few films, he admits that he constantly listens to music.

If Davies made most of his discoveries about classical music after leaving school, his love of the romantic melodies and over-the-top lyrics of popular songs dates from his earliest childhood. Indeed, he has claimed that the single biggest formative influence upon his work as a director is the American musicals that he was brought up with (Falsetto 1999: 71). He has a vast repertoire of such songs, of course, and a detailed knowledge of the works of a whole range of song writers from Cole Porter to Hoagy Carmichael, as well as immediate and perfect recall of all their lyrics. He is particularly fascinated by the ability of such songs to give ordinary people a voice for their feelings, and for that reason describes them as 'poetry for the ordinary person'. He thus recognises that a key characteristic of popular songs is their ability to straddle the public/private divide, and to be adopted by each individual listener as his or her personal property.

Echoing his twin musical passions, Davies's films combine classical and popular music in exciting and innovative ways, and reveal both his eclectic knowledge and his deep understanding of music. Given that each extract or song that we hear will have been chosen with precisely the care that characterises all aspects of his directing, and will be performing complex and multiple functions within the narrative, it is essential to recognise music's function as a key signifier in all of his work.

Music and autobiography

The films we shall be focusing on in this section are the *Trilogy: Children* (1976), *Madonna and Child* (1980) and *Death and Transfiguration* (1983); the two parts of *Distant Voices, Still Lives* (1988); and *The Long Day Closes* (1992). We have already seen that despite their radically different narrative structures, which of course reflect something of the elusive and problematic nature of time and memory, nevertheless all these films can be characterised as autobiographical. The *Trilogy* provides an essentially bleak exploration of family life and developing sexuality in relation not only to Davies's remembered past but also to a hypothesised future (in which he confronts the terror of his own and his mother's death by 'remembering' them), and Davies's alter ego, Robbie Tucker, appears variously in all three films as child, adult and old man. In *Distant Voices, Still Lives*, however, there is no alter ego, and, whilst the film's 'mosaic of memory' is fashioned from fragmented and multiple viewpoints (Davies's own and those of his family), the remembering self is marked as absence. And finally, in *The Long Day Closes*, the subjective memories articulated through Bud, Davies's younger self, are shown to be inseparable from, or even a construct of, popular culture, particularly cinema. All the films reflect the elliptical and diffuse 'stories' of memory itself so that none of them attempts a linear narrative structure. Instead, various times and places collide and merge in juxtapositions that are internal to the processes of remembering. Nevertheless, one of the most striking features shared by all these films is the central role they accord to music. To some extent this might be accounted for as a straightforward reflection of a childhood which, as Davies recalls, was filled with music (radio, films, records, family singsongs) (Falsetto 1999: 72). However, the particular prominence music is accorded in the films, as well as the multiplicity and complexity of its various functions, reveal a far greater significance, and it is this aspect of Davies's work that concerns us here.

The first observation that we can make is that popular songs totally dominate the music tracks of Davies's autobiographical films. By popular songs, in this context, I do not mean current pop music (about which Davies claims to know nothing), but the songs that predominated in his childhood and early adolescence, that is to say, during the mid-1940s to late 1950s, which is the period the narratives are, in the main, exploring. In these films we find the songs, hymns and carols that Davies would have learnt at school, as well as those he would have listened to repeatedly in family parties or in pub singsongs and, of course, the songs that featured in the films he went to, and which were repeatedly played on the radio, and hummed by his mother as she went about her chores.

Two important observations can immediately be made: the first is that the majority of the songs featured in the films are well known and will therefore tend to be recognised by at least a proportion of the audience; the second is simply the predominance and variety of the songs that are heard. While we can clearly observe that as we move through the autobiographies, from the *Trilogy* to *The Long Day Closes*, both the number and the range of songs increases, nevertheless, from the very beginning, it is clear that the songs have a vital role to play. Already in *Children*, Davies's short first film, we hear recordings of 'The Ballad of Barbara Allen', and Peggy Lee's 'The Folks Who Live on the Hill', as well as children's voices singing 'Way Down Upon the Swannee River', and the mother singing a lullaby to her son. These songs clearly reflect the enclosed and intimate world of the child, Tucker. Memories of Davies's Catholic primary school similarly explain the children's voices singing 'Hail Queen of Heaven' that we hear in *Madonna and Child*. By the final part of the *Trilogy*, *Death and Transfiguration*, we find a whole range of pub singsongs ('Abie, Abie, Abie My Boy'; 'How You Going to Keep 'Em Down on the Farm?'; 'There's a Someone to Watch Over Me'; 'If You Knew Suzie') enabling us to appreciate Tucker's gradually widening horizons, while a hymn ('Jesus Thou Art Coming') and a number of Christmas carols ('O Come All Ye Faithful'; 'We Three Kings'; 'Away in a Manger'; 'Silent Night') blend together the different times and memories of the old man's existence. It is also important to note that as we watch the opening sequence of this final part of the *Trilogy*, depicting the funeral of Tucker's mother, we hear Doris Day singing 'It All Depends On You'. This song marks a key moment since it provides both the first real acknowledgement in Davies's work of the importance of popular culture in the formation of identity and the first intimation of the possibility of salvation. For although, as we saw in the opening chapter, Tucker (unlike Davies himself) does not succeed in breaking away from this constricting and tightly circumscribed world, nevertheless the inclusion of this song, and the importance accorded to its lyrics, reveal that at last Davies is able to distance himself from the world he is portraying (a feature which can also be discerned, as we have seen, in his increasingly fluid and mobile camera). Moreover, the fact that Davies is here also using the lyrics to comment ironically upon the narrative indicates the increasingly self-conscious use of music that will characterise his subsequent work. Nevertheless, the *Trilogy* as a whole still relies to a large extent upon silence to create its particular atmosphere of stasis and despair.

However, as soon as we move to *Distant Voices, Still Lives*, we become aware of a major shift in Davies's treatment of music. This is obvious merely from noting the proportion of the film in which music is heard. Since the two sections of the film together last only some 80 minutes, the fact that 45 of these minutes contain music is little short of astounding (given that the film is not, of course, a 'musical'). Moreover, for the most part, the music we hear consists of popular songs. To clarify further the significance of this fact, it is important to understand that in

Distant Voices, Still Lives, as indeed in all his films, music is not being used as mere background support, surreptitiously shaping our emotional responses as we concentrate on dialogue and action, but is at least as important as these in creating the film's meanings. Indeed, the songs, with their combination of music and lyrics, are foregrounded in such a way as to permit them to evaluate, subvert or even replace the narrative actions that we observe. Furthermore, we can see that the films are, to a large extent, even structured by music, which also dictates their internal pace and rhythms, while their underlying meanings are, to a considerable degree, actually dictated by its presence or absence from the soundtrack. Given the inseparability of form and meaning, the stark and fundamental opposition between moments when music is heard, and those (often eerily silent) when it is not, must be recognised as a vital component of the film's exploration of the past, not least of the deeply traumatic effect on Davies's family of his father's brutality and violence. Earlier, we noticed how the opening scenes of the film appear to position the father as the central pivot around which other characters and events revolve (signified by the central positioning of his photograph within the various family groupings), and how his presence on screen is marked by his inarticulate violence or by the oppressive silence that heralds such violence. Songs and music, on the other hand, occur almost only when he is absent (although their function transcends any simplistic binary divide), and almost always in association with the mother. Only two occasions disturb this neat presence-as-absence dialectic: the first is the memory of Christmas, to which I shall return; the second is a scene in which the children secretly observe their father, listening to him singing and whistling as he grooms a horse. These two occasions, which constitute the only moments of tenderness shown by the father, are also the only two when his presence involves music. It is therefore clear that Davies understands music not only as an indicator of mobility and freedom but also in relation to the maternal, with its connotations of love and nurture. Music and silence thus serve to articulate the tensions at the heart of the film: mother, love, pleasure on the one hand; stasis, fear, violence and the Law of the Father, on the other.

The Long Day Closes, while in many ways the most personal of all the autobiographical films since it explores Davies's own subjective identity and memory, is also a complex and multilayered collage of music, songs and quotation of dialogue and images from the films of his childhood. Not surprisingly, therefore, music plays a key role, and indeed more than twenty different popular songs are heard, as well as numerous pieces of classical music. Davies himself describes the songs as articulators of his emotional autobiography, and that idea leads us usefully to a consideration of the nature of the relationship between popular songs and memory.

Music and memory

The unique ability possessed by music to access remote and hidden times, places and emotions has of course long been recognised and it is perhaps this aspect more than any other that characterises its function in classical Hollywood films where its basic role is to support and protect the narrative by affecting the emotional response of the audience. However, it is only the relatively recent recognition of hearing as one of our earliest developmental senses that has emphasised the significance of music in relation to unconscious memory, to the pre-Oedipal, pre-linguistic state, and has thus drawn attention more particularly upon the formative role of music in an individual's earliest experiences. Given that the infant hears before it sees, and can recognise the sound of its mother's voice long before it can identify her face, the association between music, particularly song, and the maternal thus appears to be established well before birth, so that the centrality of the auditory realm to the formation of subjectivity becomes clear (Rosalato 1974: 80). It goes without saying that this is a particularly interesting development in film theory, where Lacan's work on the importance of vision and the image in the formation of the subject (the mirror phase) has, not surprisingly, tended to dominate. The powerful ability of music to affect our emotions is therefore seen to emanate from its early association with the mother, and from its apparent ability to restore plenitude and the lost maternal object (Kristeva 1980: 286). And it seems to me that these ideas can be usefully developed in relation to Davies's work.

It is within this relationship between music and anteriority, particularly the close link between voice and self, or voice and mother, that the phenomenon of the popular song must be situated. It appears that for all of us, even those whose main interest is classical rather than popular music, popular songs remain firmly embedded in the mind, to such an extent indeed that they can be seen to constitute part of its 'mental furniture' (Storr 1997: 126). In the light of this, it might seem paradoxical that film, which has always been keen to exploit the emotional power of music, should generally have avoided popular songs, and yet outside the special case of the musical, such songs rarely featured in film scores before the late sixties, and even then their inclusion was unusual (Brown 1996: 564–6). The explanation, enshrined in the rules governing the role of music in classical narrative, also reflects wider issues concerning the nature of musical discourse, and the imperfectly understood relationship between it and the iconic images of film. Indeed, the very impenetrability of musical structures to the non-specialist, along with the power with which music can affect the emotional, and even the physical responses of its listeners, has tended to characterise it as a potentially disruptive element, that must be tightly contained by the narrative. Hence the traditional requirement that film music should support the dramatic impact of the narrative without drawing attention to itself; in other words, that it should be 'inaudible', or at least inconspicuous. It was Kurt London, one of the earliest theorists to tackle the issue of film music, who, in 1936, stipulated that the primary requirement of film music was that it should be 'unnoticed' (London 1936: 37), a view which was still acknowledged, albeit with some reservations, by Adorno and Eisler, in their seminal 1947 study, *Composing for the Films*. 'The composer is thus faced with a new and strange task, that of producing something sensible which at the same time can be perceived by way of parenthesis, as it slips by the listener' (Adorno and Eisler 1947: 132). This view of music's near-invisibility continued to inform film music theory for a very long time (Brown 1994: 1). In *Unheard Melodies: Narrative Film Music*, written in 1987, Claudia Gorbman lists the principles governing classical film music as Invisibility; 'Inaudibility'; Signifier of emotion; Narrative cueing; Continuity; Unity, in that order, thereby still supporting the notion that whilst music powerfully influences our emotional responses and interpretations of a film, we are not supposed to be aware of its presence; its fundamental role is to support and protect the narrative without drawing attention to itself (Gorbman 1987: 1). 'The classical narrative sound film has been constituted in such a way that the spectator does not normally (consciously) hear the film score', she comments, for example (p. 31). In practice, the main consequences of this notion were, first of all, that film music should not be complicated or 'difficult', since the attention such music demands would inevitably distract the viewers, drawing them outside the control of the narrative (Thomas 1991: 72), and secondly that 'familiar' music (into which category popular songs must be placed) should be avoided because, similarly, it 'runs the risk of drawing attention to itself as music' and, in so doing, of distancing the spectator from the film's narrative (Steiner 1937: 225). For his part, Lindgren, in commenting at length upon the 'disturbing' potential of familiar music heard within a film, suggests that its principal danger is that 'it often has certain associations for the spectator which may conflict entirely with the associations the producer wishes to establish in his film' (Lindgren

1963: 139). In other words, by bringing the spectator's own personal memories and associations into the interpretative process, not only does popular music weaken the film's narrative hold, but it also risks subverting its intended meaning and affect. Complex or well-known music was therefore avoided as potentially detrimental to the control exercised by the narrative and as a consequence, Flinn notes, despite the growing critical awareness of the centrality of its role, film music still tends to pass largely unnoticed, to have 'the rather curious distinction of being at the periphery of most people's concerns about the cinema' (Flinn 1992: 3).

Clearly, this approach is over-simplistic, for, if film music is to play any part in the text's construction of meaning, it must be to some degree 'perceived and organised by the film spectator', that is to say that it must function at a level other than the subconscious one (Smith 1996: 235). Indeed, the whole tradition of the (Wagnerian) leitmotif in its cinematic interpretation(s) depends, to some extent, upon a conscious processing of the musical information we are given. Musical themes and motifs within a film may well serve to facilitate the audience's recognition of character, place and period but, at the same time, to construct memory patterns within the narrative, while our awareness of the connotative and, in particular, the ironic use of music pinpoints that conscious processes are at work. Nevertheless, understanding these dominant principles helps to clarify reasons why, despite the ability of popular songs to bridge temporal and spatial distance, and their vivid and immediate recall of particular places or people from our past (Monaco 1987: 110), their inclusion in films was for a long time considered too great a risk. And this perceived risk was increased by the songs' ability of to 'wrap themselves around whatever emotion you happen to be carrying when you first heard them' (Potter 1993: 84–5).

What I have discovered in my work on autobiographical films in general, however, is that, within their essentially open-ended discourse, not only do directors want the memory trigger mechanism of songs to be recognised, they tend actively to seek the personal and creative involvement of the spectators. Indeed, it is arguably even a requisite of the fragmentary nature of the discourse that spectators should contribute their own individual memories. This aspect may indeed account for the widespread popularity of these films; the way in which audiences, irrespective of age, background or even nationality, respond by claiming to have seen in them a reflection of their own childhood (Davies 1992: 21). Accordingly, not only do popular songs abound in autobiographical films, but they tend to be actively foregrounded in a variety of ways which intentionally destabilise the narrative and redefine the fundamental relationship between image and music. To some extent, therefore, what Davies is doing with the songs in his films fits quite neatly into the general characteristics of the medium, and can profitably be considered alongside a wide range of autobiographical films produced across Europe in the last two decades of the twentieth century (Everett 2000b). Nevertheless, our concern here, is with the specificity of Davies's films, and the remainder of this analysis will focus on them more closely as a means of identifying at least some of the complex and multiple ways which make his treatment of music one of the hallmarks of Davies's films.

Nostalgia

Working directly on the listener's emotions, and powerfully recalling the past, music is able to promise a return to 'better, more perfect, times and memories', whilst simultaneously underlining the impossibility of any such return (Flinn 1992: 9). It is for this reason that Flinn describes the function of music as 'utopian', explaining that music refers to a world outside 'reality'; passionately longed for, but ultimately unrealisable. It is, she claims, the way that music operates a process of constant referral within a film narrative that enables it so powerfully to create feelings of nostalgia (Flinn 1992: 151–3).

It is true that the ambiguous status and the emotional energy of popular songs can provide an exceptionally potent source of nostalgia. However, autobiographical discourse, as we have seen, is about the processes of memory and does not therefore seek the closure of nostalgia, so that, even when the nostalgic potential of popular songs is exploited, this is generally done ironically and self-consciously. Dennis Potter, who, in his trilogy about the mediating effects of popular culture in Britain in the 1930s, 1940s and 1950s respectively – *Pennies From Heaven* (1978), *The Singing Detective* (1986) and *Lipstick on Your Collar* (1993) – also experimented widely with the relationship between popular song and memory, explains that it is the particular combination of ironic self-awareness and nostalgic innocence provided by such songs that enables the director to turn fiction 'inside out', to move the narrative inwards from description to process: 'you can use the power of nostalgia to open the past up and make it stand up in front of you. That is why I use popular songs' (Potter 1993: 22; 96).[1] We have already seen these processes at work in our analysis of the opening sequence of *The Long Day Closes*, where the song itself performs as a key device in establishing both the historical moment and the personal nature of the narrative. We saw that while the song ('Stardust', sung by Nat King Cole) is acknowledged as part of the personal memories of the director/protagonist and of the spectators, it also simultaneously interrogates these memories by revealing their essential artificiality, so that the self which the film strives to reflect is acknowledged, at least in part, as a construct of popular culture. At the same time, the lyrics of the song, which insistently draw our attention to its nostalgic function as 'a song that will not die', serve to distance us intellectually by making us aware of the processes at work, even as it involves us emotionally in those processes.

As a further example of the way in which the song is able to create a powerful sense of nostalgia while simultaneously distancing us intellectually, I should like to examine the Christmas sequence in *Distant Voices, Still Lives* referred to earlier in this chapter. The sequence opens with that most nostalgic of all sounds, a Christmas carol, as the camera makes a fluid, retrospective track from right to left along the narrow street. Nostagia, quite literally, transforms the landscape of memory here, for the soft-focus effect of the shot is intensified by the Christmas-card snow which magically softens the hard contours of street and houses. We see the entire family, happily gathered together around the crib, in a perfect evocation of the 'spirit' of Christmas, and then watch as the father lovingly decorates the tree and wishes the children goodnight. Later we see them as sleeping cherubs, from what appears to be his point of view, as he creeps into their bedroom to hang up their stockings. I have already mentioned this occasion as one of only two instances in which the father's presence on screen does coincide with music on the soundtrack, so it might well be tempting to read the scene as the embodiment of nostalgia: childhood as Utopia; as paradise lost.

However, the carol continues unbroken into the next scene, which depicts the children and their father sitting at the table for Christmas tea. The staging is a little theatrical, in that the chair directly in front of us is empty and, interestingly, in this scene in which the father is present, it is he and not his photograph that is positioned centrally, while on the wall immediately behind him hangs a mirror in which we can see the reflection of the back of his head: a powerful metaphor for the two sides of his personality the sequence depicts. The music stops abruptly and, in the frozen silence that replaces it, the children watch their father, first apprehensively and then with increasing terror, as he sweeps the cloth off the table in a sudden rage. By using the carol to link these two very different scenes, Davies allows nostalgia to develop and then to be destroyed from within. Childhood was not perfect, he vividly demonstrates, and, within the shift imposed by this new context, the actual words of the well-known carol take on a chilling new meaning. This midwinter world is indeed bleak, icy and frozen. It is in fact the embodiment of stasis and despair. It is the antithesis of the scene as we first perceive it, coloured by the potent nostalgia of the remembered music. However, it is important to recognise that the power of the sequence really emanates from the intense reactions this music provokes in us, the viewers, by involving us in its apparent nostalgia. Moreover, not only does the sequence contrast the open-ended mobility of music with the silence of stasis, but it also exploits the way in which music can encompass different temporalities and viewpoints, not least those of the spectators themselves.

Such notions are further explored and expanded in *Distant Voices, Still Lives*, in the chilling sequence which begins with the mother sitting on the windowsill of an upstairs window, and leaning precariously out to clean the glass. 'Please don't fall', pleads her terrified daughter. The adult voice of that daughter is then heard asking 'Why did you marry him, mam?', immediately linking the mother's visual framing and entrapment with the brutality of her husband. As the mother replies, the song begins. The song we hear this time is 'Taking a Chance on Love'. It is deeply romantic, of course, but the lyrics, centring on the notion of love as a gamble, will be savagely undermined by the images of reality that accompany them; there is no *chance* and never was. Like almost all the women in the film, the mother is doomed; we know this from the minute we see her framed by the window, for the camera allows her no possibility of freedom or escape. The frightened gazes of the children and the reflective gaze of the adult director shift effortlessly through time and space, but the mother remains trapped, a message heightened by the futile circular movements with which she later polishes the table. The particular potency of Davies's juxtaposition of music and image is heightened as the song carries us into the next scene, stopping abruptly as we see her being viciously beaten by her husband. Since the trigger for the scene is the mother's reply to her daughter's question – 'He was nice. He was a good dancer' – we again see how nostalgia is being brutally attacked from within. Indeed Davies is here highly critical of the unrealistic expectations fostered by such songs through their dishonest portrayal of romantic love. Davies thus exploits and then attacks our own nostalgic response as a way of introducing into the film deeper issues about the position of women in postwar society, and he achieves this powerfully and economically and without recourse to explanation or didacticism.

I am not, of course, suggesting that Davies is directly blaming these songs: we know how much he loves them, and their function in the films is essentially positive. But he has recognised that, through our responses to the songs, it is possible to open up new readings of the past that completely undermine the complacent indifference of nostalgia, and that, in so doing, the words of the songs play a powerful role in provoking an ongoing and wide-ranging process of reassessment.

A further example of this procedure can be provided by a further sequence in *Distant Voices, Still Lives* which we have already examined in some detail. This is the visually exquisite sequence that begins with a beautifully textured collage of gleaming umbrellas as homage to one of Davies's favourite films, *Singin' in the Rain*. To the lush and romantic strains of 'Love Is a Many Splendored Thing', the camera moves us inside the cinema and focuses on the faces of the audience as they gaze in total absorption at the screen. Most of the women in the cinema, including Davies's sisters, are in tears. In this sequence, therefore, we see homage to the power of film to capture our emotions and even transform our lives (outside the cinema, the rain was definitely of the Hollywood variety). However, yet again, we are not long permitted to wallow in nostalgia, for, as we watch the women's tears, our responses are inevitably tempered by our knowledge that for them love is less 'a many splendoured thing' than a momentary illusion (or gamble) that irrevocably leads to their exploitation and entrapment. And in the following scene, in which the song is still playing, we see the two men falling through a glass roof which, like the illusory promises of the song, shatters as they do so.

Subjectivity is of course grounded socially and historically, and again the iconic and concrete functioning of music can symbolise the emotionally experienced dimensions of other people's lives, as well as the external social relationships with which the individual is intimately involved. Thus, revealing the relatedness of human existence, songs can be used to establish a sense of community and group identity, in a uniquely powerful manner. Terence Davies has often been accused of creating a nostalgic myth of community in his repeated depictions of pub singsongs. Closer attention, however, reveals that, while scenes of family and friends singing together in the pub might appear to be reinforcing this sense of community, in fact the device of song is actually revealing the process as myth. For example, on one such occasion we see all the family and their friends and neighbours crammed together in the friendly, smoke-filled local pub. However, an unpleasant scene between Jingles and her brutish husband leads to an argument in which the women criticise the men who, of course, immediately retaliate. Tempers flare. Suddenly, the mother's voice is heard: 'Now come on, we don't want any upsets. We're here to enjoy ourselves.' The mother is therefore demanding that the appearance of enjoyment be maintained. Her advice is taken, and the group settles down to sing. The first song,

'Bye-Bye Blackbird', supports the illusion with its determined cheerfulness: 'Pack up all my tears and woe'. But there follows a spectacular battle: all the hurts and conflicts are still there, but are being articulated through the apparently anodyne lyrics of the chosen songs, thus succeeding in creating a powerful dynamic which whilst appearing to support the nostalgic version of happy working-class community spirit, actually powerfully deconstructs the myth. Ever more complex patterns, gazes and layers of meanings proliferate in the cigarette smoke. For Davies the importance of such songs was, above all, that they enabled people to express their emotions: 'You know, what they did, those songs, prior to rock and roll, they gave ordinary people a voice for their feelings' (see Chapter 8).

If *Distant Voices, Still Lives* creates a dialectic structured around despair and hope, fear and love, stasis and flux, silence and music, the conflict at its heart reflects the tensions between the patriarchal regime, signified by stasis and violence, and the nostalgic tenderness of the mother expressed through her close relationship with music. Despite the apparently weak position of the mother, it is she who, through the disruptive mobility of music, triumphs. For it is the nature of music to move through time, to change, to modulate, to escape definition, and in its constant movement we find constantly renewed hope. Of course, that hope is vulnerable perhaps even doomed; silenced by the very reality whose limitations it is responsible for revealing.

Voice

Although we have recognised the nostalgic power of the music, and the rich potential for an ironic revaluation of the past provided by the lyrics, nevertheless we still have not dealt with what is almost certainly the key feature of song, which is the complex relationship it creates between melody and words. Music, as well as being a self-contained, self-referential and intellectual medium, is also, and at the same time, a physical one; it influences such basic reflexes as heartbeat, rate of breathing and mood of the listener (Blacking 1976: vi–viii; Steiner 1992: 44). In song, where music and language function together, this basic physicality appears to be enhanced. Barthes explains this as 'the materiality of the body speaking its mother tongue', and suggests that it is this increased physicality that enables song to intensify both the memory of the original experience (*jouissance*) and the keenness of its loss. It is because song is marked by what he refers to as the *grain* of the voice that it occupies a privileged position in memory (Barthes 1977: 179–89). It is true that the significance of songs to autobiographical films appears to result largely from their complex status as both verbal and non-verbal, both music and discourse, and this too perhaps accounts for their ability to be both public and intimate, or – in Potter's terms– to move inwards from description to meaning. I should like to illustrate this idea by referring to a sequence from *The Long Day Closes*. In the first part, we see Bud and his mother and sisters at a fairground, and in the second we see Bud, at home, sitting on his mother's knee. Again the two sections are linked by a single song, 'She Moved Through the Fair', which we hear throughout. Like 'Stardust' this song was popular both during and after the 1950s, and is likely to be widely remembered. It too is accorded, at least initially, a non-diegetic status. It is heard throughout the long fairground scene, where it signifies Bud's happiness but, although this is for the child a moment of carnival, the overall atmosphere is reflective and quiet, and the slowness of the song's rhythm is echoed in the artificially slow pace at which the child and his mother walk. As we hear the words 'And then she went homeward / With one star awake / As the swan in the evening / Moves over the lake' we move back into Bud's house and into the more intimate memory of his mother singing that same song to him. Whilst we see Bud on his mother's knee as she sings to him, we hear the recorded voice, which is first joined and then replaced by that of the mother. The change of voice mirrors the gradual interiorisation of the song, its changing status for Bud, from public to personal. However, *we* can see that the mother's voice signals *her* interiorisation of the song (as she recalls her father singing it to her), and expresses *her* sadness and sense of loss. Bud, the child, is aware of her voice, and interested by the information that his grandfather used to sing this song to his mother when she was small, but unlike us he is not aware of her sadness, and does not see her tears. However, Davies, the adult, in using the song to recall his own lost childhood, reaches through it to a new awareness of his mother's sadness and of her own lost past. So the song performs multilayered functions through the increasing internalisation of its status, but, equally importantly, it is insistently foregrounded within the film, so that we, the spectators, are simultaneously involved emotionally in the process of remembering, and intellectually in the consideration of that process.

And just as the emotional impact of the melody is intensified by the presence of voice, so too it is mediated by the lyrics which, as we have seen, may well provide a commentary on, or counterpoint to, the narrative. The words can thus act as ironic distancing devices which draw attention to the gap between the adult narrator's understanding and the child's remembered perceptions. Davies's films offer and demand a rereading of the songs they contain, and, through this, an acknowledgement of the shifting relationship and distance between remembering and remembered; subject and object. The song both links and separates the different times of the narrative, and draws attention to the processes at work.

The songs in Davies's autobiographical films can therefore increase the multiple textualities of film and self by emphasising the lack of distinct boundaries between past and present, fiction and reality, screen and audience. The insecurity of their temporal and narrative status mirrors the slippage and doubling which we recognise as essential features of autobiographical discourse, the perhaps inevitable consequence of turning one's attention inwards: 'Self-scrutiny engenders self-estrangement'; the self you remember is both first and third person; both self and other (Sheringham 1993: viii). In Davies's films, popular songs largely obviate the need for distancing devices such as authorial voice-over, since they themselves provide an alternative strategy and can capture the sense of disparity that Sheringham identifies between self as historical phenomenon, and self as something outside and perhaps at odds with history. In other words, song provides the moment in the narrative when history and fiction, personal and public, present and past intersect.

If the songs in autobiographical films are placed in the foreground, and if their performance draws attention both to their position as memory trace and to the nature and process of remembering, it is because they are recognised as part of the personal act of narration of the director; in other words, they form part of the dynamic process of the creation of self: 'Writing one's story/history, is an attempt to create oneself, rather than to know oneself', writes Lejeune who, arguably, still today remains the leading theorist in this field (Lejeune 1971: 84, my translation). Davies uses songs not to *illustrate* his memory but as part of the autobiographical process which turns the song itself into a form of 'quasi-autobiography', Potter would argue, whereby even the most 'extraordinarily banal tune and nonsensical lyric' is recognised as part of the actual process of recalling and articulating the past, and thus of *creating* the self (Potter 1993: 96). Thus the positive and dynamic role of popular songs within Davies's autobiographical journey becomes clear; they can actually lead to the deeper self-awareness that enables him to move forwards, away from the past.

The Neon Bible

Self-conscious songs thus act as key signifiers in Davies's autobiographical films, not only because of their ability to recall the past so vividly but also because their combination of melody and lyrics enables them to perform as complex and multilayered signifiers within the memory processes the film articulates. At the same time they are deliberately foregrounded so as to involve the audience in the creative process. And as has been seen, the purpose of popular songs in Davies's autobiographies is not to create a nostalgic vision of the past but to use the power of nostalgia to demystify and demythologise that past. *The Neon Bible*, however, is an adaptation rather than a personal memory narrative, and we might therefore expect to find alternative strategies at work. Yet, because the novel is presented as a first-person account, is structured as an extended flashback and, like autobiography, is marked by shifting tenses and viewpoints, there are considerable areas of overlap with Davies's own experiences, and this overlap is clearly reflected by the fact that he retains many similarities in his treatment of music in this film.

Again the soundtrack is dominated by popular songs, although, with some ten different songs in all, there are fewer than in *The Long Day Closes* and *Distant Voices, Still Lives*. Again the songs are accorded both diegetic and non-diegetic functions, and again there is some overlap of these categories even within the performance of an individual song. Yet again there is an important relationship between women and music, while once more songs also function as indicators of community and of social context. As an example of the link between women and music, we could quote Aunt Mae singing George and Ira Gershwin's 'How Long Has This Been Going On?' and her moving performance of 'My Romance', by Rodgers and Hart, at the factory party. Slightly more problematically, the mother sings 'Too-ra-loo-ra-loo-ra, That's an Irish Lullaby' (composed by J. H. Shannon) in a much-criticised scene showing her vulnerability and her increasing madness. Community singing might include the townsfolk's stirring rendition of 'The Old Rugged Cross' at the Revivalist meeting, and David's class singing 'Dixie' at their graduation ceremony. Given that the songs are foregrounded, we reflect on their lyrics even as we respond to their well-known melodies, and, although for us too they serve to indicate place and time, they never function as mere background. Nevertheless there are important differences too, and these might well reflect that for all his empathising, Davies's own personal experiences are not the direct subject of the film. There is, for example, a slightly greater sense of distance or objectivity in the choice of songs that both reflects this difference and reveals Davies as someone who is trying to understand a community from outside rather than from within.

One immediate difference, of course, is that there are far fewer references in the film to popular culture, particularly the glamorous Hollywood culture that coloured Davies's own childhood. This lack reflects the narrow-minded mentality of the valley where cinema, in particular, is considered sinful and dangerous. But the irony is that it is largely through such American films as *Gone With the Wind* (Victor Fleming, 1939) that Davies himself became familiar with the music and images that serve as his template for *The Neon Bible*. It might be tempting to suggest that the use of music is less complex here than in the previous films; both 'Dixie' and 'Chattanooga Choo Choo', for example, are songs widely associated with the Deep South, so that their purpose on the soundtrack might appear to be a simple (nostalgic) re-creation of a lost place and time. However, closer attention reveals the process at work to be considerably more complex. For example, although it is true that David's class sing 'Dixie' at their graduation, both its articulation as performance (they are standing on the stage in front of an audience of friends and family) and the scenes with which it is juxtaposed suggest more subtle and critical readings. In the sequence that precedes it we hear Aunt Mae's voice asking David to recite again his favourite lines from Longfellow's 'The Day Is Done' (considered by David to be the most beautiful thing he has ever heard):

> Then read from the treasured volume
> The poem of thy choice,
> And lend to the rhyme of the poet
> The beauty of thy voice.
> And the night shall be filled with music,
> And the cares that infest the day,
> Shall fold their tents, like the Arabs,
> And as silently steal away.[2]

As he does so, his voice is first joined and then replaced by that of Mr Farney, the English teacher, before we cut to the class singing 'Dixie'. As well as showing us the interiorisation of the poem, in a way that we have seen songs function in Davies's earlier films, in this instance these shifts of voice and viewpoint also explore the notion of the outsider: Mr Farney, of course, by virtue of being a gay intellectual and, essentially, David himself. In the novel we are told that the class was made to learn this poem and to recite it at graduation, and that David could never have admitted to his fellow pupils how deeply he liked it because 'they thought it was stupid, and wanted to sing a song instead'. When Mr Farney allows them to choose a song as well, 'the class voted to sing "Dixie" (p. 101).[3] David thus does not include himself in this decision (not 'we' but 'the class'). Moreover, the abrupt transition from poem as expression of individuality to 'Dixie', as community doxology reinforces the hopelessness of David's situation; his basic feeling of difference in a community in which, as we have seen, difference is not tolerated. (And in the staging of the song as performance, we can also sense Davies's own detachment from the mores of community he is portraying.) Immediately after the graduation scene, David's sense of exclusion is reinforced by his treatment by his aunt and her lover (who make him wait alone as they make love), and then by the terrifying spectacle of his mother who, as embodiment of difference, is now completely isolated by her madness.

If there is a marked lack of the Hollywood romance and glamour in the songs we hear in *The Neon Bible*, the exception is Aunt Mae's rendition of 'My Romance' at the factory party, while the men are away at war. It is of course because the men are not present that this party can take place, and that she has at last been accepted into the community. The scene is the only relaxed social occasion in the film, and that and its status as a female event leads one to suspect that the sequence is strongly coloured by Davies's personal memories and emotions. Before singing the romantic song, Aunt Mae highlights the act as individual and as rejection of the pressures exerted upon a community in time of war, by announcing 'I tell you, it ain't going to be "God Bless America!"'. This is a significant departure from the book, where she does, in fact sing 'God Bless America!' with the crowd joining in. Davies is foregrounding her difference and perhaps reclaiming the moment for himself. As Aunt Mae sings, his camera cuts repeatedly to the group, and in particular to David and his mother who stand, isolated but smiling, on its edge. We watch the effect the song has on the mother as she (illustrating Potter's and Davies's comments about the way that songs are personalised by the individuals who hear them) internalises the lyrics and applies them to her own situation ('My romance doesn't need a thing but you') since her husband is away at war. We, of course, cannot fail to notice the irony of the song's reception, as we have repeatedly seen her being abused by her brutal husband. Nevertheless, the song creates its magic idealisation of romantic love, and the woman's eyes fill with tears as she is drawn into its world. (And yet again, the song's lyrics assume ironic status as they conjure a romance that does *not* need any help from romantic songs and music.)

If such moments of internalisation occur rarely in this film because we are not dealing directly with Davies's personal experiences, nevertheless Davies's more detached position does enable him to use songs as a powerful means of commenting upon the community. One particularly striking example is the sequence showing the Revivalist meeting in the town, a sequence we earlier considered in relation to its (ironic) portrayal as epic. It is equally interesting to note the function of music here. The beginning of the sequence is signalled by the singing of a traditional hymn, 'The Old Rugged Cross'. At first the screen is black, although, as the camera starts its movement, gradually we make out stars in the dark sky. Thus the epic dimensions of the sequence are established. The camera then pans slowly down to follow the crowds of townsfolk heading for the tent in which Bobbie Lee Taylor is to make his final appearance. We have already commented on the dramatic images of the vast tent, lit from within and with fires burning on either side, and suggested various links with the iconic *Gone With the Wind* as Davies plays with notions of the epic. As the camera moves us into the tent, we find that the powerful non-diegetic music has changed status since it is now being sung by the people themselves. This is a subtle but significant shift away from the epic and back to the personal. While the occasion is still marked as religious by the music's status as hymn, now it appears as an affirmation of a community's faith. The singing stops as Bobbie Lee is announced, and in the moment before he goes out to greet the crown we hear him gloat, 'Good crowd. Good money', a clear indication of the hypocritical and exploitative role of religion in the community. There are clear links here both with the falsely nostalgic sense of community suggested by the group singing in Davies's earlier work and with the cynically exploitative role of religion in fostering this illusion, and upholding the status quo.

I commented earlier that Davies's choice of music in *The Neon Bible* reflects the knowledge he has of the Southern States of America, and that this knowledge largely emanated from the films that he had seen at David's age. Inevitably, therefore, these films and these songs will be called upon to 'authenticate' the setting and period and, essentially, to involve us directly in the self-conscious myth-making processes of the film. Nowhere is this more vividly illustrated than in the moment at which 'Tara's Theme', from *Gone With the Wind*, surges dramatically on to the soundtrack. Here Davies is relying on our familiarity with the music and the film it represents to enable him to widen his sequence (coffins draped with flags, followed by a white sheet on a washing line), so that it introduces into the narrative wide-ranging, epic themes of war, loss and suffering, while simultaneously reminding us of the history and mythology with which the South defines its identity. In this way, the music itself performs as a metaphor through which individual and group experiences, and different times and places, meet.

David's most intimate experiences are also put into a wider social and historical context through the use of song as in the sequence depicting Aunt Mae's departure. The song in question starts as Mae gets on to the bus, continues as David waves goodbye and the bus drives off leaving him in clouds of dust and exhaust, and then accompanies his slow walk back to the dilapidated shack he lives in, and his discovery of his mother lying senseless on the floor. It ends just before she draws her last breath. The song, 'Hard Times Come Again No More', written in 1854, speaks for the weary and the dispossessed, "Tis the song, the sigh of the weary', and its themes are death and hardship. The irony of its refrain, as David faces his own hardest and most difficult times, is made infinitely more moving through its evocation of the suffering and poverty endured by slaves in the Deep South. Davies's decision to include this song is interesting, not least because of the way in which its lyrics self-consciously explore its themes in relation to music: 'There's a song that will linger / Forever in our ears; / Oh hard times come again no more'.[4]

So we can note that while songs are used in *The Neon Bible* with the now familiar purpose of modifying and extending the film's various meanings, as well as creating the emotional landscape of the period, the differences that we have discovered are particularly significant. For example, the fact that there are fewer songs by individual voices than in his earlier films, and more group singing, tells us a good deal about the nature of the community the film describes, specifically its intolerance of individuality and difference. Even the community singing we hear does not reflect the informal and unstructured atmosphere of the pub but only the controlled rituals of church or school. And while music does still occasionally reveal its relationship with the feminine (as in the case of Mae and the party), even this aspect is limited by the dictates of the dominant patriarchy. It therefore follows that the link between singing and the maternal is also weakened. In fact, the only time that David's mother sings is as an expression of madness from which David is excluded. The irony of the fact that the song happens to be a lullaby will not be lost. But we know from Mae's intimate relationship with singing that she is David's surrogate mother; his sole source of love and support. Her departure, therefore, is the more devastating: hard times have returned with a vengeance.

Even from the above brief analysis, it is clear that Davies's handling of songs is particularly innovative. It is clear that despite the similarities that can be established between *The Neon Bible* and his autobiographical films, the differences that we have identified serve to underline the extent to which the songs are central to the actual meanings of the film. Within the symbiosis of form and meaning, therefore, music is a key signifier.

Given the key role of popular songs in the autobiographical process, I have so far chosen to focus exclusively on these. However, to do so runs the risk of falsely seeming to imply that Davies relies exclusively on such music, whereas his love of classical music is no less essential to the films' composition. In *The Long Day Closes*, for example, in addition to all the popular songs, we also hear a Boccherini minuet, Kathleen Ferrier singing 'Blow the Wind Southerly' and Sir Arthur Sullivan's song, from which the title of the film is taken, 'The Long Day Closes'. However, in *The Neon Bible* there is no classical music at all, apart perhaps from an oblique reference to Dvorák's Symphony No. 9 op. 95, *From the New World*, through the townsfolk's rendition of 'Goin' Home' during the Revivalist meeting. (Although this song has now acquired the status of a traditional air in American culture, Art Tatum, who originally popularised it, simply set words to the nostalgic theme from the second movement of Dvorák's *From the New World*).[5] If classical music otherwise plays no part in the film it is because it is simply not tolerated by the community. (We will see a reversal of this situation in *The House of Mirth*, which deals with a community entirely isolated from popular culture, so that in this case exclusively classical music is heard.) However, *The Neon Bible* does contain one single work for solo instrument, 'Perfida', composed by Alberto Dominguez and made popular by Glenn Miller, whose version features in the film. The tune is used to represent wartime culture outside the valley, as well as being closely associated with David since it accompanies the scenes of him alone on the train. Its performance by a solo instrument is therefore linked to his ultimate isolation and marginalisation.

The House of Mirth

That Davies has finally moved away from autobiography in his adaptation of Edith Wharton's *The House of Mirth* is strikingly indicated by the film's fundamentally different treatment of music. Music is heard on only twelve occasions throughout, and there are no popular songs (although, as we shall see, there is one coded reference to a song from Davies's childhood). However, the sparser music track in no way indicates that music is accorded a lesser role, nor is its treatment any less innovative than in his earlier films. Thus, for all its apparent restraint, the role of music in articulating the film's various meanings remains seminal.

It has become clear, through studying Davies's other films, that music tends to be associated with the feminine, particularly the maternal voice, and to be used in stark opposition to silence which is thereby linked to stasis, violence and the Law of the Father. Moments of extreme mobility, on the other hand, frequently articulated through lyrical tracking shots, are not merely accompanied by music but appear actually to be motivated and given shape by it. Music offers freedom and escape, and is thus linked with implications of creativity and joy. The very fact that music is heard so infrequently in *The House of Mirth* reflects the closed and claustrophobic society that Lily inhabits and, by focusing our attention instead on minute everyday sounds, its very absence serves to reinforce our awareness of Lily's entrapment. Nevertheless, when music is heard, it occupies the same prominent position that we have consistently noted, that is to say that it never acts as mere narrative support or simply to provide background texture. Instead, as one of the prime signifiers in the film, its role is to provoke the thoughtful and creative response of the spectator.

The music Davies uses in this film is almost entirely classical in origin, with a preponderance of the baroque. Only nine different pieces of music are included, three of these being from Mozart's comic opera *Così fan tutte* (1790): the Overture, which we hear during the opera sequence; the first aria of the opera, 'La mia Dorabella', which we hear as Lily leaves the opera house and gets into the carriage with Gus Trenor (the music's abrupt ending as she enters his house thus prepares us for the terrible and potentially violent situation which will develop) and 'Soave sia il vento', the beautiful, lyrical trio, chosen by Davies for his transition shot.

As we saw in the last chapter, Davies's decision to use *Così fan tutte* is significant for a number of reasons. In the novel, Wharton does not reveal the name of the opera since it is the occasion rather than the music that she is concerned with. This means Davies had considerable freedom of choice. His decision to use a Mozart opera was undoubtedly influenced by the opera scene in *Letter From an Unknown Woman* which, we noted, was one of his templates in making *The House of Mirth*. (Ophuls, of course, uses *The Magic Flute* in his film.) Davies explains that the deciding factor in selecting *Così fan tutte* was his determination to use 'Soave sia il vento' for his transition sequence, and that it therefore made sense to use that opera throughout. Certainly, this coherence, along with the greater importance he places on the opera itself (not least by directly linking it to the scene in which Gus Trenor compromises Lily), reinforces its central role within the narrative, and, accordingly, prepares us to expect that this work will contribute additional layers of meanings. In other words, we should be prepared to look further to unravel some of the other reasons that make *Così fan tutte* particularly appropriate for this role.

One of the reasons why Mozart enjoyed experimenting with the Italian comic opera tradition, or *opera buffa*, was the potential it offered for matching language to music, for, as he wrote to his father, the words 'can be perfectly expressed by the music' (Rosen 1971: 288), and the seamless match of language and music in *Così fan tutte* would certainly be a factor in delighting Davies, as would 'the complete appropriateness of the tonalities' (Einstein 1971: 461). But while its musical quality is universally praised, certain critics have been less fulsome in their response to its plot, which recounts an experiment conducted by an elderly philosopher, Don Alfonso, to prove to two young men that their sweethearts would not remain faithful, were the men away at war. Blom, for example, refers disapprovingly to 'the palpable absurdities of the libretto' (Blom 1962: 153). However, such judgement ignores the basic traditions of the *opera buffa* form which is structured by a complex interplay of mask, disguise and reality. In his fascinating analysis of the classical tradition in music, Charles Rosen suggests that in fact the tropes of the *opera buffa*, as epitomised in *Così fan tutte*, provide valuable insight into eighteenth-century notions of psychology, specifically the notion that the outward personality is a mask behind which, as a sort of *tabula rasa*, lies an individual's real identity waiting to be formed by experience (Rosen 1971: 315). What is particularly interesting about these ideas is their continuing relevance to the world of *The House of Mirth*, given that here too characters consistently hide their real feelings under the appropriate social persona, and that beneath her mask and trappings Lily is indeed vulnerable to manipulation by more intelligent and cleverer characters. For this reason alone, *Così fan tutte* is well suited to provide a central and multiple point of reference in the film. Moreover, the essentially closed worlds of both *Così fan tutte* and *The House of Mirth* serve to link the works still further, as does their shared, and perhaps equally tender exploration of the vulnerability of their female subjects who, in both, are positioned as potential victims of the male gaze. But it is perhaps, above all, the artificiality and self-consciousness of Mozart's work that renders it so entirely apt; the world it constructs aims not to be true to life but to a particular view of human nature which is created and explored through formal theatrical and musical devices, while the irony and 'tone' of the opera, like its musical virtuosity and richly polyphonic passages, suggest endless parallels with the work of Davies himself.

Nowhere perhaps is this relationship more effectively revealed than in the transition sequence in *The House of Mirth* which we have already discussed at some length. This sequence, which Davies has described as 'just me and Mozart', explores music and film as movement through time and space. In the aria, we hear the voices of the two young women as they bid a tearful farewell to their lovers who, they believe, are sailing off to war, and wish them a safe voyage. Not only, therefore, is the song actually dealing with the theme of journey, but it is also about love and tenderness, hope and loss, the very emotions that we imagine Lily might be feeling as she leaves for her trip. However, the lyrical and tender voices of the two women are joined, from time to time, by the ironic comments of Don Alfonso who, in setting up the experiment, is also controlling the women's destiny, and here again the parallels are obvious since Lily too is being manipulated here. The camera's lyrical tracking across water is entirely motivated by the trio, and it is the music that dictates both the pace and length of the sequence. Moreover, camera and music together create sensations of openness and freedom that have been conspicuously lacking in the film until this point. Indeed, if, as we have suggested, the oppressive silence of the interior shots increases the feeling of the impossibility of escape, and serves to create the self-contained, self-obsessed nature of Lily's world, then the sudden transition from stasis to movement (through both music and camera), and from rain and darkness to sunlight and sparking water, is electrifying in its sudden articulation of escape and hope. The perfect match of music and image creates in this sequence one of those sublime moments of epiphany at which Davies excels.

It has already been noted that during the opening credits and the shots of Lily arriving at Grand Central Station we hear an excerpt from the Oboe Concerto in D minor by Alessandro Marcello (1684–1750), an Italian composer, philosopher and mathematician. This same music is repeated at the end of the film as Lily takes her fatal dose of chloral, and continues to be heard as Selden discovers her body and holds her, at last admitting his love. It is also heard in the scene in which they kiss for the first time, so that it is becomes intimately associated with the film's most powerful subtext: Lily and Selden's unfulfilled love. As an example of Davies's thoughtful approach to music, we noted in the previous chapter that when the Marcello is heard for the second time, in the scene where Lily and Lawrence kiss, it has been transposed to a different key and arranged for string quartet, and that this very subtle modulation that we hear contributes further intensity and delicacy to the scene, as well as indicating the care with which Davies handles music as signifier throughout.

Excerpts from two other string quartets are also heard, in what we initially assume to be a diegetic context, although we do not actually see the musicians. The first of these occasions is the Van Osburgh wedding in which the third movement of Haydn's *Lark* Quartet Op. 64, No. 5 in D major is played in the background, and the second is the sequence in

Monte Carlo where we hear the Rondo from Rossini's third String Quartet. These works are easily understood as the sort of music which would have been performed at just such occasions, while their form and style again foreground the balance and control of the main characters' emotions.

However, here too, the choice of music has further significance. While the operas of Gioacchino Antonio Rossini (1792–1868) actually mark a move away from the baroque, significantly, his five string quartets, which are classified among his juvenilia, were written at a time when his greatest influence and model was indeed the music of Mozart. It may also be significant that, as his mother was a leading performer in comic opera in Bologna, Rossini had from an early age been familiar with the musical and dramatic traditions of the form. The quartet therefore brings together the two major musical themes of *The House of Mirth* and at the very least reveals the acute susceptibility of Davies's ear.

Franz Joseph Haydn (1732–1809) is recognised as one of the leading composers of the late baroque period, along with Beethoven (1770–1827) and Mozart (1756–91). Composed in 1790, the *Lark* Quartet dates from his mature period and reveals both his continuing originality and his complete mastery of the medium. It also contains evidence of the fruitful exchange of ideas that was taking place between Mozart and Haydn at this period (Geiringer 1964: 914). The quartet acquired its name because of the quality of its soaring principal melody for solo violin, high on the E string, suggesting images of escape away from the more earthbound rhythms of the other instruments. Rosen also notes the daring originality of the widely spaced musical registers which give the quartet a new harmonic range and a new openness of sonority (Rosen 1971: 141). In such terms, it is easy to relate the music both to the form of Davies's own film and to the character of Lily, particularly since it is still playing as she makes her appearance in a 'Tableau Vivant', dressed as 'Summer', by Watteau (1684–1721). It is important to remember that in the novel Lily appears as Sir Joshua Reynolds's painting of 'Mrs Lloyd', so that, while undoubtedly retaining the terms in which we perceive her, 'it was as though she had stepped, not out of, but into Reynolds's canvas' (p. 196), Davies does not retain the same painting or even the same artist in his film. That Watteau should be his choice is thus particularly interesting, not least since he is widely seen as a painter who is less concerned with representing his period than with exploring what lies beneath its surface (another extension of the play of masks), as well as one who was able to accept the shiny veneer of eighteenth-century Versailles, its court life and court manners, 'without being seduced by it' (Newton 1964: 205). Newton also suggests that in

Watteau's essential detachment we can find reflections of the baroque composers of the time, not least Mozart and Haydn.[6]

Two of the remaining compositions included by Davies are unusual, relatively unfamiliar, and intensely interesting. The first of these, from the fourth movement of *Rothko Chapel: Why Patterns?* by the twentieth-century American composer Morton Feldman (1926–87), is heard as we see Lily drinking chloral for the first time. The extreme delicacy of the music blends with (initially, unseen) women's voices, grows in intensity, along with their chattering, as we cut to the room where we see them at work trimming hats, and then fades out again, ominously, just before Lily's dismissal. The second piece, heard as the film nears its end, is 'Shtiler, Shtiler' ('Quiet, Quiet'), a song by Alexander Volkoviski Tamir (with words by Shmerke Kaczerginski and Avraham Shlonsky). Why might these two works have been included? What do they contribute to the proliferating meanings of the film?

'Shtiler, Shtiler' is an Estonian Resistance song, dating from the Second World War. At level of subtext, therefore, it reflects both Lily's determination to fight and, however briefly, to resist her fate. This act of resistance, which Davies articulates by having Lily attempt to confront the Dorsets with the letters she possesses, is of course ultimately futile. And whatever the origin of the music, its prime function here, where it is heard in a complex collage of sounds emanating from both within and outside the sordid boarding house, is to reinforce our knowledge of the hopelessness of her struggle. That Lily is trapped in her situation is thus made clear from the domestic sounds that contain her: ticking clocks, creaking floorboards, unknown footsteps that negate music's potential for mobility and escape. And as if to highlight such implications, the music itself is firmly contained; it is unable to offer a sense of escape since it too is trapped. We hear it as if being played on an old cylinder gramophone in a nearby room; the crackling and faint scratching of the music positions it firmly inside and thus contains it.

The composer Morton Feldman was greatly influenced by the music of John Cage and fascinated by notions of chance, with which he experimented repeatedly in his own work. He was also a highly spatial composer, exploring ways in which musical structures can be spatial as well as temporal, and *Rothko Chapel: Why Patterns?* provides a fascinating example of this. It was composed as a tribute to the artist Mark Rothko (1903–70), to be performed in the chapel that Rothko had created as a place of contemplation for people of all faiths, and for which he had painted fourteen large canvases. Feldman wanted his composition to recreate both the octagonal space of the chapel and the way that Rothko's images go right to the edge of his canvas. It is not difficult to assess the relevance of these factors to *The House of Mirth*, obviously because the role of chance in deciding Lily's fate is considerable, but also because Feldman's experiments with time and space recall those of Davies himself, whose fundamental belief in the close relationship between film and music they seem powerfully to support. Music is used by Davies to open up spaces in the narrative, as we have seen, whether here, where it leads to the beautiful set of the milliners' workshop, or when, as in the transition shot, it simply transports us through both space and time. And of course we have repeatedly noted how, in all of Davies's films, music deepens and extends narrative space through the proliferating layers of meaning that it contributes.

Yet there is another angle from which these last two works could be viewed. Both were written by Jewish composers and both contain specific references to Hebrew culture and tradition which reflect and transcend historical experiences. It seems possible to argue not only that Davies refused to include anti-Semitic references in his film because he found them unjustifiable, but that he actually sought (whether consciously or not) to compensate indirectly for Wharton's prejudice through the possible unravelling of another of the film's many subtexts.

The remaining piece of music that we hear is an excerpt from Borodin's String Quartet No. 2 in D Major, which is played on two occasions. Alexander Borodin (1833–87) was a Russian composer and member of the group known as 'The Five'. His compositions include two symphonies, three string quartets, one opera and a number of songs and piano pieces. The inclusion of this melody might well seem surprising for it is lush and romantic, in striking contrast with the dominantly baroque music found in the rest of the film. When we first hear it, in the scene in which Lily and Selden kiss each other for the second (and last) time, its romantic cadences powerfully create the depth of their passion and suggest that their careful emotional control is at risk. The music is heard faintly in the background as the couple sit on a concealed bench in the garden, and it thus both suggests the celebrations going on inside the house and reveals their momentary escape. The music pauses as they kiss, again suggesting that, for a brief moment, their surroundings have ceased to exist, but is heard again as Lily draws back, regaining her self-control, and lightly rests her head on Selden's shoulder. The significance of the words they then exchange is clear: to Selden's comment that the only way he can help Lily is by loving her, Lily replies, 'love me, but don't tell me'.

However, yet again we can identify a deeper and more personal level at which this music is working. This particular melody has been known and loved by Davies since childhood, although then he had no idea that it originated in a classical work. Davies, like so many others, learnt the tune as a popular song of the 1950s, entitled 'And This Is My Beloved'. Using Borodin's music, the song had been written for the musical *Kismet*, reaching popularity initially as a stage show (1953), but known to Davies through its screen version directed by Vincente Minnelli in 1955 (and starring Howard Keele). The film contained a number of other songs whose melodies similarly originated in Borodin's music, including 'Stranger in Paradise', and 'Baubles, Bangles and Beads'. Thus, by including the melody that, as a child, he had known as 'And This Is My Beloved', Davies is tapping directly into his own memories, as well as introducing into the film the notions of romantic love that he repeatedly addresses in his autobiographical works. And although the decision to use Borodin's original score removes the cloying sickliness of the lyrics (and of course avoids the anachronism that would otherwise result), nevertheless the words will be lurking somewhere in the background of his (and to some extent, our) readings. Romantic love has no place in Lily's world, and, although Davies has been highly critical in his earlier works of some of the consequences of its portrayal by Hollywood in the 1950s, nevertheless, he is saying, romantic love is precisely what we desire at this moment. For inevitably he (and we), at least momentarily, long for the 'happy ending' it might afford.

A happy ending, however, will most definitely not be provided for Lily, and thus the second time we hear the melody, as the final credits scroll over the freeze frame of her dead body with Selden kneeling beside her, our sense of tragedy and loss is vividly reinforced. As we watch, all the colour gradually leaches out of the image, in a mesmerising process that contrasts strikingly with the earlier romantic image of the bright red chloral leaking from the bottle on to the white sheets, as well as reintroducing a sense of distance, both ironic and temporal. As Lily's increasingly insubstantial image fades from the screen, in a perfect response to her emergence through the clouds of steam at the start, we are reminded that this is after all just a story, and that Lily has existed as much in our imaginations as on the screen, for she has no substance.

Film as music

It is therefore clear that music is one of Terence Davies's most passionate interests, and that, as such, it influences his film-making as much as his life. He claims the symphonies of Mahler, Bruckner, Shostakovich and Sibelius as his template, and American musicals as his most formative early influence (Kennedy 1988: 17–18; Falsetto 1999: 71). He repeatedly discusses both his own work and that of other directors in musical terms, using musical references, and along with a number of other directors, including Bergman, Tarkovsky, Duras, Robbe-Grillet and Carax, he also frequently argues that film is closer to music than to any other art form.

In turn, the musical analogy provides a particularly apt critical approach to Davies's elliptical and innovative cinema. This is primarily, of course, because of his insistence on the indivisibility of form and content in his work, which in some way therefore approximates to the entirely self-contained discourse of music, but also takes account of his films' attempts to explore the sensations, memories and desires that lie beyond language, and that cannot directly be expressed or represented. As we have seen, Davies believes that cinema does have the power to achieve this, but, when we look at the means he uses, we automatically find ourselves referring to elements such as unresolved cadence, undertone, and nuance that we might most easily analyse in relation to musical composition. It is equally possible to argue that the essential structure of Davies's films is musical (in contradistinction to the linear structure of classical narrative, for example), and that the patterns of images, themes and rhythms that recur in shifting combinations and modulated forms throughout all his work construct meaning in a musical, rather than a narrative, sense. The simple fact of resiting and redefining the role of music itself in his films, moving it away from the role of support to that of signifier in its own right, immediately impacts upon every other element of the film. Traditional hierarchies of meaning are constantly deconstructed in Davies's films since music and images are equivalent signifiers functioning independently and in harmony to transport us backwards and forwards through time and space, and into the deeply hidden interstices of memory and desire.

Barthes maintained that the best way of understanding modernist (and modern) culture was by studying the relationship between music and other art forms, and of course there have been numerous attempts to do just that: critics have approached film, writing, painting and sculpture in relation to musical structures (Barthes 1995: 819). However, it is the link between film and music that must surely seem the most appropriate, particularly since both are indissolubly linked in our minds with time and movement. Music is above all a temporal art and this fact, suggests Storr, links it not only to film but to fundamental human experiences: 'Its patterns exist in time and require duration for their development and completion. Although painting and architecture and sculpture make statements about relationships between space, objects and colours, these relationships are static. Music more aptly represents human emotional processes because music, like life, appears to be in constant motion' (Storr 1993: 26). However, he also argues that, although music does indeed structure time, our perception of it as movement is basically an illusion. What he means is that a tune is really a succession of separate tones although we actually hear it but as a pattern or development which creates the illusion of movement. He thus suggests that this perception reflects a fundamental link between hearing and spatial orientation since we find it impossible to separate our perception of sound, he says, from a perception of space and movement. And he thus concludes that music exists only in time, but we can think of time only in terms of space (Storr 1993: 171–3). Similarly, we might argue, the concept of moving images in film also rests upon an illusion. What we see on the screen is a series of still images which, when projected at a precise rate (twenty-four frames per second), are interpreted by the brain as continuous movement. Nevertheless, the sensation of movement is fundamental to our intellectual perception and our emotional response to both music and film. The inevitable disjuncture imposed by editing, the gaps between the images, is overcome by our tendency to link events that follow each other in quick succession to form a coherent pattern in our minds, in just the way that we link the separate musical tones to form a melody. In these terms, it is clear that rhythm is absolutely fundamental to both, since it organises (and is itself organised by) all the other elements which create and shape our perception and understanding. And in both film and music, rhythm is used to create mood and tension and to structure and maintain our perception of time and movement.

Davies's conviction that film is closest of all to music is clarified and developed by his explanation:

> Notes and chords on their own don't mean anything. They only mean something when you juxtapose them with something else. Shots on their own don't mean anything. Once you start to juxtapose them, they gather a meaning, and that's why they're so close. And that's why they're so visceral. What you look at, you have to respond to with your emotions. You can extrapolate a meaning later but you've got to initially respond to it ... It's like smell, it's instant. You either respond to it or you don't.
> (Chapter 8)

His account thus takes account of the illusory nature of movement in both film and music, and highlights the central importance of rhythm and editing in the creation of meaning. But he also introduces a further and equally fundamental similarity which is that, if the editing is right, if the tune and harmonies work, they will affect you and involve you emotionally, in the first instance. For it is only if they do so that they will carry you with them on the journey that they articulate.

Davies thus seems to pinpoint two fundamental, and yet fundamentally opposed, responses: the immediate visceral response that grabs the listeners or spectators and involves them emotionally and imaginatively, and the intellectual response of evaluating, understanding, considering. Both responses are necessary in his films just as they are in music, and for director and composer much of the challenge lies in the ability to create them concurrently. For if music both structures time and intensifies emotion and feeling, it is because it is at the same time intellectual and obscure, a 'symbolic language of the unconscious mind whose symbolism we shall never be able to fathom' (Ehrenzweig 1975: 164–5), and yet direct and powerful in its ability to manipulate our emotions, and even to affect us physically. Like music, Davies's films take us on journeys through time and space, and the ultimate destination of these journeys is of course the self, for it is yet another paradox that the movement which appears to lead us through different times and spaces, ultimately returns us to our own thoughts and emotions, and to our shared need to reach into these through the images and sounds that we encounter.

Notes

1 The works were television serials written by Dennis Potter, who also played a collaborative role in the directing. They were particularly innovative in their non-naturalistic device of using lip-synced popular songs as a means of exploring the emotions and the conscious and unconscious memories of the characters.
2 These lines from the poem are quoted in full in the novel (p. 101), leading us to assume their significance for John Kennedy Toole, and Davies chooses to accord equal importance to them in the film. Since Henry Wadsworth Longfellow (1807–82) is one of the best loved of all American poets, it would have been normal for his work to be familiar to American schoolchildren, and it is quite possible that Toole himself remembered learning these lines in that context. As far as Davies is concerned, Longfellow played an important role as one of the earliest American writers to draw inspiration from native American themes, and to write in his poems about American landscape, history and traditions. As well as revealing a good deal about David through his response to the beauty of its images, therefore, the poem also acts as another pointer to place and time.
3 Unlike the previous case, John Kennedy Toole did not think it necessary to quote the words of 'Dixie' since the song itself is so well known. It was written by Daniel D. Emmett in 1859 while he was performing in New York as one of 'Bryant's Minstrels'. In 1860, the troupe gave a performance in New Orleans, where the song received a rapturous reception and was quickly adopted by the people as their own. It became the inspirational anthem of the Confederate Army (despite having been written by someone from Ohio). For Davies, its inclusion on the soundtrack provides another powerful indicator of the history and identity of the South.
4 Both the melody and the lyrics of this song were composed by Stephen C. Foster (1826–64), who also wrote 'My Old Kentucky Home' and 'Swanee River'. He is known above all for his great contribution to American folklore.

MUSIC AND TIME   199

5 Antonín Dvořák (1841–1904) is in many ways an obvious and interesting composer to have chosen since during the three years he spent in New York as head of the National Conservatory (1892–95), he travelled extensively, exploring all aspects of American culture and music. Whilst he was often thought to have included existing American tunes in his symphony, he himself denied this repeatedly as a lie, instead claiming, 'I tried to write in the spirit of those national American melodies'. In fact the matter is still far from settled. He did, however, help to develop Americans' pride in their own culture, and urged them to explore their own cultural roots rather than looking back to Europe for inspiration (Stefan 1964).

6 It is no less interesting, of course, to consider the significance of Davies's decision to use 'Summer' as the actual painting, for the ripe beauty of the season inevitably also foretells its imminent decay, and this suggestion may relate both to the destiny of Lily herself and to the sense of nostalgia that Newton has identified in Watteau's work; the feeling that 'nothing lasts ... oblivion is just around the corner' (Newton 1964: 206).

References

Adorno, T. and Eisler, H. (1947), *Composing for the Films*, London: Dennis Dobson.
Barthes, R. (1977), 'The grain of the voice', in *Image, Music, Text*, New York: The Noonday Press. Translated by Stephen Heath.
Barthes, R. (1995), 'Analyse musicale et travail intellectuel', in *Oeuvres complètes*, vol. 3, Paris: Editions du Seuil, pp. 819–20. The article originally appeared in *Le Monde*, 2 March 1978.
Blacking, J. (1976), *How Musical Is Man?*, London: Faber & Faber.
Blom, E. (1962), *Mozart*, London: J. M. Dent and Sons Ltd.
Brown, R. (1994), *Overtones and Undertones: Reading Film Music*, Berkeley, Los Angeles and London: University of California Press.
Brown, R. (1996), 'Modern film music', in Nowell-Smith, G. (ed.), *The Oxford History of World Cinema*, Oxford: Oxford University Press, pp. 558–66.
Davies, T. (1992), *A Modest Pageant*, London: Faber and Faber.
Dixon, W. W. (1992), '*The Long Day Closes*: an interview with Terence Davies', *Cineaste* 19/2–3, December, 20–3.
Ehrenzweig, A. (1975), *The Psychoanalysis of Artistic Vision and Hearing*, third edition, London: Sheldon Press.
Einstein, A. (1971), *Mozart*, London: Panther.
Everett, W. (2000a), 'An art of fugue? The polyphonic cinema of Marguerite Duras', in Williams, J. S. (ed.), *Revisioning Duras: Film, Race, Sex*, Liverpool: Liverpool University Press.
Everett, W. (ed.) (2000b), 'Songlines: alternative journeys in contemporary European cinema', in Buhler, J., Flinn C. and Neumeyer, D. (eds), *Music and Cinema*, Hanover and London: Wesleyan University Press, pp. 99–117
Falsetto, M. (1999), *Personal Visions: Conversations with Independent Film-makers*, London: Constable.
Flinn, C. (1992), *Strains of Utopia: Gender, Nostalgia, and Hollywood Film Music*, Princeton: Princeton University Press.
Geiringer, K. (1964), 'Haydn', in Sabin, R. (ed.), *The International Cyclopedia of Music and Musicians*, London: J. M. Dent and Sons Ltd, ninth editition, pp. 911–20.
Gorbman, C. (1987), *Unheard Melodies: Narrative Film Music*, Bloomington: Indiana University Press.

Gorbman, C. (1998), 'Film music', in Hill, J., and P. Church Gibson (eds), *The Oxford Guide to Film Studies*, Oxford: Oxford University Press, pp. 43–50.
Kennedy, H. (1988), 'Familiar haunts', *Film Comment* 24/5, September–October, 13–18.
Kristeva, J. (1980), *Desire in Language*, New York: Columbia University Press.
Lejeune, P. (1971), *L'Autobiographie en France*, Paris: A. Colin.
Lindgren, E. (1963), *The Art of Film*, second edition, New York: Macmillan.
London, K. (1936), *Film Music*, London: Faber & Faber.
Monaco, P. (1987), *Ribbons in Time*, Bloomington and Indianapolis: Indiana University Press.
Newton, E. (1964), *European Painting and Sculpture*, London: Penguin.
Potter, D. (1993), *Potter on Potter*, London: Faber & Faber.
Rosalato, G. (1974), 'La voix entre corps et langage', *Revue Française de Psychanalyse* 38, January, 75–94.
Rose, S. (1992), *The Making of Memory*, London and New York: Bantam Press.
Rosen, C. (1971), *The Classical Style: Haydn, Mozart, Beethoven*, London: Faber and Faber.
Sheringham, M. (1993), *French Autobiography – Devices and Desires*, Oxford: Clarendon Press.
Smith, J. (1996), 'Unheard melodies?', in Bordwell, D. and Carroll, N. (eds), *Post-theory: Reconstructing Film Studies*, Madison: University of Wisconsin Press, pp. 230–47.
Stefan, P. (1964), 'Antonin Dvorák', in Sabin, R. (ed.), *The International Cyclopedia of Music and Musicians*, London: J. M. Dent and Sons Ltd, ninth edition, pp. 576–9.
Steiner, M. (1937), 'Scoring the film', in Naumberg, N. (ed.), *We Make the Movies*, New York: Norton, pp. 216–38.
Steiner, G. (1992), *Heidegger*, London: Fontana.
Storr, A. (1993), *Music and the Mind*, London: Harper Collins.
Thomas, T. (1991), *Film Score: The Art and Craft of Movie Music*, Burbank: Riverwood Press.
Toole, J. K. (1989), *The Neon Bible*, New York: Grove Press.
Wharton, E. (1995), *The House of Mirth*, New York: Simon & Schuster. First published in 1905.

Close-up: an interview with Terence Davies 8

> What we call the beginning is often the end
> And to make an end is to make a beginning.
> The end is where we start from. And every phrase
> And sentence that is right ... is an end and a beginning,
> Every poem an epitaph.
>
> ('Little Gidding')

The following text is an edited transcription of an interview or conversation that I had with Terence Davies, at the RIBA, London, on 21 March 2001. The conversation lasted several hours, and only a portion was recorded. This text covers the majority of that section, although I have respected Davies's request that certain elements should not be reproduced. I have indicated the places where sizeable elements of the text have been cut.[1]

Davies on his own films

W.E. *Do you have any particular favourite films or moments in your films and, if so, do these tend to change as you make subsequent films, or as you get older?*

T.D. Yes, I think so. I do like the transition from *Distant Voices* to *Still Lives* over the water, with the Benjamin Britten. I'm very proud of that because it goes from fire to water to birth and there's something sort of primal about that, which I just feel is right. I like the Tammy sequence in *The Long Day Closes*. I like the sheet in *The Neon Bible*. I like the transition from New York to Monte Carlo in *The House of Mirth*, but also, in *The Long Day Closes*, because I love Kathleen Ferrier, I like that sequence with her voice, because I love that voice. I can remember as a child, just before I left primary school, on Thursday afternoons we were allowed to listen to the radio. It was a brown, bakelite radio. It was switched on and I can still hear the announcer saying: 'And now Miss Kathleen Ferrier singing "Blow the Wind Southerly".' And we would sit and listen to her. It brings that back with such vividness. And it is such a great, great voice. And I like the sequence that goes with it. Those things still give me pleasure. I still get pleasure from one or two lines. I like Curly's wife who says, 'Who's that supposed to be?', and when he says, 'Edward G. Robinson', she says, 'It sounds more like Cardew Robinson'. And the other bit I like is when her child says, 'I'm hungry', and she says, 'Well eat someone!' I like that. So there are little bits like that that I like.

Can you run them through your mind at will?

Yes.

And yet, as you commented earlier, you can't bear to rewatch your films.

Well I tried to recently, and it was, I just thought 'God!' They seemed so clumsy. I just found it all a bit ponderous really. It just seemed ... it might have been the mood I was in, they just felt very lifeless. But as I say, it's also very hard not to remember the production difficulties. And I know that should not have any bearing on it, but it does, and it's also hard not to remember when someone was horrible to you, because there's always someone who is. [Conversation about some of the problems he encountered on set in the making of *Distant Voices, Still Lives* and *The Long Day Closes*; on the personal tensions that can develop; and on the difficulties that can arise when working with child actors, which Davies asked me not to reveal.]

Do you have the feeling that the film you are currently working on is always the most important one for you?

Yes, because I always think it'll be the last one I do.

I'm really interested to know what happens in your head to all the other films you've made, when you are making a new one. Are they still there as an unconscious subtext, or do you make a conscious effort to get rid of them as though to start afresh with a blank screen? Because you do quote and requote yourself so frequently. Your films often quote earlier films.

But I don't really see those quotes, you see, I don't. It's like when people talk about style. In a way I can't dissect it because it's so instinctive. And if there are echoes, and of course there must be, because in any body of work there's going to be echoes and self-quotes, I'm not aware of it, being the film-maker But when I'm making a film, when I'm writing it, that's the new film. And I write that. But inevitably, you know, I know at some point there's going to be a long track, and it's going to go from left to right or from right to left, or whatever and there's going to be something over it, you know. I mean, will I ever be free of it?

What about, for example, the various shots of the stairs in all the autobiographical films? It seems to me, for example, that when you see Bud on the stairs, at the beginning of 'The Long Day Closes', your reading has built into it complex layers of memory such as the mother being beaten beside the staircase in 'Distant Voices, Still Lives'. The spectator builds up new levels of understanding of a given scene by recognising elements from earlier films, and this increases the spatial and temporal depth of the film.

Well, I wasn't really aware of that. I just remember spending a long time in the parlour, in the kitchen, on the stairs, when I was a child. I just remember it. That's what I did. I mean like being in the bedroom ... I just remember it vividly.² And those things ... As soon as you came in the house there were the stairs. Because it was a very small house. I wasn't aware at all, not even subconsciously, that I was doing that. I just remember that's what the house was like. And I did spend a lot of time looking and listening to my family. That's what I did. Because when you are the youngest of ten, seven surviving, you don't very often get the chance to speak. I mean, you just listen.

I loved that house. We had nothing, but I loved it so much, you know, because we were all together. And there were times when I was in there on my own, when they all went to the pub. And I just waited for them to come home. I'd just sit and wait, that's what I did. And it was one of my nieces, actually, who said, 'I didn't realise just what a lonely childhood you had'. And I said, 'It didn't feel lonely'.

The Neon Bible

When you made 'The Neon Bible', were you aware of the similarities between its world and the world you had been exploring through your own memories? Was that what attracted you to the story?

Yes. I was still working on experimentations with time and memory, and that's what really attracted me, because the book is told all in flashback. And I think it's a transitional work, from telling my own stories and my obsessions with the nature of time and memory and to telling somebody else's story. It *is* a transitional work. I think it is a failure, because it doesn't always work. But I couldn't have made *The House of Mirth* without having made *The Neon Bible*. It's a transitional work. If you like, it's my equivalent of the Shostakovich Fourth Symphony and the Sibelius Fourth Symphony, both of which are transitional works. But it doesn't really work, does it?

Were you annoyed by the press reports which implied that you were simply remaking Liverpool in the Bible Belt?

I found that was very hurtful because I didn't think that it was a fair criticism. I think it's a fair criticism to say that the film doesn't quite work, and it doesn't work, I think, for the reasons I've just given. It's neither one thing nor the other. But those comments did hurt, and I think the worst thing was that someone said, 'Well of course, it's understandable that it should meet with such box office apathy'. That hurt, because that's dismissive. No one sets out to make a bad film. Nobody. And it did seem a harsh thing to say, but I'm the first one to admit that I too think it's a failure.

What fascinates me about the film is the way that you create the rhythms and atmosphere of the Deep South; that there's a rhythmic change.

A lot of people would say that I don't achieve that. There are elements I'm proud of. I'm proud of the tent. Going down the street. That's terrific. I am proud of that. I know it's my little version of *Elmer Gantry*, but 'see if I care?', I say.[3] And those people in the town who sang for me in the tent were terrific, and I'm very proud of that. Although there is a beat missing somewhere in the tent, but I don't know where it is.

Music

Whenever I analyse your films, I find myself drawn to the musical analogy. It seems to me that structurally they are closely linked to music. This includes the way that they modulate. The way that they have themes, for example, that appear again and again, but always in a slightly different key, or with different intervals. You keep insisting that form is content, and that you can't distinguish the two. And that is completely true in music, as is always true in your films. Do you support my thinking about your films in terms of music?

Yes, I think you're right, and it's a huge compliment, because my template in fact has always been symphonies, and I've always said, whenever I've spoken to students, 'If you want to learn about emotional structure, you listen to a symphony. You learn more if you do that than by reading anybody else's screenplay because you respond emotionally to what you hear. And even if you can't read music, even if you are not a musician, you can follow a musical argument because you follow it emotionally.' My great templates are the symphonies of Bruckner and Sibelius. So they were always in the back of my mind somewhere as a model of how you begin and how you develop as a symphonic artist. And I do think that film is closest of all to music. Notes and chords on their own don't mean anything. They only mean something when you juxtapose them with something else. Shots on their own don't mean anything. Once you start to juxtapose them, they gather a meaning, and that's why they're so close. And that's why they're so visceral. What you look at, you have to respond to with your emotions. You can extrapolate a meaning later but you've got to initially respond to it. And that's the way we deal with music. It's like smell, it's instant. You either respond to it or you don't. When I worked with Wilfred Brambell (who was a smashing man), he hated Britten; thought it was tuneless. But I said to him, 'It is full of the most glorious tunes'. And he said, 'Not for me. It's just boring.' And I have this same block with Wagner. The thought of listening to Wagner is really purgatory. *The Ring* goes on for days. I'm sorry. You think 'life's too short and so am I!' And I can't listen to it. I just cannot listen to it. But other people love it, love it. I think when you respond to something, whatever it is, no matter what it is, it has some sort of echo within you. And it's the echo you recognise. You may not know what the echo is, but that's irrelevant. You recognise it. The first time I listened to Bruckner, it was the Seventh and Eighth Symphonies. (On 78s, would you believe? Because that's all that was in the library.) I was knocked out. The first time I went to a concert to hear Sibelius Five, I don't think I came down for about three weeks. I thought it was one of the most electrifying experiences ... particularly those six chords that end it. God! And you recognise something like that; you pick it up ... music, poetry, anything. And I can't always tell you intellectually what it means, but I know what it means here, in my heart. And then it stays with you for ever.

And it becomes part of you so that the next thing you listen to, that earlier experience is there as well?

That's right. At times there are things that you can't appreciate. You know they're true. They find this echo in you, whatever this echo is. But it's only later that it dawns on you just exactly what it means. And then, very often, your understanding, your appreciation is so deep, has deepened so much, that you may not even be able to bear them. There are certain sonnets that I almost can't read. Simply because they are so beautiful that I'd start to cry. Because it's only now that I really know their true meaning. 'Like as the waves make towards the pibled shore.'[4] How can you read that without weeping? 'Being your slave' is another.[5] How can you not, not, just weep? 'But like a sad slave stay and think of nought / Save where you are, how happy you make those ...' It's just, it's heartbreaking. But I wouldn't be without it.

You've talked a lot about symphonies. You also talked earlier about chamber music, particularly Shostakovich quartets. Do you find in them the same sort of intensity?

Certainly. Where the symphonies are concerned, Five and Ten are the great achievements, I think. I think possibly that Ten is an even greater achievement than Five. It has such a wonderful kind of courage. But I suppose what it is about the string quartets is that they are so private. That was the only way Shostakovich was allowed to express himself, because the regime didn't mind what you wrote in string quartets. It just minded what you wrote in symphonies because they were so much more public. And so he had to toe the party line.

But the quartets are like sonnets, aren't they? They impose that restraint within which you must work?

Indeed. And everything is distilled. I mean, number Eight which, as you know, was for his wife, his first wife, who had died, is desperately sad. But number Thirteen, where, in the silence, they just tap the belly of the instrument and nothing else, and it's like fate knocking on the door. But not the fate that Tchaikovsky has in his Fourth or Fifth Symphony, but just this gentle knocking: 'And there you will die.' I mean, terrifying.

Can we perhaps move now to popular songs? I am fascinated by your use of popular songs in your autobiographies, particularly by their power to transcend nostalgia, perhaps to move through it towards something else, so that they reveal something new about a past moment.

Yes, but it's only a certain type of popular music that works like that. I mean, modern popular music I detest, with a passion. My interest in popular music declined with the coming of Elvis Presley and rock and roll. I simply wasn't interested. I really like the popular music before that, songs that were meant to be sung, and lyrics which were clever or witty. That gave you enormous pleasure because of their wit. Or actually, their beauty. There's a wonderful ... I remember finding, but I didn't have the money to buy it (which has always irked me), 'The Complete Cole Porter', which gave the original lyrics to his songs. And there was one, I've never heard it recorded, the opening stanza is 'Ravel is chasing Debussy. The aphid is chasing the pea. The gander is chasing the goosey. But nobody's chasing me.' It's called 'Nobody's Chasing Me'. [Laughs.] But you know, you hear these songs and sometimes they were really poetic. 'Someone to Watch Over Me', it's a perfect poem. Some of the Hoagy Carmichael songs are heartbreaking because they're so beautiful. You know, what they did, those songs, prior to rock and roll, they gave ordinary people a voice for their feelings. And I didn't realise then that, when people sang these songs, they were singing something that was deep inside them. They just happened to like that song, and they thought they were singing it just because they liked it. But really they were saying much more. I didn't realise this until after I'd finished *Distant Voices, Still Lives.* When those people, and my family, sang those songs in the pub (I know because I was there), they were of course

singing what they felt in their hearts, and some songwriter, way over in America, had given them the ability to express that through song. I don't think popular music does that now. That's not its function now.
But also some of these songs rose to the level of art. What I love about 'Tammy', two things: its incredible romance, but also those terrible lyrics: 'I'd sing like a violin, if I were in his arms', that's just fantastic. But what's so fantastic is it's so bad that it's good. Like, you know, 'Love is a many splendoured thing. It's the April rose that only grows in the early spring.' But it's so terrible it's almost good. But, but then you go and see, in the mid-fifties, something like *All that Heaven Allows*, and what have they done on the soundtrack? They've taken a Liszt *Etude de Concert*, and they've orchestrated it, and it's so right. As they did, of course, for *Letter From an Unknown Woman*.[6] And everyone, as soon as they heard that tune, they may not have known that it was based on an étude by Liszt. It didn't matter, it got them, like that, in their heart [sings] ... you're lost, aren't you? As soon as you hear it, you're lost.

The songs are very powerful in your films when ordinary people sing them. Particularly, for example, the moment in 'The Long Day Closes', where 'She Walked Through the Fair' moves the narrative from the fairground to the house, and shifts from the recorded version to the mother's own voice.

It's true. They were just wonderful, especially when they're sung by untrained voices, because there's a sense of the most wonderful truth. You know, there's a modern pop song – I don't know how old it is – 'Wind Beneath My Wings', and it is very sentimental.[7] My sister Maisie sang it. And she has a very good voice. (My mother had a very good voice. I'm the only one in the family who sings in X flat.) And it's sentimental, but it was incredibly moving, because her voice was untrained but she sang it with her heart. And that's the difference. The only songs you get like that now are really confined to Country and Western, and most of them are just sentimental. I mean, 'Stand By Your Man'. Why? is the immediate thing that I want to ask. [Aside: 'Stand by your *ottoman*.' Laughs.]

Another thing that is very interesting is the way you can use these songs as a potent tool for irony and anger, I mean, 'Taking a Chance on Love', in 'Distant Voices, Still Lives', and so on. It seems to me that as a child you believed the songs were what life was going to be about, but as an adult, of course, you are aware that they aren't remotely related to life. That life isn't like this. And the songs are at the same time a sorce of succour and yet, I don't know, perhaps they are cheating you somehow.

I don't know. I mean, when I wrote that sequence, I just thought I knew it was a good juxtaposition. I didn't know why. Because very often you don't at the time. You just think 'I know this is right'. Even then the irony wasn't lost on me, but I didn't really think about it, I just knew it was right. It was only afterwards that I thought actually this is quite powerful. Because it is such a romantic song and he's doing such unromantic things.

But I suppose what I love most about the songs is what we have just been talking about. They are the poetry for the ordinary person, and their ability to express their feelings through a song, which I've always found terribly moving. It just moves me beyond measure. But they do also create this romantic tyranny, the idea that this is what life can be like. And of course it can't, it can't. Because real love is not like that.

Romantic love is simply different. Real love is, I think, never, never, never judging, and saying 'you may do things that I don't approve of, and I might not like them, or I may not think they are very honourable, but I actually just love you. I just love you.' And I didn't realise that until very very recently.

[Another lengthy omission.]

The love which your films explore occurs between mothers and children, or is expressed or experienced by the women.

Yes. But that's how I experienced it, you know; that's how *I* experienced it. And so, the films just reflect that. The danger in marriage is that love just becomes a kind of habit. But real romantic love, you know, can hold out a panacea, but it can also reinforce a tyranny, a romantic tyranny. I suppose that's why the songs are so powerful, because they do those two things.

Were the songs in your autobiographies, such as 'The One and Only Boy for Me', songs which you actually remember your mother singing to you?

All those songs she's given in all the films, those were songs that she used to sing.

You said earlier that the song or the music should never dictate the length or the speed of a shot and that that's why your sweater shot went wrong, because it's really too long. But it seems to me that the music and the visual and narrative rhythms in your films are intricately related. How does this work?

The difficulty is that you can sometimes want a shot to last longer than it should, simply to fit the music, and that is the danger. And I think I have fallen into that trap sometimes. No, the shots have a life, and there's a point when they decay, and you've got to get out of the shot then. That's what's wrong with *The Neon Bible*. We leave too many shots in that have decayed, I think. And that's my fault, nobody else's. It's entirely my fault. But no, once you map out what the shot should be in any sequence, then they have a moment when they're right, and then there's a moment when they die, you've got to get out of them. And the music should not then extend them beyond their life, and sometimes that's quite difficult to work out. Sometimes it's very difficult. Especially when the sequence is long. But within the sequence they will reach a point where they begin to decay. And then there's no more interest in them, and you've got to get out immediately. And that's always hard when the sequence is long, like the Tammy sequence; like the transition from New York to Monte Carlo. Those sequences are actually quite long. And you have to be very careful that you don't let each shot overstay its welcome.

Can you talk a little about your use of music in 'The House of Mirth'? It seems that some critics confused the fact that you were using other sounds more, and music less, with the idea that this implies that music was not so important in that film. To me the music is still central, and absolutely perfect. Could you tell me something about how you came to choose the various baroque composers and pieces?

Well the music is terribly important; it is in all my films, but it just wasn't necessary to have lots of music in *The House of Mirth*. What was important was the actual sounds that you hear. These are crucial. The clock ticking, and the fact that you hear a hackney cab go by, you know. She [Lily] plays the piano. Stops. Nothing. Silence. A clock, a doorbell ... that's it. I find that as musical as using music. But when I began writing the film – I go to a gymnasium three times a week, because I think you need to be fit, especially making films, you really do – (I did have this kind of pathetic thought that I would become butch and manly. Sad really. But there you go.) and someone put this compilation disc on. Mostly they play pop music which is pretty tedious. 'What's that?', I asked, and my trainer said 'I'll go and get it'. And it was the Marcello. And you always know when something's right. And I knew it was right. The reason I chose quite a lot of baroque music is that, of course, it is in strict metre, which is perfect for the strict metre of their lives, so that you get this beautiful music but it's restricted. It's never vulgar. You know, fantastic, but it's restrained. That's why, of course, the Trio from *Così fan tutte* is so moving. Because what they're singing about is so emotional, and the music is so beautifully restrained. And it's a *fabulous* tune, isn't it? You know, isn't it a fabulous tune? And I remember when we set the first shot up, which was in the dining room, and we just played that, it electrified everybody. But then the same thing happened with 'Tammy' [in *The Long Day Closes*]. It electrified the crew. It just electrified them. I can't tell you the effect it had.

Did you always know you were going to use 'Tammy' for that shot?

Yes. Well I mean, when I wrote it, I had these bits of paper on the floor, and I was the camera ... I was going like this [imitates looking down through the camera], and I thought, 'but it's got to be 'Tammy'. 'I'd sing like a violin if I were in his arms.' Fabulous!

The perspective of the camera

The crane shot at end of 'Children' gives us a little perspective of the child's life. But you are still caught. You can't escape. Whereas in the 'Tammy' shot in 'The Long Day Closes', the camera just soars and looks down from a great height, and you know you're actually summing up this childhood at that stage. You've got enough distance to be able to do it.

That is just what I was doing. And it works. And the other bit I was proud of is Christ on the cross. Because it took me nine hours to shoot. But I was very proud of that.

Was the origin of that image actually something you did imagine as a child? Nails piercing flesh?

I was aware of that image because, you know, being Catholic, then you would be. But going to see *The Robe* in 1953, you actually see the hand with a nail through it.[8] But it's basically in soft focus, so you can't see very much. And then, when I was writing it, I obviously knew that picture by Dalì,[9] which is actually incredibly sexy. He's got an incredibly sexy body, and it's really beautiful, and I said to myself, remembering all that we were taught about Christ being crucified, seeing that shot in *The Robe*, and seeing that picture, I thought what if they all combined. And then if at the end he shouts at him. That never happened as a child, but I just felt that it was right at that moment. And of course, he confuses the labourer on the wall with Christ.

Once your camera begins to move more freely, towards the end of the 'Trilogy', I have the sense that you, Terence Davies, are moving away from the guy who is stuck there in that film, with his foreseeable future, with its repetition of time past in time present. And that you are breaking away. And it seems that the fact that you have made the decision, that you are making films, that you will survive, is shown by your freer camera.

Well, perhaps that's right. I've never thought of it like that. Perhaps what it is is that one becomes distant and therefore the camera becomes freer. I've never thought of it like that. Because in many ways you do move away, but you don't leave it emotionally. I'm still very much that child. I'm still very much that man in that office thinking 'I'm going to die here. I'm going to die.' Because I *hated* what I was doing. Ironically I was very good at it, and I hated doing it. And there's an element in me, still now, that feels that someone will come along – and I've said it as a joke, but I really do believe it – that someone will come along and say,

'No, it's the other Terence Davies that should be making films. You should be back in the office.' And I know I said it rather frivolously before, but I really do mean this with all my heart, I don't think that I look like a film-maker. I see other directors, and they've got this kind of patina of, I don't know what it is, it's not confidence. Confidence is too feeble a word. They've got a patina, that makes you think, 'yes, they look like a film director', and I don't. I look in the mirror and I think, this red face, this white hair, this body covered in a library pallor, it's very depressing.

You look like a film director to me! Not that I'm sure what a film director looks like.

Oh neither am I, but you know what I mean. They seem to sort of have it. They have a way of behaving. Someone described it as having a glass wall in front of them. And they do. I don't have the glass wall. Because I don't know how it's acquired.

So that makes you a sincere film director?

I don't know. It might make me a worse one. It might make me really naive, and at fifty-five to be that naive is almost not naivety, it's almost stupid. I wish I had that patina, whatever it is. It's like actors. Actors have a something. As soon as they come in a room, even if no one told you, you think they're actors because they have got a something. [Lengthy omission.]

Texture and image

One thing that fascinates me is the way that you texture shots, and I mean by texturing, both your light and shadow, and your camera distance, but also your texturing with sounds and music and all the rest. It seems to me that your sense of detail and your texturing is something that very few other directors ever achieve. Is this something you think about?

Yes, I think about it a lot. I remember being on a jury, two years ago, I think, at BAFTA, and I was talking about this very thing. And they said, 'Is it because you don't like the detail?' And I said, 'No, you misunderstand me. I'm not talking about the detail, I'm talking about texture.' Sometimes you don't need to see what you're looking at. You need texture in the shadow, but you don't *need* other things. And if you do that, you add something enormous for the actors to play *in*, not against but inside of. You know, I mean, if, for instance (and it seems to me like dead obvious), you know, the track around when they're reading the will in *The House of Mirth*, of all those faces, there are two that you don't see. Completely, you just don't see them, but that throws into relief those faces you do see. But that seems to me to be exciting, that you have these deep shadows behind them. This light which is diffused, because my favourite painter is Vermeer, because I love light falling on a subject, and that light diffusing, I just think it's ravishing to look at. And then you've got the light behind them, and then texture in their clothes. And then, you know, that's all you need. And then they do just a tiny gesture. I can tell you exactly what I told Gillian Anderson for that shot, I said, 'All you do is open your lips. That's all you do.' And I knew it was right, because that's all that's needed, because she'd have to show her disappointment, but she'd have to do it in such a way that nobody else would see it. And you do that by a small gesture. The lips parting. You don't need anything else. But to get to that, you've in fact built it up by texture. That's all you've done. And I love that more than anything else, when I see that. And that's why I think, it's one of the many reasons that I love *Letter From an Unknown Woman*. You know the wonderful texture that's there. When she's in the opera box, and she says: 'I know he's out there, I can feel his eyes on me.' God! It's just sensational. Or when she goes back with her husband and it's in a room full of swords. I mean you just know that he's going to challenge Louis Jourdan to a duel. And the film doesn't have to spell it out. All you have to do is see it. And I love that so much, that coffee house they go into. God, it's just ... it's full of texture, that's all it is, it's texture, and that's what makes something rich. Richness can also be created by lack. It can be completely sparse but still full of texture.[10] When Shelley Winters leaves the spoons and goes out into the fog, and there's hardly any texture there; that's what makes it *full* of texture.

I wonder if you could talk about the beautiful images of trains and wheels that open 'The Neon Bible', and of course, 'The House of Mirth'?

Yes, there are those moments, but also they are tempered by things which a viewer can't know. Like for instance, when I was in America doing *The Neon Bible*, the one thing I did notice, was the size of the trains. They're huge. They are much bigger than ours. So that's the problem we had with the beginning of *The House of Mirth*. Our trains are too small. So they built it out of plaster and wood, that's what it's made of, and in an odd sort of way, that gives me enormous pleasure, knowing that that's what it is, and you believe it's a train. You do. And I do love her coming out of the steam. I'm very proud of that. But there are other things that give me enormous pleasure. The fact that the big scene between Lily and Bertha Dorset is played against candles that just ripple in the background, I love that. But a lot of the time, because I've seen *The House of Mirth* two hundred times, I can't respond any more. Or I can't respond with any kind of a fresh eye. My eye is too tired. You know, if I go back to it in five years' time, I may be able to. One thing I do do, I notice the faults of all the films. That's why I can't watch them. And I remember getting a recording of the Sixth Symphony of Vaughan Williams, at the end of which there's a little speech by Vaughan Williams, saying 'I must thank Dr Boult, and the London Philharmonic Orchestra, and the lady harpist, because they made me realise, all my faults rose to the surface, which they gallantly covered'. And when I did try and look at one of the films about two weeks ago, I had to switch it off. Two reasons: first, I just got upset because of the memories (it was *The Long Day Closes*, as a matter of fact) of my mum, and I thought I can't watch it. But I just looked and thought, 'Oh God, it's so slow and it's so ponderous'... But do you know what I mean? But part of it is because of remembering Mum, and it's so painful, it's like my heart being stirred.

But it's such a gorgeous memory of her. It's so positive.

But I'll never see her again. I'll never hear her voice again. We used to speak, every day, six o'clock, she'd ring me or I'd ring her. We only said the same old things but just not to be able to hear her voice or just hold her. It's worse than any pain. I'll never get over it. Never. I'll miss her until the day I die, and I can't watch it for that reason. I just can't. So there are very very mixed feelings about *Distant Voices, Still Lives* and *The Long Day Closes* because they open up so many wounds. But I do see their faults too.

Adaptation

I'm generally really hesitant about adaptations. So many of them end up as bad films. But I was completely fascinated by what you did in 'The House of Mirth', because you never fall into heritage mould, and because you are never self-indulgent. And it struck me that one of the reasons why the film is so successful is to do with your feelings for the rhythms of the text and your own stylistic sparseness or restraint. Everything you do visually seems to spring from the rhythms of the text. Am I making any sense?

Yes, because I love the book so much and I wanted to do it well. But what gave me enormous pleasure was to be able to say what is it about these encounters that they tell you. And what they tell you, all the encounters between Lawrence and Lily, is that at some point one of them says the wrong thing which the other misinterprets. Every time; it happens every time. And you've got to tease that out, as well as getting rid of a lot of stuff that is not right, because you haven't got that time in a film, it can be much more succinct. But what actually gave me enormous pleasure was having to write dialogue in Wharton's style which she did not write. That gave me enormous pleasure. Enormous pleasure. Because I've got quite a good imitative ear and I think she'd be actually proud of that. I think she'd be proud of that. So it was a mixture of trying to be true to the text, while trying to make it into a film.

What I don't like about most period pieces is that they are lit so that you can see all the frocks and all the decor just because an awful lot of money has been spent on it. That's not interesting. I mean there are shots in *An Ideal Husband*[11] and *An Ideal Husband* is virtually unwatchable – like *The Winslow Boy*[12] – where you think 'we're looking at this simply so that we know they spent a lot of money on the decor and their frocks', and that's not interesting. It's simply not interesting. What is interesting is making texture out of what you look at with light and shadow, and the things which are around them, and the space through which they move, but always getting the tone. Every great novelist has a tone. And Edith Wharton has a tone and you have to keep to that. But you have to pare it down because you can't have it at the length at which she can have it in the book. And there are things in the book which are grossly sentimental which had to go. She has no idea how the lower orders live. Her idea of not having enough money was only being able to afford two riding habits a year, and that's literally true. But I think if you listen to the text, really listen to the text (when you're reading it you have to listen to it as well). I've always said content dictates form, and it will tell you what is right, and then it's left to your own imagination, to have to think, well right, how do I make that idea cinematic. Like, I mean, beginning the film with New York 1905, and ending it with New York 1907. I can't tell you the fight I had about that. Those two years in which it happened have got to be marked, and I was really determined. They're like emotional bookends and I was determined. I had to fight for that.

The tiniest gestures. The erotic quality of these gestures when they are together.

In that scene in the woods, the one thing I'm very very proud of is her hand going into his, and then she withdraws it. But it tells you a lot. And when they're in the apartment, the smoke ... them smoking, it's very powerful. And I just said – that wasn't written in the script – I said when they do that, we've got to go into a close-up shot. We've just got to, because we can't stay further away from them than this. We've got to have it. Things like that. It is about gesture, but small, small. I was very concerned about gesture, because something that I was very good at when I was an actor was gesture. And I'd say, 'no, your hand's got to be like that', and I'd say, 'if it's like that, believe me, trust me, it will be all right'. And then they would. But I know when it's right. Like Dan

Aykroyd at one point went like this [gestures, smoothing the side of his hair], and I said 'You've got to keep that in, because it looks as though you're saying "dull, boring, next", without ever saying it.' You know. So all those things are crucially important, but you've got to listen to the text. You've got to listen to the voice of the text. Because it does have a voice, and, if you betray that, then you betray the entire thing. And I think that's what happens with a lot of adaptations of that period. The voice is not listened to. It's just never never listened to. And you must not modernise the characters. Often directors try to play the women as modern women; but they're not modern women. These women in *The House of Mirth* are women from 1905 to 1907, they are not modern, and they wouldn't think in a modern way. How could they? You cannot apply the same feminist principles. It would be like, in a hundred years' time, when society has no doubt gone through a radical change and they set something in the late 1990s or early twenty-first century, people will say, 'Did they really think like that?' You don't know what's going to happen in a hundred years' time. How can we know?

That's what always angers me about things set in the 1950s, because they always get it wrong. The one thing I said when we were preparing for my films (because I always do a lot of tests before we shoot) was that the look has to be right. What people had in those days were not things dating from the 1950s, but things that went back to the 1920s, particularly furniture, because they couldn't afford new, because the credit restrictions weren't lifted until the mid-1960s. So if you couldn't afford to buy anything new, you made do with what you had. We had, until we got a little suite in 1958, we had a utility suite that my mother and father had bought in 1944. My grandmother, my father's mother, lived two doors down, had a big sideboard in mahogany which she had bought at the turn of the century. because that's when she got married. Because, as you say, when you see most of these adaptations, you think, because they're made by thirty-year-olds who don't know the period, they don't realise that they didn't look like that. They didn't have that. They didn't.

Poetry and film

I know you love language and writing, I know you love poetry. We've already talked a lot about T. S. Eliot in relation to the 'Trilogy'. I'm just wondering about your ideas of poetry in film. Because your film is poetry. You have described it somewhere as 'the poetry of the everyday', which I thought was beautiful. But I wonder what you would see as poetry in a film.

I suppose I do love the poetry of the ordinary, because I find that so moving. I learnt that from Chekhov, when I first discovered Chekhov. I suppose when something is done with a kind of white-heat sincerity, then it is beautiful. It doesn't have to look physically beautiful. It doesn't. It can really be rather ragged. I mean I have huge reservations about the Bill Douglas *Trilogy*, but Part 3 opens with a series of wonderful images which are beautiful, they just are, and you know they've come from deep within him, and that's why it's so deeply felt. But then I would always go back to the template of music where something is so deeply felt that it's almost not felt at all. There's a moment in Bruckner, in the slow movement, when out of the huge *tutti* the main theme returns just on violins and it's [sings], it's like a long, long echo, and it's just heartbreaking. When you see or hear that it's with such instant recognition that you can't not be moved by it, and you can be moved by it even as a child, when you may not know why it moves you, but there's something in it that does, and you are aware of it, however dimly. I suppose what I think of as beautiful in film is that which has that kind of sincerity and immediateness, but also immense power. Shelley Winter's body in the water in *Night of the Hunter*. I mean, have you ever seen such a beautiful image of death in your life? And it's kind of chilling, but exquisite at the same time, you know. There's something wonderful about those moments. Look at how extraordinary the interiors are in *Cries and Whispers*, all red, you know.[13] Incredibly oppressive, but with a kind of almost repellent beauty. A sickly beauty, because it's about a woman dying of cancer in those enclosed spaces. But then, what does he do? Because he's a great film-maker he ends it in the open. They're all in white, in the garden, and she says, the woman who's died, 'This is happiness. This is perfection'. Oagh ... it's devastating after what you've just seen. And you know, it's also incredibly beautiful and terrifying when the body comes alive. I mean, that's really frightening. So it's when it's deeply deeply felt, that's the beauty of it. My particular bag, if you like, is just the ordinary things happening. I find ordinary things happening just extraordinary, *because* they're just ordinary, you know. That's why when you see it in films, when they didn't do it particularly well, for instance, like *It Always Rains on Sunday*, you know, the Three Compasses pub, wonderful.[14] And when they go back home, those very high beds with the bolster. I love that. And I love the fact that the woman goes out with the baby from the shop and says (she's married to Sidney Tafler), she says, 'I'm just going for a bit of fresh air. Don't worry, I'll get it wholesale.' I love that. I love that. But it has a kind of visual poetry. And look at the beauty of the black and white images in *Kind Hearts and Coronets*.[15] I *remember* the film in colour! But it's just black and white. You know they are all different sorts of visual poetry, but you can tell when it's true somehow. Even in films that are not particularly good, there will be a moment like, for example, the ending of *A Kid for Two Farthings*, where they are walking down the street, and St Paul's is in the background.[16] It's impossible to see, from the East End, like that. And they just walk down towards it, seen through the eyes of a child. It *could* have been like this. My house, the front of my house did not open, but I felt it could have. But it's not something which is factually true.

Self, time and representation

Some of your earlier remarks suggest that you still feel as much an outsider as you did in your twenties and thirties. Is this really the case?

I don't feel part of life. I always felt as though I were a spectator. When I was a child, it didn't matter, because I wasn't really aware of it. I was happy just to listen and watch. I was perfectly happy to do that. Because they all told such wonderful stories. I mean, it was fantastic to listen to, and there was so much to discover. But now I don't feel that I am part of anything. I feel very lonely a lot of the time. I do things on my own a lot, so no I don't feel I belong. It's as though everyone has the key and I don't have it. I know people don't have the key, but they seem to, and I don't have, I've never had it.

And do you feel an outsider in the film world as well?

Oh God, yes! I certainly don't feel part of it. I never felt part of it. I don't like it either, all that hype and phoniness, you know. I can't do with that, no. I used to go to these film parties. I don't go any more. I found them pretty unbearable. Unless I go with a couple of friends or someone I can have a good laugh with. But if I go on my own, all my humour evaporates, and I just think it's a lot of phoney people just jockeying for position, and that's not why I make films. It's not why I do it. Although there must be an element of vanity in it. There must be. It might be 'Love me! Love me! Love me!', you know, it might be that. Bit sad really.

How do you respond when critics constantly ask you where you see yourself in the British canon?

All I can say is I don't see myself anywhere. I don't feel part of it.

I could situate you within a broader European context, alongside directors with similar attitudes, similar feelings about the nature of film and so on. But you don't see yourself in these terms either?

No, because I don't speak their language, and it's the one thing that I do feel sorry about. There are a certain number of films that I love. I couldn't live without Bergman's *Fanny and Alexander*,[17] and his *Cries* and *Whispers* is heartbreaking; so powerful. Yes, I think Bergman is one of the greatest directors ever. I really like Derek Jarman's *War Requiem*,[18] and I love the Swedish film *My Life as a Dog*.[19]

'Distant Voices, Still Lives' is a memory narrative based on stories and memories that had been handed down to you. A number of critics have, mistakenly I believe, implied that in this film Tony actually represents you. Is this in any way correct?

Well no, I do not appear in *Distant Voices, Still Lives*, but there are certain memories of mine, like my sister's friend Monica. She was a joy. She's in the film because I remember her so vividly. She was full of life, and very very funny, and could get round my father. She was the only person who could get round my father. She could charm him, 'Oh go on, Mr D., don't be dead miserable', 'Oh, all right then, go on'. She could get round him. But she was funny. Like she'd read her father's medical book and come in and say, 'I've got a brain tumour, I know I have'. And he'd say to her, 'You're healthier than I am'. 'But I've got a tumour, I know. I just know I've got one.'

She has an uncanny ability to get round him. She's not afraid of him, which makes a big difference.

But also she was jolly and funny. It's very difficult, for even the most heard-hearted people to resist humour. It's very difficult. I mean we'd open the door and she'd say, 'It's leukaemia', and we'd say, 'It's not'. And then she'd say, 'Are you sure, Mr D.?', and my father wasn't a doctor, and he'd say, 'Of course I'm sure, Mick. You haven't got leukaemia.' She'd say, 'Ok', and then she'd get to the door and say, 'You would tell me if it was wouldn't you?'

I love the shot when Mick and Eileen come home from the dance and stand outside the front door with their fags.

It was a wonderful period for women, I mean, for their clothes, their appearance. They looked so sensational, they just did. They looked sensational. All you need to see in that scene is their dresses. You don't need anything else. You don't need to see them go to the dance. You know they've been there.

I am always impatient with critics whose responses to 'The Long Day Closes' were that it was altogether too happy, and that in it you were admitting neither your suffering nor the fact that you were gay. I can't think they can have looked at the film. It strikes me that the way you have internalised these problems in that film is enormously powerful

But even one of my friends said she didn't get it. For me, anyway, at that point, it's not that he recognises the fact that he's gay; it's recognising that there's something wrong, and that's all. Because at eleven, how can you know more? And when I said to this friend, 'but when he sees the labourer on the wall, looks down, and moves back', and she said, 'Oh I didn't get that at all'. And she's very intelligent. She said, 'That's too elliptical, I just didn't get it'. But what hurt most about those sorts of criticism was they were criticising the film for what it ought to have been rather than what it was. And that seems to me to be unfair because that's not what criticism is. It's like the other thing that was levelled at it. That it has completely no sense of the political. 'Why wasn't the Suez Canal mentioned?' Well, at the age of eleven, I didn't even know where the Suez Canal was.

I have argued precisely that point in conferences. What do you know at that age? And people were also unfairly critical of the scene in which you run screaming to your sisters when a coloured man came to the door.

But that's what happened. That's exactly what happened. Because in Liverpool in 1966, you hardly ever saw coloured people. You didn't, honestly, that's the truth.

And with such reactions people condemn you. But that's the way it was. That's the way we responded.

Well it was a very little community. A very tightly knit community.

Yes. When my sister, my elder sister, got an American boyfriend, all the street came out to look at him and hear him speak. They literally did. Because the only American accents you'd hear was in the movies, and people knocked on the door and said 'Is he there?' And he'd have to come out and say, 'Hi' or whatever, and they'd think, 'It *is* an American'. But in the end you've just got to say I've re-created it as it was. If people don't like it, or think it's bad, then there's nothing I can do. It would be almost like saying, 'Why does the mother stay with him?' 'Because', you can say, 'because that's what they did then'. There was nothing like women's refuges or anything like that. The nearest you could get was a separation.

Even today, most battered women don't go off to refuges. They stay, for whatever reasons.

So has anything changed? And then you've got the priest coming round on a Friday saying, 'Mrs Davies, this is your cross and you've got to bear it'. And in those days, a working-class, naive woman thinks, 'Oh well if the priest has said it, it must be true'. Another response I've had is that the teacher wouldn't be as cruel as that. And I replied, 'Oh but he was. Mr Nicholls was. He was.'

We've all known a Mr Nicholls at some point in our school days.

Soon after I made the film, another teacher who was at the school at that time came up to me and said who he was. (I didn't recognise him.) And he said, 'Oh he wasn't such a bad man'. I said, 'Well, he was to us'. To be caned for every mistake you made in English is not the way to teach English.

And to cane new pupils, to terrify them just to show who's the boss.
And people don't realise that that's what a lot of those men were. They were from the military. They thought that the way you made men of boys was to terrify them. That's what they thought. And, if they thought you were sissy, they really despised you.

When I was at primary school, that's where my imagination was allowed to be expressed, although there were one or two martinets there. But going up to secondary school was a real real trauma. But in an odd way it didn't kill something in me. What it did, funnily enough, I was thinking about it the other day, I've got a pretty good memory; it's not photographic, but it's pretty good. One of my brothers was in the army, John, I think it was, and he loved comedy radio shows like *Round the Horne*. So I'd listen to it twice and I'd remember it and write it down and then I'd send it to him. That way, I discovered I could make people laugh, and that was a joy, that did help, because I found that I could make people laugh at school, and that was a joy. And going back even to when I was making *Distant Voices, Still Lives*, listening to all those old *Round the Horne* programmes got me roaring with laughter. Especially Julian and Sandy. Wonderful! There was one that I listened to, for some reason Kenneth Horne had to go to a solicitor, 'I've just taken articles and he's just taken frequently', he said. 'Well I would like you to act for me', he said. 'Oh, we've got a criminal practice.' 'Yes, but apart from that can you do it? Can you act for me?' [The dialogue is performed with all the voices. Davies collapses with laughter.]

I loved your geography lesson on erosion.
Well, I've never forgotten that. I've never forgotten. I got that from a book, you know that was published. I just found a book to give you the definition because I'd long since forgotten the precise definition. But I remember that lesson. I remember clearly.

Is this lesson your comment on the erosion of innocence?
Yes, that probably is true. I think it probably is true because where it began actually was seeing the labourer on the wall. [Clicks fingers.] In that instant everything changed. I was never the same again. Because I knew I wasn't supposed to feel this for another man. And I just knew it.

What makes me so angry is that it was impossible for you to talk about your sexuality. For you to see it as normal and natural.
You couldn't. You couldn't. They didn't even talk about heterosexual sex. Imagine talking about this. No, it just wasn't possible. But the misery it's caused. It's caused so much misery. And I hate it. And it's like being in the thrall of something all the time. You know, I just hate it. It's awful. Because it never never stops. It's like alcoholism; you never get rid of it.

It should be possible for you to see it positively now.
But I can't, because I see it as having ruined my life. Because it has. It just has.

What drew you to 'The Neon Bible'? What made you choose that novel?
I was still very much wrapped up in time and memory, and I just responded to it. As soon as I read the first chapter, I knew where the camera should be. That's why. And it was about that era, that moment in your life when you're still a child but on the cusp of being a man. And all those things, where you're still a kind of innocent in the world. But also it was all the things that I had seen in films, that were interesting to me as a foreigner not being an American, about the deep South, like *Elmer Gantry* and films like that. All those things which I do find fascinating. And that era I love. I love the 1940s and 1950s. It seems to me that the great golden age of Hollywood is the 1940s and 1950s, not the 1930s, you know, not for me any way. And so I love that era. And of course I love the music, you know.

Music and memory

And so the ideas for the music for 'The Neon Bible' came from your earlier film experiences?
Yes, but also, you know, you want to create the wartime world and you just play Glenn Miller, and it's instant [snaps fingers]. You want to create an eighteenth-century ballroom, you play Boccherini. And everyone knows where they are. It's instant. And so it involved all my interests. Also I do think it's a good book for a sixteen-year-old to have written. But above all I was still experimenting with time and memory. What I hope to do in future is perhaps a mixture of the two, to tell something linearly but with memory. That would be interesting.

And difficult.
Difficult, yes. But if it's easy, what's the point in doing it? You have to feel you're being challenged by what you do because that's where the interest lies. If you just repeat the same thing, then it's not interesting. And that's what hurt about *The Neon Bible*. People saying I had just repeated the same thing. That did hurt. Because I did feel that that was unfair.

Clearly the narrative has close links with your personal experiences. There are close links. You can see that you are using your own experience as a way of getting right into that other experience. But David's experience is also fundamentally different from the one you've been exploring in the earlier films.
I think it is. And I do think things which are rather touching have been missed. You know, I think it's very touching when he's with that

girl in the cinema and then afterwards, looking at those empty houses. And you think, surely you can be touched by that. It's so innocent. They're still innocent. But few people seemed to see that, or to be touched by it.

There's an amazing sense of community once the men go off to war. A community that suddenly hangs together. It's particularly clear in that wonderful dance scene where they sing and dance and there's a sense of healing. Of course, you have linked music and women again. It seems that for you music is entirely linked to female or maternal experiences.

Well, I suppose it is because I just remember being brought up, really, by my mum and my sisters. I mean, I loved my brothers but, you know, I didn't know anything about football. I wasn't into sport. I just wasn't. And I really loved my sisters and their friends. Particularly on Fridays, when I went to buy their make-up and all that, I loved it so much. And I always felt intrinsically more at ease with women, and I love their camaraderie. I love their small talk because usually it's funny and lively. It can be bitchy as well. But it can be very funny. Whereas men's small talk is rather dull. I don't know about politics. I don't know about sport. It's just very difficult. But women always find something they can say. Even just listening to them. I've overheard some of the most wonderful things women have said. I remember the first time I was in Dublin, I went to this tea shop in a corner street, and I sat down and I had my tea and these two women were sitting behind me and one said to the other [the story is told complete with Irish accent]: 'Well I wouldn't say that she was nasty, but they do say that she can change an apricot into a lemon just be smiling at it.' [Laughs.] And the other woman: 'Well, there ye are.' [More laughter.] Or you go through Liverpool and you hear two women and one says to the other [accent now switches to Liverpool]: 'O God, look at the gob on this one!' [Infectious laughter swamps the tape.] And you think, it could only be here, and it could only be between women.

This atmosphere came over powerfully in the dance scene.

In doing that scene, you know, when that woman goes like this and knocks Mae over she actually knocked her over. And those two women caught her. When we were doing the scene, there were two women there who did the Jitterbug really well. And I said, 'but you'll have to do it less good', I said, 'because I'm looking at you all the time instead of them', I said. 'You're ever so good.'

What about the shots of the child with the moon? The repeated shots of the child stretching his hands up?

I don't know where that came from. I suppose it's when you are a child you think you can touch it. Especially if the moon is low and big.

You think you can touch it. But I have no idea where it came from.

It struck me that the small townness in the 'The Neon Bible' was really pretty much like the small townness of your bit of Liverpool. Again, an enormously enclosed community.

Yes, I'm sure that was one of the reasons that drew me to it. They would know everybody. Everybody would know them. And going into town was a big thing. Just like being taken to town pictures was a big thing.

That terrifying idea of having to think exactly what your father thought.

But there that would have been much more the case than here. Here it was in a way just as sinister, but more subtle. It was not what your family thought but what the Church said, and you were told: 'This is your place so be grateful. And know your place.' And that's what we accepted then. Now people don't accept that and that's a good thing. But what has also gone out of the window is compassion for other people and knowing that the world does not revolve around you.

Finance and production

'The House of Mirth' was a novel you'd always loved and wanted to film, wasn't it?

Yes.

And was it hard to find somebody who would support you?

Yes it was. Very. It took six years.

Were you already working on the script by then?

Yes. I got the money promised by Channel 4 when David Aukin was there, and then things became really rather complicated because he then left, and Paul Webster took over. And so we had to go back and say, 'Look you know this is your predecessor's baby. If you don't want to continue with it you must tell us.' And he said, 'No, I want to continue with it'. And then we heard that Dustin Hoffman was doing a version of it in which he would play Lawrence Selden, directed by John Schlesinger with a script by Frederic Raphael. And we went back again to Channel 4 and said, 'Look, this is on the cards you know. Should we stop?' And to give them their due, they said, 'No, carry on'. But it was touch and go for a while.

What is it about that novel that captured your imagination so much?

I suppose, it's primarily about a woman, and I grew up on what used to be called 'The Woman's Picture'. And I know you can't say that any more, but that's what they were called. You know, *All that Heaven Allows, Magnificent Obsession, Love Is a Many-Splendored Thing*, that's what they were called.[20] And I wanted to try, not to make films like that, but they influenced me. But *The House of Mirth* is a great tragedy. A great modern tragedy. And Lily herself is a great tragic heroine, of course.

Lily is a woman who sacrifices herself for her own integrity.

But she discovers that integrity. She doesn't know that it's there at the beginning. And that's what the journey is. And that's what's fascinating. But also, you know, I think Lily learns courage as she learns she has integrity.

Did you sense a link between the courage and integrity of Lily Bart and that of your mother?

That's an interesting idea. I never though of my mother as having integrity. But she did have courage. But she also had a stoicism which I've inherited, and what's so ironic (God will have his little joke) is that I've inherited her stoicism and I've inherited my father's tenacity. But also I've inherited his temper. I'm not afraid of anything or anyone when I lose my temper. And I don't like to lose it often.

What sort of things make you lose it?

Cruelty, bullying, manipulation. I get really angry about that. And someone telling me what to do. Turns round and tells me my job. Because I know my job.

So did you lose your temper about the poster [for 'The House of Mirth']?

Yes. I did lose my temper over the poster. I said, 'I'm not having some crappy poster', I said. 'Forget it. I'll fight you tooth and nail over it.' And I did. And then when it came out, to give the woman at Channel 4 her due, I've got to say this, she said, 'You were right. Several of my friends have seen this and they think it's a wonderful poster.' And I said, 'That's really generous of you to come up and say that. And I'm sorry I shouted at you. I didn't mean to but it means a lot to me. Please accept my apologies, because I hate doing that. But it just seemed as though everyone wanted to get out some crappy poster. I won't have that. I won't have it. Imagine if I'd just gone on the set and given you a crappy film. Would you have liked it? The answer is no.'

The future

Are you excited about making your next film? Do you have moments of lying in bed at night thinking, 'Yes, this is going to be good'?

Not at the moment. I'm still going through that process of thinking 'Oh God ... what have I let myself in for?' But I can tell you exactly when it will change: as soon as I've got an opening. Once I get the opening, I think, 'OK I've got the opening now!' And that always excites me. It *always* excites me. And then, it's true (you'll have to withdraw what I said earlier) you do forget the pain of the last one and all the difficulties. You do forget it. What I want to return to now is the magic of going on the set and thinking, 'We're on a film set!' And I know probably what will happen, because it always seems to, I'll be driven on to the set, and I'll see people waiting by the catering van for their breakfast and that will be it and I'll think, 'Oh God! We're on a film set.'

Notes

1 I should like to express my gratitude to Terence Davies, not merely for agreeing to talk to me, but also for his generosity in continuing our conversation for the best part of a day. The discussion was completely fascinating, and I felt extremely privileged.
2 Earlier in the conversation, Davies had vividly described lying in bed and listening to the everyday sounds of the household waking up; the sounds he replicated in the opening sequence of *Distant Voices, Still Lives*.
3 *Elmer Gantry* (Richard Brooks, USA, 1960).
4 This is Sonnet 60. In it, Shakespeare is exploring the nature of time, and it is easy to see how the sonnet would particularly fascinate Davies. After considering time as flux, as is seen in the following lines, Shakespeare then contrasts that ephemerality with the durability of art.
>Like as the waves make towards the pibled shore,
>So do our minutes hasten to their end,
>Each changing place with that which goes before,
>In sequent toile all forwards do contend.
5 Sonnet 57 is intensely romantic and clearly has very emotional meanings for Davies.
6 *Letter From an Unknown Woman* (Max Ophuls, USA, 1948).
7 The song was actually written by Larry Henley and Jeff Silber for the soundtrack of the extremely sentimental film *Beaches* (Garry Marshall, USA, 1988), although Davies was not aware of this.
8 *The Robe* (Henry Koster, USA, 1953).
9 The painting Davies refers to is *Christ of Saint John of the Cross*, painted in 1951 and owned by the Glasgow Art Gallery and Museum. The painting, a dramatic view of the crucified Christ from above, was initially inspired by a dream Dalí had and by a drawing of Christ by the Spanish mystic Saint John of the Cross.
10 *Night of the Hunter* (Charles Laughton, USA, 1955).
11 *An Ideal Husband* (Alexander Korda, UK, 1947; Oliver Parker, UK/USA, 1999).
12 *The Winslow Boy* (Anthony Asquith, UK, 1948; David Mamet, USA, 1999).
13 *Cries and Whispers* (Ingmar Bergman, Sweden, 1972).
14 *It Always Rains on Sunday* (Robert Hamer, UK, 1947).
15 *Kind Hearts and Coronets* (Robert Hamer, UK, 1949).
16 *A Kid for Two Farthings* (Carol Reed, UK, 1955).
17 *Fanny and Alexander* (Ingmar Bergman, Sweden, 1982).
18 *War Requiem* (Derek Jarman, UK, 1988).
19 *My Life as a Dog* (Lasse Hallstrom, Sweden, 1985).
20 *All that Heaven Allows* (Douglas Sirk, USA, 1955); *Magnificent Obsession* (Douglas Sirk, USA, 1935); *Love Is a Many-Splendored Thing* (Henry King, USA, 1955).

Terence Davies filmography

The *Trilogy*

Part 1: *Children* (1976)

Director: Terence Davies
Screenplay: Terence Davies
Producer: Peter Shannon
Executive producer: Geoffrey Evans
Editors: Sarah Ellis, Digby Rumsey
Production assistant: Rick Thomas
Director of cinematography: William Diver
Assistant cameraman: Chris Evans
Assistant director: Dave Wheeler
Continuity: Anna Mayson Pachachi
Sound recordist: Digby Rumsey
Cast: Philip Mawdsley (Tucker as a boy), Nick Stringer (Father), Val Lilley (Mother), Robin Hooper (Tucker at 24), Colin Hignet (Bully), Robin Bowen (Bully), Harry Wright (Teacher), Philip Joseph (Teacher), Trevor Eve (Man in shower), Linda Beckett (Neighbour), Bill Maxwell (Doctor), Elizabeth Estensen (Nurse), Malcolm Hughes (Man in bedroom), Katherine Fahey (Neighbour), Marjorie Rowlandson (Neighbour), Ann Kiesler (Soloist), Stella Dickson (Cor anglais soloist).
Music: 'The Folks Who Live on the Hill', by Oscar Hammerstein, Jerome Kern, performed by Peggy Lee; 'Way Down Upon the Swanee River', by Stephen Collins Foster, children's choir; 'The Ballad of Barbara Allen', traditional folk song, sung by Ann Kiesler
A British Film Institute Production

Part 2: *Madonna and Child* (1980)

Director: Terence Davies
Screenplay: Terence Davies
Producer: Mike Maloney
Director of cinematography: William Diver

Editor: Mick Audsley
Assistant cameraman: Sergio Leon
Assistant director: Kees Ryninks
Continuity: Victoria McBain
Sound recordist: Antoinette de Bromhead
Grip: Tim Rolt
Dubbing editor: Geoff Hogg
Cast: Terry O'Sullivan (Tucker, middle-aged), Sheila Raynor (Mother), Paul Barber (Tattooist), John Meynall (Priest), Brian Ward (Man in club), Dave Cooper (Tattooed man), Mark Walton (Second man), Mal Jefferson (Man in toilet), Lovette Edwards (Woman in office), Rita Thatchery (Woman in office), Eddie Ross (Man in office)
Music: 'Hail Queen of Heaven', taken from 'The Hymns of the Breviary and Missal', children's voices
A National Film School Production

Part 3: *Death and Transfiguration* (1983)

Director: Terence Davies
Screenplay: Terence Davies
Producer: Claire Barwell
Executive producer: Maureen McCue
Director of cinematography: William Diver
Editor: Mick Audsley
Art director: Miki van Zwanenberg
Make-up adviser: Fae Hammond
Continuity: Helena Barrett, Carine Adler
Sound recordists: Mohammed Hassini, Charles Patey, Mark Frith
Cast: Wilfred Brambell (Tucker as an old man), Terry O'Sullivan (Tucker, middle-aged), Iain Munro (Tucker at 11), Jeanne Doree (Mother), Chrissy Roberts (Nurse), Virginia Donovan (Nurse), Carol Christmas (Nun), Angela Rooks (Ward Sister), Brian Gilbert (Doctor), Katharine Schofield (Nurse), Ron Metcalfe, Lisa Parker, James Wilde, Ron Jones, James Culshaw, Marie Smith, Jim Penman, Gerry Shaw, Mandy Walsh (Neighbours), Paul Oakley (Boy at window), Children from The McKee School
Music: 'It All Depends on You', by DeSylva, Brown, Henderson, performed by Doris Day; 'Abie, Abie, Abie My Boy', sung by group; 'How You Gonna Keep 'Em Down on the Farm?' sung by group; 'There's a Someone to Watch Over Me', George Gershwin; 'If You Knew Suzie', Renee Craig and Steve Delehanty, sung by group; 'O Come All Ye Faithful, traditional carol, children's voices; 'We Three Kings of Orient Are', traditional carol, children's voices; 'Away in a Manger', traditional carol, children's voices; 'Silent Night, Holy Night', traditional carol, children's voices: 'Jesus Thou Art Coming", children's voices; 'You're Still the Only Boy in the World', sung by Mother
A Greater London Arts production in association with the British Film Institute

Distant Voices, Still Lives (1988)

Director: Terence Davies
Screenplay: Terence Davies
Producer: Jennifer Howarth
Executive producer: Colin MacCabe
Director of cinematography: William Diver
Editor: William Diver
Art directors: Miki van Zwanenberg, Jocelyn James, Carine Adler
Camera: Patrick Duval
Costume designer: Monica Howe
Cast: Freda Dowie (Mother), Pete Postlethwaite (Father), Angela Walsh (Eileen), Dean Williams (Tony), Lorraine Ashbourne (Maisie), Sally Davies (Eileen as a child), Nathan Walsh (Tony as a child), Susan Flanagan (Maisie as a child), Debi Jones (Micky), Chris Darwin (Red), Marie Jelliman (Jingles), Andrew Schofield (Les), Anny Dyson (Granny), Jean Boht (Aunty Nell), Pauline Quirk (Doreen), Matthew Long (Mr Spaull), Frances Dell (Margie), Roy Ford (Uncle Ted)
Music (*Distant Voices*): 'I Get the Blues When it's Raining', sung by Mother: 'There's a Man Goin' Round Takin' Names', performed by Jessye Norman; 'Limelight', solo harmonica; 'In the Bleak Midwinter', traditional carol, choir; 'Roll Along Kentucky Moon', sung by Aunty Nell; 'A little Bit of Cucumber', sung by Granny; 'When Irish Eyes are Smiling', by Ernest Ball, Chauncey Olcott, George Graff, sung by Father; 'Taking a Chance on Love', Latouche, Fetter, Duke, performed by Ella Fitzgerald; 'Barefoot Days', sung by Mother; 'Roll Out the Barrel', sung by Eileen; 'Cos I Love Ya That's a Why', Guy Mitchell and Cindy Carson; 'S'wonderful', by George Gershwin, sung by Jingles; 'Ragmop, Ragmop', by George Gershwin; 'Buttons and Bows', by Jay Livingstone and Ray Evans; *Pastoral Symphony*, Symphony No. 3, by Ralph Vaughan Williams
Music (*Still Lives*): 'A Hymn to the Virgin', Benjamin Britten, unaccompanied choir; 'With a Song in My Heart', Rodgers and Hart (*Family Favourites* theme tune); 'The Finger of Suspicion', Dicky Valentine; 'The Birthday of the Little Princess', sung by Maisie; 'Brown-skinned Girl', sung by Eileen, then group; 'Oh, My! What a Rotten Song', sung by group; 'Dreamboat', sung by Doreen; 'I Want a Girl', sung by Tony, then group; 'Mississippi Honeymoon', sung by Maisie, then group; 'We're All Together Again, So Here We Are', sung by group; 'Bye-bye Blackbird', Henderson, Dixon, sung by Monica; 'I Want to Be Around', Jonny Mercer, sung by Eileen; 'I Love the Ladies', sung by group; 'The Road to Anywhere', sung by group 'I Will If You Will So Will I', sung by group; 'Barney Google', sung by Maisie; 'Love is a Many-Splendored Thing', soundtrack from *Guys and Dolls*; 'Galway Bay', Tommy Riley on harmonica; 'From the Candy Store on the Corner', sung by Eileen; 'Thanks to You', sung by Mother; 'Oh Mein Papa', played by Eddie Calvert; 'O Waly, Waly', unaccompanied soprano; arrangement by Benjamin Britten
A British Film Institute Production, in association with Channel 4 and ZDF

The Long Day Closes (1992)

Director: Terence Davies
Screenplay: Terence Davies
Producer: Olivia Stewart
Executive producers: Ben Gibson, Colin MacCabe
Director of cinematography: Michael Coulter
Editor: William Diver
Production designer: Christopher Hobbs
Art director: Kate Naylor
Costume designer: Monica Howe
Music director: Robert Lockhart
Music supervisor: Bob Last
Executive in charge of production: Angela Topping
Production co-ordinator: Lesley Stewart
Production manager: Chris Harvey
Location managers: Andrew MacDonald, Jeff Bowen
Casting: Doreen Jones
Assistant directors: Gus Maclean, Tommy Gormley, David Gilchrist
Cloud photography: Chris Plevin, Jeremy Kelly
Camera operator: Harriet Cox
Cast: Marjorie Yates (Mother), Leigh McCormack (Bud), Anthony Watson (Kevin), Nicholas Lamont (John), Ayse Owens (Helen), Joy Blakeman (Frances), Denise Thomas (Jean), Patricia Morrison (Amy), Tina Malone (Edna), Jimmy Wilde (Curly), Robin Polley (Mr Nicholls), Peter Ivatts (Mr Bushell), Gavin Mawdsley (Billy), Kirk McLaughlin (Labourer/Christ), Marcus Heath (Black man), Victoria Davies (Nun), Brenda Peters (Nurse), Karl Skeggs (Albie), Lee Blennerhassett (1st Bully), Peter Hollier (2nd Bully), Jason Jevons (3rd Bully)
Music: 'Stardust', by Hoagy Carmichael, Mitchell Parish, performed by Nat King Cole; 'If You Were the Only Girl in the World', by Nat Ayers, Clifford Grey, sung by Mother; 'At Sundown', by Walter Donaldson, performed by Doris Day; 'Blow the Wind Southerly', performed by Kathleen Ferrier; 'The Carousel Waltz', by Richard Rodgers; 'She Moved Through the Fair', by Hughes and Collum; male singer, then Mother; *A Shropshire Lad*, Rhapsody for Orchestra, by George Butterworth; 'O Come All Ye Faithful', traditional carol, children's voices; 'Once in Royal David's City', traditional carol, children's voices; 'Silent Night', traditional carol, children's voices; 'White Christmas', by Irving Berlin, performed by Bing Crosby (from the soundtrack of *Holiday Inn*); 'The Cokey-Cokey', by Jimmy Kennedy, sung by group; 'Auld Lang Syne', traditional, sung by group; 'Faith of our Fathers Sanctify My Breast', by Robert King, piano with children's voices; 'Tantum Ergo', by Corinth and Webbe, children's voices; 'Once in Love with Amy', by Frank Loesser, sung by John and Kevin; 'My Foolish Heart', by Victor Young, Ned Washington, sung by John and Kevin; 'Me and My Shadow', by Al Jolson, Dave

Dreyer, Billy Rose, sung by Mother; 'Ae Fond Kiss', by Robert Burns; 'Over the Banister', by Hugh Martin, Ralph Blane, performed by Judy Garland; 'Civilisation (Bongo, Bongo, Bongo)', by Bob Hilliard, Carl Sigmond; 'On a Slow Boat to China', by Frank Loesser; 'When I Leave the World Behind', by Irving Berlin, sung by Curley; 'I Don't Know Why (I Just Do)', by Frank Ahlert, Roy Turk, sung by Edna; 'We're a Couple of Swells', by Irving Berlin, sung by Bud and Helen; 'O You Beautiful Doll', by Seymore Brown, Nat Ayler, sung by Curley; 'Tammy', by Jay Livingstone, Ray Evans, performed by Debbie Reynolds (from the soundtrack of *Tammy and the Bachelor*); 'If I Had My Life to Live Over', by Joe Jaffe, Henry Tobias, Larry Vincent, sung by Mother; Minuet in G, Opus 11, No. 5a, G275, by Boccherini; Symphony No. 10, Gustav Mahler; 'The Long Day Closes', by Sir Arthur Sullivan, choir

Film clips: *The Ladykillers, The Happiest Days of Your Life, Meet Me in St Louis, The Magnificent Ambersons, Private's Progress, Great Expectations*
Radio clips: *Lift Up Your Hearts, Ray's a Laugh*
Film Four International in association with the British Film Institute

The Neon Bible (1995)

Director: Terence Davies
Screenplay: Terence Davies, based on the novel by John Kennedy Toole
Producers: Elizabeth Karlson, Olivia Stewart
Executive producers: Nik Powell, Stephen Woolley
Director of cinematography: Michael Coulter
Editor: Charles Rees
Production designer: Christopher Hobbs
Art director: Philip Messina
Costume designer: Monica Howe
Music director: Robert Lockhart
Set decoration: Kristen Toscano Messina
Casting: Ali Farrell
Assistant director: Cas Donovan
Sound mixer: Thomas Varga
Special effects: Lisa Reynolds
Cast: Gena Rowlands (Aunt Mae), Jacob Tierney (David aged 15), Drake Bell (David aged 10), Diana Scarwid (Sarah), Denis Leary (Frank), Leo Burmester (Bobbie Lee Taylor), Frances Conroy (Miss Scover), Peter McRobbie (Reverend Williams), Joan Glover (Flora), Bob Hannah (George), Tom Turbiville (Clyde), Dana Dick (Jo Lynne), Virgil Graham Hopkins (Mr Williams), Jill Jane Clements (Woman), Aaron Frisch (Bruce), Sharon Blackwood (Mrs Watkins), Charles Franzen (Tannoy), Sherry Velvet, Stephanie Astalos-Jones (Testifiers), Ian Shearer (Billy Sunday Thompson), Duncan Stewart (Head Boy)
Music: 'How Long Has This Been Going On?', by George and Ira Gershwin, sung by Aunt Mae; 'My Romance', by Rodgers and Hart, sung by Aunt

Mae; 'Too-ra-loo-ra-loo-ra, That's an Irish Lullaby', by J. H. Shannon, sung by Mother; 'The Old Rugged Cross', sung by group; 'Dixie', by Daniel D. Emmett, sung by school group; 'Chattanooga Choo Choo', by Mack Gordon, Harry Warren, sung by group; 'Tara's Theme' from *Gone With the Wind*, composed by Max Steiner; 'Hard Times Come Again No More', by Steven Foster; 'Going Home', words by Art Tatum, melody from Dvořák's Symphony No. 9, Opus 95, *From the New World*; 'Perfida', composed by Alberto Dominguez, performed by Glenn Miller
Artificial Eye/Mayfair/Scala/Channel 4

The House of Mirth (2000)

Director: Terence Davies
Screenplay: Terence Davies, based on the novel by Edith Wharton
Producer: Olivia Stewart
Executive producers: Bob Last, Pippa Cross
Director of cinematography: Remi Adefarasin
Editor: Michael Parker
Production designer: Don Taylor
Art director: Kate Naylor
Costume designer: Monica Howe
Music director: Adrian Johnston
Conductor: Terry Davies
Wardrobe supervisor: Ann Taylor Cowan
Co-producer: Alan J. Wands
Production co-ordinator: Mandy McKay
Production manager: Wendy Broom
Unit manager: Tony Hood
Cast: Gillian Anderson (Lily Bart), Dan Aykroyd (Gus Trenor), Eleanor Bron (Mrs Peniston), Terry Kinney (George Dorset), Anthony LaPaglia (Sim Rosedale), Laura Linney (Bertha Dorset), Johdi May (Grace Stepney), Elizabeth McGovern (Carry Fisher), Eric Stoltz (Lawrence Selden), Penny Downie (Judy Trenor), Pearce Quigley (Percy Gryce), Helen Coker (Evie Van Osburgh), Mary MacLeod (Mrs Haffen), Paul Venables (Jack Stepney), Serena Gordon (Gwen Stepney), Linda Marlowe (Madame Regina), Lorelei King (Mrs Hatch), Anne Marie Timoney (Miss Haines), Claire Higgins (Mrs Bry), Ralph Riach (Lord Hubert Dacy), Brian Pettifer (Mr Bry), Philippe de Groussouvre (Ned Silverton), Trevor Martin (Jennings the Butler), David Ashton (Lawyer), Lesley Harcourt (Mattie Gormer), Mark Dymond (Paul Morpheth), Pamela Dwyer (Edith Fisher), Kate Wooldridge (Parlour maid), Graham Crammond (Clerk), Roy Sampson (Dorset butler), Alyxis Daly (Landlady), Joanne Bett, Mary Goonan, Gowan Calder, Morag Siller (Millinery girls)
Music: Alessandro Marcello, Oboe Concerto in D minor, slow movement, performed by the Ferenc Erkel Chamber Orchestra; Mozart, *Così fan*

tutte, Overture, performed by Orchestra and Chorus 'La Petite Bande'; 'La mia Dorabella'; 'Soave sia il vento', Slovak Philarmonic Chorus; Haydn, *Lark* Quartet, Opus 64, No. 5 in D major, third movement, performed by the Hagen Quartet; Rossini, String Quartet No. 3, Rondo; Alexander Borodin, String Quartet No. 2 in D major (the melody is set to the words 'And This Is My Beloved', in *Kismet*); 'Shtiler, Shtiler', song by Alexander Volkoviski Tamir, words by Shmerke Kaczerginski and Avraham Shlonsky, sung by Melanie Pappenheim: Morton Feldman, *Rothko Chapel: Why Patterns?*, fourth movement

Granada Film Limited, in association with The Arts Council of England / FilmFour / The Scottish Arts Council / Showtime / Glasgow Film Fund. A Three Rivers Production developed with the support of the MEDIA Programme of the European Union Supported by the National Lottery through the Arts Council of England and the Scottish Arts Council

General filmography

Asquith, Anthony: *The Winslow Boy* (UK, 1948)
Balasko, Josiane: *Gazon maudit / French Twist* (France, 1995)
Bergman, Ingmar: *Viskingar och Rop / Cries and Whispers* (Sweden, 1972)
Bergman, Ingmar: *Fanny och Alexander / Fanny and Alexander* (Sweden, 1982)
Boorman, John: *Hope and Glory* (UK, 1987)
Boulting, John: *Private's Progress* (UK, 1956)
Brooks, Richard: *Elmer Gantry* (USA, 1960)
Carax, Leos: *Les Amants du Pont Neuf / The Lovers on the Pont Neuf* (France, 1990)
Clair, René: *Entr'acte* (France, 1924)
Collard, Cyril: *Les Nuits fauves / Savage Nights* (France, 1992)
Curtiz, Michael: *Casablanca* (USA, 1942)
Delvaux, André: *Rendez-vous à Bray / Meeting at Bray* (Belgium, 1971)
Donen, Stanley: *Singin' in the Rain* (USA, 1952)
Douglas, Bill: *The Bill Douglas Trilogy* (UK, 1978)
Duras, Marguerite: *India Song* (France, 1975)
Fleming, Victor: *Gone With the Wind* (USA, 1939) (Other directors: Sam Wood, William Cameron Menzies, George Cukor, Reeves Eason)
Godard, Jean-Luc: *JLG/JLG* (France, 1996)
Godard, Jean-Luc: *Vivre sa vie / My Life to Live* (France, 1962)
Greenaway, Peter: *A Zed and Two Noughts* (UK, 1985)
Greenaway, Peter: *The Draughtsman's Contract* (UK, 1982)
Hallstrom, Lasse: *Mit Liv som Hund / My Life as a Dog* (Sweden, 1985)
Hamer, Robert: *It Always Rains on Sunday* (UK, 1947)
Hamer, Robert: *Kind Hearts and Coronets* (UK, 1949)
Jackson, Mick: *A Very British Coup* (UK, 1988)
Jarman, Derek: *Caravaggio* (UK, 1986)
Jarman, Derek: *War Requiem* (UK, 1988)
Jordan, Neil *The Crying Game* (UK, 1992)
King, Henry: *Love Is a Many-Splendored Thing* (USA, 1955)
Korda, Alexander: *An Ideal Husband* (UK, 1947)
Koster, Henry: *The Robe* (USA, 1953)

Laughton, Charles: *Night of the Hunter* (USA, 1955)
Launder, Frank: *The Happiest Days of Your Life* (UK, 1950)
Lean, David: *Great Expectations* (UK, 1946)
Loach, Ken: *Cathy Come Home* (UK, 1966)
Mackendrick, Alexander: *The Ladykillers* (UK, 1955)
Malle, Louis: *Au revoir les enfants* (France, 1987)
Mamet, David: *The Winslow Boy* (USA, 1999)
Mankiewicz, Joseph L.: *Guys and Dolls* (USA, 1955)
Minnelli, Vincente: *Kismet* (USA, 1955)
Minnelli, Vincente: *Meet Me in St Louis* (USA, 1944)
Moretti, Nanni: *Caro Diario/Dear Diary* (Italy, 1994)
Ophuls, Max: *Letter From an Unknown Woman* (USA, 1948)
Parker, Oliver: *An Ideal Husband* (UK/USA, 1999)
Perec, Georges: *Récits d'Ellis Island: histoires d'errance et d'espoir / Ellis Island Revisited: Tales of Vagrancy and Hope* (France/USA, 1979)
Petit, Chris: *Radio On* (UK, 1979)
Pevney, Joseph: *Tammy and the Bachelor* (USA, 1957)
Potter, Dennis: *Pennies From Heaven* (UK, 1978)
Potter, Dennis: *The Singing Detective* (UK, 1986)
Potter, Dennis: *Lipstick on Your Collar* (UK, 1993)
Potter, Sally: *The Gold Diggers* (UK, 1983)
Potter, Sally: *Orlando* (UK/Italy/France/Netherlands/Russia, 1992)
Ray, Man: *L'Etoile de mer / Starfish* (France, 1928)
Reed, Carol: *A Kid for Two Farthings* (UK, 1955)
Renoir, Jean: *La Règle du jeu / The Rules of the Game* (France, 1939)
Resnais, Alain: *Nuit et brouillard / Night and Fog* (France, 1955)
Resnais, Alain: *Hiroshima mon amour* (France, 1959)
Robbe-Grillet, Alain: *L'Eden et après / Eden and After* (France, 1971)
Sandrich, Mark: *Holiday Inn* (USA, 1942)
Scorsese, Martin: *The Age of Innocence* (USA, 1993)
Sirk, Douglas: *Magnificent Obsession* (USA, 1955)
Sirk, Douglas: *All that Heaven Allows* (USA, 1955)
Straub, Jean-Marie and Danièle Huillet: *Chronik der Anna Magdalena Bach / Chronicle of Anna Magdalena Bach* (Italy/West Germany, 1968)
Syberberg, Hans-Jürgen: *Hitler: A Film from Germany* (Germany, 1977)
Tornatore, Guiseppe: *Nuovo Cinema Paradiso / Cinema Paradiso* (Italy, 1989)
Truffaut, François: *Les 400 coups / The 400 Blows* (France, 1959)
Vigo, Jean: *Zéro de conduite / Zero for Conduct* (France, 1932)
Welles, Orson: *The Magnificent Ambersons* (USA, 1942)
Wilder, Billy: *Some Like It Hot* (USA, 1959)
Wyler, William: *The Little Foxes* (USA, 1941)

Select bibliography

Adorno, T. and Eisler, H. (1947), *Composing for the Films*, London: Dennis Dobson.
Andrew, G. (1989), *The Film Handbook*, Harlow, Essex: Longman.
Barker (1988), 'Distant Voices, Still Lives', *Monthly Film Bulletin* 55/657, October, 294.
Barthes, R. (1977), *Image/Music/Text*, New York: The Noonday Press. Translated by Stephen Heath.
Barthes, R. (1984), *Camera Lucida: Reflections on Photography*, London: Jonathan Cape. Translated by Richard Howard.
Barthes, R. (1993), *Oeuvres complètes*, vol. 1, Paris: Editions du Seuil.
Baxter, B. (1988), 'Distant Voices, Still Lives', *Films and Filming* 400, January, 14–15.
Bergman, I. (1994), *Images: My Life in Film*, London: Bloomsbury. Translated by Marianne Ruuth.
Boorman, J. (1987), *Hope and Glory*, London and Boston: Faber and Faber.
Brooks, P. (1976), *The Melodramatic Imagination: Balzac, Henry James, Melodrama, and the Mode of Excess*, New Haven and London: Yale University Press.
Brown, R. (1994), *Overtones and Undertones: Reading Film Music*, Berkeley, Los Angeles and London: University of California Press.
Brown, R. (1996), 'Modern film music', in Nowell-Smith, G. (ed.), *The Oxford History of World Cinema*, Oxford: Oxford University Press, pp. 558–66.
Caughie, J. (1992), 'Halfway to paradise', *Sight and Sound* 2/1 (NS), May, 11–13.
Clair, R. (1970), *Cinéma d'hier, cinéma d'aujourd'hui*, Paris: Gallimard.
Constanzo Cahir, L. (2001), '*The House of Mirth*: an interview with director Terence Davies and producer Olivia Stewart', *Literature/Film Quarterly* 29/3, 166–71.
Cook, P. (1985), *The Cinema Book*, London: BFI.
Cott, J. (1988), 'Godard: born again filmmaker', in Sterritt, D. (ed.), *Jean-Luc Godard Interviews*, Jackson: University Press of Mississippi.
Danks, A. (1998), 'The art of memory: Terence Davies' *Distant Voices, Still Lives*', *Metro* 116, 53–4.

236 SELECT BIBLIOGRAPHY

Davies, T. (1984), *Hallelujah Now*, London: Penguin Books.
Davies, T. (1992), *A Modest Pageant*, London and Boston: Faber and Faber.
Davies, T. (2001a), 'Four songs at twilight', *Guardian*, 13 October, Saturday Review, 4.
Davies, T. (2001b), Commentary on the film by the director included as one of the 'Special Features' on the DVD recording of *The House of Mirth*, London: Granada Film Limited and FilmFour Limited.
Deleuze, G. (1989), *Cinema 2: The Time-image*, London: Athlone Press. Translated by Hugh Tomlinson and Robert Galeta.
Dick, B. (1990), *Anatomy of Film*, second edition, London: St Martin's Press.
Dick, E., Noble, A. and Petrie, D. (eds) (1993), *Bill Douglas: A Magic Lanternist's Account*, London: British Film Institute/Scottish Film Council.
Dixon, W.W. (1992), '*The Long Day Closes*: an interview with Terence Davies', *Cineaste* XIX/2-3, December, 20-3.
Dixon, W. W. (1994), '*The Long Day Closes*: an interview with Terence Davies', in Dixon (ed.), *Re-viewing British Cinema 1900-1992: Essays and Interviews*, New York: State University of New York Press, pp. 249-59.
Doane, M.A. (1984), 'The Women's Film: Possession and address', in Doane, M. A., Mellencamp, P. and Williams, L. (eds), *Re-vision: Essays in Feminist Film Criticism*, Frederick, MD: The American Film Institute and University Publishers of America.
Durgnat, R. (1992), '*The Long Day Closes*', *Sight and Sound* 2/2 (NS), June, 44.
Ehrenzweig, A. (1975), *The Psychoanalysis of Artistic Vision and Hearing*, third edition, London: Sheldon Press.
Eley, G. (1995), 'The family is a dangerous place: memory, gender, and the image of the working class', in Rosenstone, R. (ed.), *Revisioning History: Film and the Construction of a New Past*, Princeton: Princeton University Press, pp. 17-43.
Eliot, T. S. (1959), *Four Quartets*, London: Faber and Faber.
Elsaesser, T. (1987), 'Tales of sound and fury: observations on the family melodrama', in Gledhill, C. (ed.), *Home Is Where the Heart Is: Studies in Melodrama and the Woman's Film*, London: BFI, pp. 43-69. First published in 1972 in *Monogram* 4.
Elsaesser, T. (1988), 'Games of love and death or an Englishman's guide to the galaxy', *Monthly Film Bulletin* 55/657, October, 290-3.
Everett, W. (1995), 'The autobiographical eye in European film', *Europa, An International Journal of Language, Art and Culture* 2/1, Spring, 3-10.
Everett, W. (1996), 'Timetravel in European film', in Everett, W. (ed.), *European Identity in Film*, Exeter: Intellect, pp. 103-11.
Everett, W. (2000a), 'An art of fugue? The polyphonic cinema of Marguerite Duras', in Williams, J. S. (ed.), *Revisioning Duras: Film, Race, Sex*, Liverpool: Liverpool University Press, pp. 21-35.
Everett, W. (2000b), 'Songlines: alternative journeys in contemporary European cinema', in Buhler, J., Flinn, C. and Neumeyer, D. (eds), *Music and Cinema*, Hanover and London: Wesleyan University Press, pp. 99-117.

SELECT BIBLIOGRAPHY 237

Everett, W. (2001a), 'Film', in Jolly, M. (ed.), *Encyclopedia of Life Writing*, London and Chicago: Fitzroy Dearborn, pp. 323–4.

Everett, W. (2001b), 'Close-up': an interview with Terence Davies, London, February 2001. (See Chapter 8.)

Falsetto, M. (1999), *Personal Visions: Conversations with Independent Filmmakers*, London: Constable.

Finney, A. (1996), *The State of European Cinema: A New Dose of Reality*, London and New York: Cassell.

Fischer, L. (1989), *Shot/Countershot: Film Tradition and Women's Cinema*, Princeton: Princeton University Press, and London: BFI/Macmillan.

Flinn, C. (1992), *Strains of Utopia: Gender, Nostalgia, and Hollywood Film Music*, Princeton: Princeton University Press.

Foucault, M. (1986), 'Of other spaces', *Diacritics* 16/1, Spring, 22–7. Translated by Jay Miskowiec,

Friedman, L. (ed.) (1993), *British Cinema and Thatcherism*, London: UCL Press.

Fuller, G. (2001), 'Summer's end', *Film Comment* 37/1, January/February 2001, 54–9.

Gilmore, L. (2001), 'Trauma', in Jolly, M. (ed.), *Encyclopedia of Life Writing: Autobiographical and Biographical Forms*, vol. 2, London and Chicago: Fitzroy Dearborn, pp. 885–7.

Gledhill, C. (2000), 'Rethinking genre', in Gledhill, C. and Williams, L., *Reinventing Film Studies*, London and New York: Arnold, pp. 221–43.

Gorbman, C. (1987), *Unheard Melodies: Narrative Film Music*, Bloomington: Indiana University Press.

Gorbman, C. (1998), 'Film music', in Hill, J., and Church Gibson, P. (eds), *The Oxford Guide to Film Studies*, Oxford: Oxford University Press, pp. 43–50.

Gusdorf, G. (1956), 'Conditions et limites de l'autobiographie', reprinted in Olney, J. (ed.) (1980), *Autobiography: Essays Critical and Theoretical*, Princeton: Princeton University Press, pp. 28–48.

Harvey, D. (1989), *The Condition of Postmodernity: An Enquiry into the Origins of Cultural Change*, Oxford: Blackwell.

Hattenstone, S. (2000), 'First steps in show business', *Guardian*, 6 October, Review, 2–4.

Hayward, S. (1993), *French National Cinema*, London: Routledge.

Hayward, S. (1996), *Key Concepts in Cinema Studies*, London and New York: Routledge.

Heath, S. (1981), 'Narrative space', in *Questions of Cinema*, London: Macmillan, pp. 19–75.

Higson, A. (1998), 'British cinema', in Hill, J. and Church Gibson, P. (eds), *The Oxford Guide to Film Studies*, Oxford: Oxford University Press, pp. 501–9.

Higson, A. (1995), *Waving the Flag: Constructing a National Cinema in Britain*, Oxford: Clarendon.

Hill, J. (1999), *British Cinema in the 1980s*, Oxford: Clarendon Press.

Horne, P. (2000), 'Beauty's slow fade', *Sight and Sound* 10/10, October, 14–18.
Hunt, M. (1999), 'The poetry of the ordinary: Terence Davies and the social art film', *Screen* 40/1, Spring, 1–16.
Jackson, K. (2000), *'The House of Mirth'*, *Sight and Sound* 10/11, November, 53–54.
Jenks, C. (ed.) (1995), *Visual Culture*, London and New York: Routledge.
Jivani, A. (1997), *It's Not Unusual: A History of Lesbian and Gay Britain in the Twentieth Century*, London: Michael O'Mara Books Limited, by arrangement with the BBC.
Keighron, P. (1991), 'Condition critical', *Screen* 32/2, Summer, 209–19.
Kemp, P. (1996), 'Alexander Mackendrick', in Nowell-Smith, G. (ed.), *The Oxford History of World Cinema*, Oxford: Oxford University Press, p. 371.
Kennedy, H. (1988), 'Familiar haunts: Terence Davies's *Distant Voices, Still Lives*, *Film Comment* 24/5, September–October, 13–18.
Kirkham, P. and O'Shaughnessy, M. (1992), 'Designing desire', *Sight and Sound* 2/1 (NS), May, 13–15.
Koshar, R. (1995), '*Hitler: A Film from Germany*', in Rosenstone, R. (ed.) (1995), *Revisioning History: Film and the Construction of a New Past*, Princeton: Princeton University Press, pp. 155–73.
Kristeva, J. (1980), *Desire in Language*, New York: Columbia University Press. Translated by Thomas Gora, Alice Jardine and Leon S. Roudiez.
Lejeune, P. (1971), *L'Autobiographie en France*, Paris: A. Colin.
London, K. (1936), *Film Music*, London: Faber and Faber.
MacCabe, C. (1999), *The Eloquence of the Vulgar*, London: BFI.
McFarlane, B. (1996), *Novel to Film: An Introduction to the Theory of Adaptation*, Oxford: Clarendon Press.
McFarlane, B. (2000), 'It wasn't like that in the book', *Literature/Film Quarterly* 28/3, 163–9.
Monaco, P. (1987), *Ribbons in Time*, Bloomington and Indianapolis: Indiana University Press.
Mulvey, L. (1977/78), 'Notes on Sirk and melodrama', *Movie* 25. Reprinted in Mulvey, L. (1989), *Visual and Other Pleasures*, London: Macmillan.
Neale, S. (1981), 'Art cinema as institution', *Screen* 22/1, 11–39.
Nochimson, M. (2001) '*The House of Mirth*', *Cineaste* 26/2, 41–3.
Nowell-Smith, G. (1987), 'Minnelli and melodrama', in Gledhill, C. (ed.), *Home is Where the Heart Is: Studies in Melodrama and Women's Film*, London: BFI. First published in *Screen* 18/2, Summer 1977.
Orr, J. (1993), *Cinema and Modernity*, Oxford: Polity Press.
Orr, J. (1998), *Contemporary Cinema*, Edinburgh: Edinburgh University Press.
Orr, J. (2000), *The Art and Politics of Film*, Edinburgh: Edinburgh University Press.
Petrie, D. (ed.) (1992), *Screening Europe: Image and Identity in Contemporary European Cinema*, London: BFI.
Petrie, D. (2000), 'The New Scottish Cinema', in Hjort, M. and Mackenzie, S. (eds), *Cinema and Nation*, London and New York: Routledge.

SELECT BIBLIOGRAPHY 239

Potter, D. (1993), *Potter on Potter*, London: Faber and Faber.
Powrie, P. (2000a), 'On the threshold between past and present "alternative" heritage', in Ashby, J. and Higson, A., *British Cinema, Past and Present*, London and New York: Routledge, pp. 316–26.
Powrie, P. (2000b), 'The "family portrait": Trauma and the *punctum* in *Distant Voices, Still Lives* (1988)', in Everett, W. (ed.), *The Seeing Century: Film, Vision, and Identity*, Amsterdam: Rodopi, pp. 20–35.
Radstone, S. (1995), 'Cinema/memory/history', *Screen* 36/1, Spring, 34–47.
Ricoeur, P. (1985), *Temps et récit*, Paris: Seuil.
Rosalato, G. (1974), 'La voix entre corps et langage', *Revue Français de Psychanalyse* 38, January, 75–94.
Rose, S. (1992), *The Making of Memory*, London and New York: Bantam Press.
Sheringham, M. (1993), *French Autobiography – Devices and Desires*, Oxford: Clarendon Press.
Singer, B. (1995), 'Modernity, hyper-stimulus, and the rise of popular sensationalism', in Charnley, L. and Schwartz, V. R. (eds), *Cinema and the Invention of Modern Life*, Berkeley: University of California Press, pp. 72–99.
Smith, J. (1996), 'Unheard melodies?', in Bordwell, D. and Carroll, N. (eds), *Post-theory: Reconstructing Film Studies*, Madison: University of Wisconsin Press, pp. 230–47.
Smith, S. (1987), *A Poetics of Women's Autobiography: Marginality and the Fictions of Self-representation*, Bloomington: Indiana University Press.
Sontag, S. (1979), *On Photography*, London: Penguin Books.
Sorlin, P. (1996), *Italian National Cinema, 1986–1996*, London: Routledge.
Steiner, M. (1937), 'Scoring the film', in Naumberg, N. (ed.), *We Make the Movies*, New York: Norton, pp. 216–38.
Sterritt, D. (ed.) (1998), *Jean-Luc Godard Interviews*, Jackson: University Press of Mississippi.
Sterritt, D. (1999), *The Films of Jean-Luc Godard: Seeing the Invisible*, Cambridge: Cambridge University Press.
Storr, A. (1997), *Music and the Mind*, London: Harper Collins.
Street, S. (1997), *British National Cinema*, London and New York: Routledge.
Taubin, A. (2001), 'The Age of Innocence: dread and desire', in Vincendeau, G. (ed.), *Film/Literature/Heritage*, London: BFI, pp. 61–5.
Thomas, T. (1991), *Film Score: The Art and Craft of Movie Music*, Burbank: Riverwood Press.
Tibbetts, J. C. and Welsh, J. M. (1998), *The Encyclopedia of Novels into Films*, New York: Facts on File.
Toole, J. K. (1980), *A Confederacy of Dunces*, London and New York: Penguin.
Toole, J. K. (1989), *The Neon Bible*, New York: Grove Press.
Updike, J. (1989), *Just Looking: Essays on Art*, London: André Deutsch and Penguin.
Valéry, P. (1988), *Regards sur le monde actuel*, Paris: Gallimard (Folio Essais).

Vincendeau, G. (ed.)(2001), *Film/Literature/Heritage. A Sight and Sound Reader*, London: BFI.
Wagstaff, P. (2000), 'The dark side of utopia: word, image, and memory in Georges Perec's *Récits d'Ellis Island: histoires d'errance et d'espoir*', in Everett, W. (ed.), *The Seeing Century: Film, Vision, and Identity*, Amsterdam: Rodopi, pp. 36–48.
Wharton, E. (1995), *The House of Mirth*, New York: Simon and Schuster. First published in 1905.
White, A. (1993), 'Remembrance of songs past', *Film Comment* 29/3, May/June, 12–15.
Wiblin, I. (1997), 'The space between: photography, architecture and the presence of absence', in Penz, F. and Thomas, M. (eds), *Cinema and Architecture: Méliès, Mallet-Stevens, Multimedia*, London: BFI.
Williams, C. (ed.) (1996), *Cinema: The Beginnings and the Future*, London: University of Westminster Press.
Williams, L. (1998), 'Melodrama revised', in Browne, N. (ed.), *Refiguring American Film Genres: Theory and History*, Berkeley: University of California Press, pp. 42–88.
Williams, T. (1993), 'The masochistic fix: gender oppression in the films of Terence Davies', in Friedman, L. (ed.), *British Cinema and Thatcherism*, London: UCL Press, pp. 237–54.

Index

Note: film titles can be found under directors' names; page numbers in *italics* refer to illustrations.

adaptation 7–8, 15, 110–19, 122, 127, 134–56 *passim*, 162, 164–6, 183, 188, 213, 215
Age of Innocence, The 20, 137–8, 141, 146, 155, 162, 165–6, 234
see also Scorsese; Wharton
Aykroyd, Dan 215, 231
alienation 49, 77–8, 93, 145
alter ego 11–12, 77, 170
America 14–26 *passim*, 35, 42, 52, 100–2, 107, 110, 112, 114, 120–2, 127–38 *passim*, 145, 156–7, 160, 163, 166, 169, 184–6, 188, 193, 195, 198–9, 207, 212, 219, 221
Anderson, Gillian 15, 20–3, 160, 166, 212, 231
Angelopoulos, Theo 27, 30
architecture 6, 42, 44–8, 50, 66, 71, 104, 138, 153, 196
art 2, 4, 24, 28–31, 53, 60–1, 64, 82, 89, 96, 98, 107–9, 138–9, 148–9, 168, 171, 182, 196, 207, 225
autobiography 12, 14, 31, 63, 65, 74, 77–80, 90, 95, 101, 107–8, 110–11, 141, 165, 169, 172, 183, 188

Bach, Johann Sebastian 27, 168
Balasko, Josiane 45
French Twist 45
baroque 130, 157, 193
Barthes, Roland 74–6, 81, 125, 135, 180, 196, 199
Bergman, Ingmar 2, 15, 27, 30, 32, 35, 52, 58, 112, 161, 196, 217–18, 225, 233
Cries and Whispers 27, 161, 216, 225, 233

Fanny and Alexander 217, 225, 233
Boccherini, Luigi 96–7, 188, 221, 230
Boorman, John 12, 43, 54, 80, 233
Hope and Glory 12, 43, 54, 80, 233
Borodin, Alexander 194–5, 232
Brambell, Wilfred 21, 205
Bresson, Robert 15, 30, 52, 61, 161
Britain 1, 7, 9, 11, 17, 20, 28, 30–1, 33, 44, 53, 58, 60, 88, 100, 109, 136, 176, 237
British 1, 2, 7, 9, 13–14, 21, 28–34, 42, 52, 54, 56–63, 80–2, 89, 109, 130, 135, 147, 166, 217, 226–8, 230, 233
British Film Institute (BFI) 13–14, 18, 24, 30, 32–4, 54, 57–8, 82, 165–6, 226–8, 230
Britten, Benjamin 168, 201, 205, 228
Brooks, Richard 157, 165, 225, 233
Elmer Gantry 162, 204, 221, 225, 233
Bruckner, Anton 168–9, 195, 204–5, 216
brutality 10, 50, 90, 111, 172, 178
budget 18–20, 58, 122, 129, 150

Cage, John 193
Carax, Leos 27, 33, 196, 233
Lovers on the Pont Neuf, The 27, 233
Carmichael, Hoagy 169, 206, 229
Catholic 9–11, 17, 24, 35–6, 43, 47, 49, 51, 86, 100, 104, 111, 171, 210
childhood 9, 11–16, 22, 26, 36–40, 43, 46, 50, 52, 59, 86, 95–117 *passim*, 126–8, 134, 154, 169–70, 172, 175, 177, 181, 184, 188, 194, 203, 210
Children 6, 10, 12–14, 17, 22, 24, 34–6, 38–40, 43, 46, 49, 52, 169, 171, 210, 226

242 INDEX

cinema 1–9 passim, 29–31, 38, 45, 47, 56–57, 59, 60–3, 65, 75, 78–80, 87–9, 92–3, 100–21 passim, 125, 127–8, 130, 133, 137, 143, 147, 152, 154, 165–6, 170, 175, 179, 184, 196, 222
Cinemascope 25, 100, 113, 122, 130–1
city 11, 35, 43–5, 51–2, 94
Clair, René 27, 32, 233
claustrophobia 148, 157, 161
close-up 35, 43–4, 66, 71, 73, 91, 105, 125, 143, 146
Cocteau, Jean 138
Cole, Nat King 100, 169, 176, 206, 229
Collard, Cyril 45
Savage Nights 45
colour 25, 27–8, 32, 45, 75–6, 116, 129–30, 151, 153, 156, 195, 216
Così fan tutte 155, 163, 164, 189, 190, 209
Coulter, Mick 24–6, 229–30
Coventry 13–14, 42
culture 4, 14, 21, 52, 59, 88, 100, 102–3, 121, 130, 139, 161, 170–1, 176–7, 184, 188, 194, 196, 199
cultural 2, 8, 16, 21, 41, 52, 57, 59, 60, 77, 88, 100, 102, 111, 121, 130–1, 134, 137, 139, 154, 184, 188, 194, 196, 199
Curtis, Ralph 138, 159
Curtiz, Michael 233
Casablanca 155, 233

Davis, Bette 18, 117, 128
Day, Doris 171, 227, 229
death 10–11, 14, 36–7, 40, 45, 70, 74, 76, 98, 110, 113–14, 119, 133, 135, 141, 150, 156, 165, 170, 187, 216
Death and Transfiguration 6, 14, 35–6, 45, 53, 169, 171, 227
Delvaux, André 27, 233
Meeting at Bray 27, 233
desire 31, 35, 45, 61–2, 134, 142, 151, 157–8, 163–4, 195–6
despair 10, 35–7, 40, 44, 50–1, 53, 78, 141, 153, 157, 165, 171, 178, 180
dialogue 4, 18, 28, 68, 118–19, 143–4, 147, 149–50, 153, 172, 214, 220
diegetic 106, 118, 122, 183, 191
dislocation 40, 50–1, 145
Distant Voices, Still Lives 2, 6, 7, 10, 14, 19, 22, 25, 28, 30, 31, 53–82 passim, 83, 86–8, 90–1, 95, 102–3, 109, 160, 169–72, 178–80, 183, 202–20 passim, 228
domestic 39, 43, 45, 51, 56, 59, 66, 87, 107, 121, 157, 159–60, 193
Dominguez, Alberto 124, 188, 231
Donen, Stanley 233
Singin' in the Rain 79, 179, 233
Douglas, Bill 29–32, 60, 88–90, 156–7, 216, 225, 233–4
Bill Douglas Trilogy, The 29, 88, 216, 233
Duras, Marguerite 8, 27, 32–3, 78, 196, 199, 233
India Song 233
Dvorak, Antonin 231

Eady Levy 57, 80
Ealing Comedies 2, 52, 97, 101, 109
Eliot, T. S. 3, 6, 34, 37–8, 41, 48, 53–5, 61, 86, 96, 110, 136, 167, 215
Four Quartets, The 3, 6, 34, 37, 54–5, 86, 96, 110, 136, 167
entrapment 45, 103, 111, 122–4, 139, 141–2, 151, 153, 178–9, 189
epic 113, 122, 129, 130–3, 186
erosion 11, 92–4, 104, 107, 220
escape 13, 29, 31, 35–6, 42–4, 51, 65, 68, 96, 102–3, 105, 111, 116–17, 122–4, 127–8, 134, 139, 142, 151, 153–4, 164, 178, 180, 189, 191–4, 210
Estonia 140, 193
Europe 7, 20, 31–3, 82, 116, 130, 136, 176, 199
European, 2, 8, 14, 19, 20, 24, 27–8, 30–3, 45, 52, 60–1, 63, 80–2, 116, 130, 136, 166, 176, 199, 200, 217, 232
expressionist 48, 156

family 9–11, 35–6, 56–8, 60, 62–3, 65, 68, 70–8, 81–2, 86, 91, 101–2, 104, 106, 112, 114, 116, 123, 157, 166, 170–2, 177, 179, 184, 203, 206–7, 223
father 9–11, 14, 21–3, 33, 36–7, 43, 49, 51, 56, 68, 70–6, 78, 80–1, 86–7, 91–2, 102, 110–23 passim, 132–3, 138, 150, 166, 172, 177, 181, 190, 215, 218, 223
Feldman, Morton 140, 163, 193–4, 232
female 10–11, 16, 49, 71, 78, 121, 127, 128, 142, 156–8, 160, 185, 190, 222
feminine 25, 66, 86, 91, 97, 104, 157, 187, 188
Ferrier, Kathleen 188, 201–2, 229
Fleming, Victor 129, 184, 233
Gone With the Wind 26, 113, 120–1, 128–33, 135, 184, 186, 231, 233

INDEX 243

Foucault, Michel 41, 54, 237
France 12, 28, 32, 40, 45, 80–1, 138–9, 142, 145, 200, 233–4, 238
freedom 51, 104, 116, 121–4, 131, 138, 151, 153–4, 157, 172, 178, 189, 191
Fuller, Morton 109, 111, 135–6, 138, 166
funding 14, 20, 57–8, 80, 107, 144–5

gay 16–17, 33, 45, 51, 134, 184, 218
gaze 30, 38, 65–6, 69, 73, 78, 92, 106, 120–1, 128, 143, 146–8, 151, 159, 161, 164, 178–9, 190
gender 44–5, 63, 139
genre 64, 96, 98, 108, 156–9, 166
Gershwin, George and Ira 183, 227–8, 230
gesture 22–3, 66, 71–2, 144, 159, 212, 214
Gide, André 138
Glasgow 144–5, 232
Godard, Jean-Luc 8, 30, 56, 58, 80–2, 108–9, 233
 JLG/JLG 80, 108, 233
 My Life to Live 81, 230, 233
Grable, Betty 117, 128
Greenaway, Peter 30, 57, 96, 233
 Zed and Two Noughts, A 57, 233
Guinness, Alec 101, 106

Hallelujah Now 8, 14, 16, 32
Hallstrom, Lasse 12, 225, 233
 My Life as a Dog 12, 218, 225, 233
Hamer, Robert 106, 225, 233
 It Always Rains on Sunday 216, 225, 233
 Kind Hearts and Coronets 106, 216, 225, 233
Harlow, Jean 32, 54, 128
Harvey, David 41, 54
Haydn, Franz Joseph 191–3, 199, 200, 232
Hayworth, Rita 117, 128
Heath, Stephen 41, 54, 81, 199, 229, 235
heritage 29, 31, 33, 137, 147, 213
history 26, 30, 33, 35, 42, 46, 48, 61–2, 88, 109, 112, 114, 130, 166, 182, 186, 198
 historical 25–6, 30, 33, 35, 41–2, 46, 48, 60–2, 64, 88, 90, 100, 109, 111–12, 114, 129–30, 139, 142, 166, 176, 182, 186–7, 194, 198
Hollywood 2, 20, 30, 38, 79, 100, 107, 122, 127–8, 140–1, 156, 167, 173, 179, 184–5, 195, 199, 221
home 11, 14, 36, 43, 45, 49, 51, 87, 93, 99, 102–3, 113, 138–9, 165, 181, 203, 216, 218

homosexuality 17, 36, 43, 49–50, 53, 77, 92, 121
House of Mirth, The 2, 6–7, 9, 15, 19–24, 26–7, 32–3, 42, 81, 85, 111, 119, 121, 124, 135–68 *passim*, 188–92, 194, 200–1, 203, 209, 211–13, 215, 223–4, 231
 see also Wharton
Howarth, Jennifer 1, 53, 228
Howe, Monica 24, 60, 82, 228–31

identity 5–6, 14, 16–17, 24, 29, 31, 38, 40, 44–6, 51–2, 61, 77–80, 87–90, 92, 96, 99, 101–3, 106–8, 125, 127, 133–4, 142, 150–1, 154, 158, 160, 171–2, 179, 186, 190, 198
image 38, 47, 50–3, 63, 66, 69, 73, 75, 96, 97, 108, 123–6, 132, 145, 165, 173, 176, 178, 191, 195, 210–11, 216
imaginary 37–8, 40, 47, 95–6, 99, 106, 116, 126
Irish 9, 132, 183, 222, 228, 231
irony 40, 57, 88, 94, 98, 111, 116, 141, 154, 184–5, 187, 190, 207–8
Italian 12, 107, 109, 114, 123, 138, 190, 191, 234
Italy 12, 114, 123, 138, 234

James, Henry 138, 141, 165, 227–8
Jarman, Derek 30, 57, 218, 225, 233
 Caravaggio 30, 57, 233
 War Requiem 218, 225, 233
Jordan, Neil 30, 233

King, Henry 79, 100, 156, 176, 225, 229, 233
Kodály, Zoltan 27
Korda, Alexander 225, 233
 An Ideal Husband 214, 225, 233
Koster, Henry 100, 225, 233
 The Robe 100, 108, 210, 225, 233
Kristeva, Julia 92, 109, 173, 200

Lacan, Jacques 32, 173
Laughton, Charles 234
 Night of the Hunter 216, 225, 234
Launder, Frank 98, 234
 Happiest Days of Your Life, The 230, 234
Law of the Father 9, 11, 32, 72, 78, 92, 104, 127, 172, 189
Lean, David 165, 234
 Great Expectations 165, 230, 234
Lee, Peggy 117, 123, 171, 186, 226, 229

Lejeune, Philippe 108, 182, 200
lesbian 33, 45
Liszt, Franz 207
Liverpool 9, 13, 15, 23, 25, 33, 35–6, 42–6, 51–2, 56, 59, 66–7, 87, 105, 111, 116–17, 126–7, 199, 203, 219, 222–3
Loach, Ken 60, 77, 234
  Cathy Come Home 77, 234
Long Day Closes, The 2, 6, 7, 9, 11–12, 14, 16–17, 19, 22, 24–6, 29–30, 32, 39, 53, 63, 68, 72, 77, 80, 84, 86–122 passim, 126, 133–5, 154, 165, 169–70, 172, 176, 181, 183, 188, 199, 201–3, 207, 209–10, 213, 218, 229–30
Longfellow, Henry Wadsworth 116, 134, 184, 198
love 7, 9–11, 22, 40, 69, 79–80, 92, 103, 110, 119, 123, 128, 142, 147–8, 155–6, 168–9, 172, 178–80, 185, 187, 188, 191, 194–5, 201, 205, 207–8, 212–22 passim
lyrical 4, 6, 79, 152, 155, 189, 191

MacCabe, Colin 18, 26, 33, 57, 58, 82, 160, 166, 228–9
Mackendrick, Alexander 97, 101, 109, 234
  Ladykillers, The 97, 101, 109, 234
Madonna and Child 6, 13–14, 35–6, 39–40, 44–5, 50, 93, 169, 171, 226
Magic Flute, The 155, 189
Mahler, Gustav 195, 230
Malle, Louis 32, 234
  Au revoir les enfants 32, 234
Mankiewicz, Joseph L. 79, 234
  Guys and Dolls 79, 228, 234
Marcello, Alessandro, 162–3, 191, 209, 231
maternal 9, 40, 49, 72, 80, 91–2, 172–3, 187–8, 222
Mediterranean 146, 152
melodrama 121, 156–60, 162, 165–6, 235–6
melody 78, 97, 100, 106, 180–1, 183, 192, 194–5, 197–8, 231–2
memory 8–9, 14, 16, 25, 29–48 passim, 53, 55–6, 63–72, 75–6, 80, 86–90, 94–5, 99, 100–2, 106–7, 109–11, 115, 119–22, 125–6, 132–4, 167, 170, 172–3, 175–7, 180–3, 196, 203, 213, 218, 220–1
Miller, Glenn 124, 188, 221, 231
Minnelli, Vincente 102, 166, 195, 234
  Kismet 195, 232, 234

mirror 60, 65, 73, 77, 173, 177, 211
mise-en-scène 4, 30, 75, 155, 157–8, 160
mobility 39, 44, 52, 69, 70, 106, 118–22, 124, 152, 154, 171–2, 172, 178, 180, 189, 193
modern 31, 141–2, 166, 196, 206–7, 215, 224
modernity 31, 141–2, 157, 166, 196, 206–7, 215, 224, 239
Modest Pageant, A 8, 32, 54, 70, 81, 199, 236
Monroe, Marilyn 159
Monte Carlo 42, 152–3, 192, 201, 209
Moretti Nanni 108, 234
  Dear Diary 108, 234
mother 9–10, 13, 15, 22, 32, 34, 36–7, 40, 44–5, 49–51, 55–6, 66–9, 71–2, 77–8, 81, 86–7, 91–2, 95, 101, 103–4, 110–33 passim, 142, 170–3, 178–81, 183, 185, 187, 192, 203, 207–8, 215, 219, 224
movement 18, 27, 39, 41–2, 44, 70, 72, 76, 96–9, 102, 105–6, 118, 122, 125, 126, 131, 135–6, 145, 151–4, 162, 180, 186, 188, 190–1, 193, 196–8, 216
Mozart, Wolfgang Amadeus 152–3, 155, 163–4, 189–90, 192–3, 199–200, 231
music 2–8, 10, 15–16, 18–19, 23, 25–6, 28, 36, 40, 50, 53, 55, 64–6, 68–9, 72, 75, 79–80, 86–7, 91–2, 96–100, 102–25 passim, 130, 144, 147, 149, 152–5, 161–3, 167–99 passim, 204–9, 211, 216, 221–2
musicals 2, 101–2, 127, 169, 195
myth 55, 117, 123, 179, 180
mythical 55, 117, 123, 130, 134, 179, 180

Neon Bible, The 2, 6–7, 14–15, 22, 24–6, 84, 110–13, 117–18, 121–2, 127, 129–37, 154, 168, 183–8, 200–3, 208, 212, 221, 223, 230, 239
New York 15, 33, 54, 81–2, 109–10, 135–6, 138–40, 145, 152, 155, 163, 165–6, 198–201, 209, 214, 235–40
nostalgia 29, 31, 60, 71, 88–9, 97, 100–3, 106, 176–9, 183, 199, 206

opera 155, 163–4, 189–90, 192, 194
  opera buffa 190
Ophuls, Max 155, 189, 225, 234
  Letter from an Unknown Woman 155–6, 207, 212

painting 96, 161, 192, 196, 199

INDEX 245

Paris 32, 45, 80, 82, 109, 135, 138, 199–200, 235, 238–9
patriarchal 11, 104, 121, 141–2, 155, 180
Perec, Georges 76, 82, 234, 240
  Ellis Island Revisited: Tales of Vagrancy and Hope 76, 82, 234, 240
perspective 39, 41, 43–5, 51, 55, 77, 105, 123, 157, 159, 210
Petit, Chris 57, 234
  Radio On 57, 234
Pevney, Joseph 106, 234
  Tammy and the Bachelor 106, 230, 234
photography 21–2, 24, 47, 70–81 *passim*, 113, 129, 172, 177
poem 4, 94, 96, 184–5, 198, 201, 206
poetry 4, 7, 32, 38, 60, 82, 109, 115–16, 119, 138, 168–9, 205, 208, 215–16, 238
popular culture 4, 14, 52, 102–3, 130, 161, 170–1, 176–7, 184 *see also* culture
popular song 16, 92, 99, 161, 167, 169–76, 182–3, 188, 195, 198, 206 *see also* song
Porter, Cole 169, 206
Postlethwaite, Pete 22, 228
postmodern 41, 61, 108, 134, 158
Potter, Dennis 176, 198
  Pennies from Heaven 176, 234
  Singing Detective, The 176, 234
Potter, Sally 30, 57
  Gold Diggers, The 57, 234
  Orlando 30, 234

realism 2–5, 28–9, 31, 39, 46, 52, 59–64, 88–90, 98, 102, 108, 120, 147, 149
realist 28, 31, 42, 59, 60, 63, 89, 101
reception, 1, 6, 28, 59–60, 88, 137, 145, 185, 198
Reed, Carol 225, 234
  Kid for Two Farthings, A 106, 216–17, 225, 234
Renoir, Jean 142, 234
  Rules of the Game, The 142, 165, 234
Resnais, Alain 2, 30, 40, 76, 234
  Hiroshima mon amour 40, 234
  Night and Fog 76, 234
Reynolds, Debbie 106, 230
rhythm 18, 27–8, 32, 70, 76, 97, 115, 181, 197
Ricoeur, Paul 108, 109, 239
Robbe-Grillet, Alain 27, 196, 234
  Eden and After 27, 234
romantic 79, 100, 102, 106, 128–30, 139, 147, 162–3, 169, 178–9, 185, 194–5, 208, 225

Rossini, Gioacchino Antonio 192, 232
Rothko, Mark 140, 163, 193, 232
Rowlands, Gina 22, 113, 230
Rutherford, Margaret 98

salvation 10, 42, 49, 53, 103, 127–8, 139, 153, 171
Sandrich, Mark 102, 234
  Holiday Inn 102, 229, 234
Sargent, John Singer 15, 21, 26, 160, 165
school 10–13, 17, 32, 34, 36, 43, 45–9, 66, 86–7, 91–5, 103–5, 114–16, 120, 138, 169–71, 187, 219–20, 231
Scorsese, Martin 20, 137, 146–8, 155, 158, 165, 234
  see also Age of Innocence, The
self-conscious 12, 24, 31, 50, 60, 62, 64, 65, 70, 78, 88, 89, 95, 98, 108, 111, 119, 122, 124–5, 133–4, 143, 146, 154, 158, 171, 186
sexuality 10, 16–17, 35, 45, 50–1, 62, 77–8, 86, 90, 92–3, 111, 158, 170, 220
shooting script 18–19, 22, 110
Sibelius, Jean 168–9, 195, 203–5
sight 16, 39, 51, 132, 146, 153
Sight and Sound 25, 29, 32–3, 81–2, 88, 109, 112, 135, 166
signifier 162–3, 169, 187, 191, 196
silence 6, 10, 16, 27, 55, 68–9, 72, 148, 159, 161, 167, 171–2, 177–8, 180, 188, 191, 206
Sirk, Douglas 156–7, 166, 225, 234, 238
  All That Heaven Allows 156, 207, 223, 225, 234
  Magnificent Obsession 156, 223, 225, 234
society 13–15, 24, 26, 61–2, 116, 121, 138–42, 148, 151, 154–5, 157–8, 160, 164–5, 178, 189, 215
song 39, 68–9, 73, 91–2, 98–101, 106, 140, 169, 171, 173, 176, 177–85, 187–8, 191, 193, 195, 198, 206–8, 225, 232
Sontag, Susan 73–5, 81–2, 239
soundtrack 18, 50, 95, 98, 101, 103, 106, 161, 167, 177, 183–4, 184, 186, 207, 225, 228–30
space 4, 25, 31, 34, 40–55 *passim*, 66, 69–71, 77, 80, 86–7, 92, 95, 97, 99, 102–4, 106, 108, 119, 125–7, 134, 148–54, 178, 190, 193–4, 196–8, 214
spatial 10, 35, 37–8, 40–1, 43, 45, 49, 52, 56, 64–5, 70, 80, 95–6, 99–

100, 105–6, 119–21, 131, 154, 163, 175, 193, 197, 203
spectator 4, 6, 10, 12–13, 22, 34, 37–8, 44, 46–7, 51, 66–7, 72, 93, 95, 98–9, 124–5, 134, 145–7, 154, 158, 161, 164, 174–5, 189, 203, 217
stasis 36, 39, 49, 70–2, 76–7, 79, 103, 112, 115, 124–5, 161, 171–2, 178, 180, 189, 191
Steiner, Max 129, 174, 180, 200, 231, 239
Straub, Jean-Marie and Danièle Huillet 27, 30, 234
    Chronicle of Anna Magdalena Bach 27, 234
Stravinsky, Igor 163
style 53, 73, 100, 118, 149, 158, 192, 202, 214
subjectivity 15, 25, 46, 52, 59, 64, 90, 91, 158, 173
    subjective 12, 15, 25, 40–4, 46, 52, 55, 59, 64, 90–1, 100, 102–3, 106, 125–6, 158, 161, 170, 172–3
Sullivan, Sir Arthur 98, 108, 188, 227, 230
Syberberg, Hans-Jürgen 81, 234
    Hitler: A Film from Germany 81, 82, 234, 238

Tamir, Alexander Volkoviski 140, 193, 232
Tarkovsky, Andrey 27, 196
Tchaikovsky, Piotr Ilyitch 206
Technicolor, 26, 117, 128–30
texture 25–6, 28, 87, 152–3, 159, 162, 189, 211–12, 214
time 1–5, 10–14, 18, 25–42 *passim*, 45–7, 52–3, 55–60, 64–5, 67–72, 74–6, 86–102, 106, 108, 110–11, 115, 119, 121–2, 125–6, 129–32, 134–40, 143, 149–53, 155, 158, 161–5, 167, 169–70, 174–5, 177–8, 180, 183–5, 187, 190–8, 203, 205, 207, 210, 212–13, 215–17, 219–22, 225
Toole, John Kennedy 14, 110, 113–14, 117–18, 120, 122–3, 126–7, 129, 131, 135, 198, 200, 230, 239
    Confederacy of Dunces, A 14, 113, 135, 239
    see also *Neon Bible, The*
Tornatore, Guiseppe 12, 234
    Cinema Paradiso 12, 234

trace 27, 35, 59, 107, 112, 182
tracking shot 4, 112, 189
transition 14, 20, 37, 86, 99, 104–5, 146, 151–5, 164, 185, 189–91, 194, 201, 209
trauma 36, 39, 47, 70, 72, 76–7, 79, 220
traumatic 36, 39–40, 47, 70, 72, 76–7, 79, 87, 104, 172, 220
Trilogy, The 7, 14, 35, 46, 53, 170, 226
Truffaut, François 12, 30, 80, 94, 234
    400 Blows, The 94, 234

Under Milk Wood 8
United States 7, 14, 111, 130, 139
Updike, John 160, 166, 239

Valéry, Paul 1, 80, 82, 239
Verlaine, Paul 154
Vermeer, Jan 26 159–61, 212
Vienna 155, 160
viewpoint 42–3, 52, 56, 65–6, 73, 90, 94–5, 105, 108, 115, 130, 132, 146–7, 184
Vigo, Jean 12, 31, 234
    Zero for Conduct 234
violence 10–11, 48, 51, 57, 68, 71–2, 76–7, 87, 91–3, 104, 172, 180, 189
voice-over 49, 100, 118–20, 125–6, 146–7, 153, 165, 182

Wagner, Richard 205
    Ring, The 205
    Wagnerian 175, 205
Watteau, Antoine 161, 192, 193, 199
Welles, Orson 97, 234
    Magnificent Ambersons, The 97, 230, 234
Wharton, Edith 7, 15, 24, 111, 119, 135, 137–44, 146, 148–9, 152–5, 158–9, 163, 165–6, 188–9, 194, 200, 214, 231, 239–40
    see also *Age of Innocence, The*; *House of Mirth, The*
Wilder, Billy 158, 159, 234
    Some Like It Hot 158, 234
Wyler, William 156, 234
    Little Foxes, The 156, 234

X Files, The 20, 22, 160
    see also Anderson

EU authorised representative for GPSR:
Easy Access System Europe, Mustamäe tee 50,
10621 Tallinn, Estonia
gpsr.requests@easproject.com

www.ingramcontent.com/pod-product-compliance
Ingram Content Group UK Ltd.
Pitfield, Milton Keynes, MK11 3LW, UK
UKHW021832140426
5217IPUK00021B/1398